# Understanding English Grammar

# Understanding English Grammar
## A Linguistic Approach

Ronald Wardhaugh

BLACKWELL
Oxford UK & Cambridge USA

Copyright © Ronald Wardhaugh, 1995

The right of Ronald Wardhaugh to be identified as author of this work has been
asserted in accordance with the Copyright, Designs and Patents Act 1988.

First published 1995

Reprinted 1996 (three times), 1997

Blackwell Publishers Inc
350 Main Street
Malden, Massachusetts 02148, USA

Blackwell Publishers Ltd
108 Cowley Road
Oxford OX4 1JF, UK

*Library of Congress Cataloging in Publication Data*
Wardhaugh, Ronald
Understanding English grammar: a linguistic approach/Ronald Wardhaugh
p.   cm.
Includes bibliographical references and index.
ISBN 0-631-19641-2 - ISBN 0-631-19642-0 (pbk)
1. English language - Grammar.  I. Title.
PE1112.W29   1995
428.2'4 - dc20                                                        94-13007

*British Library Cataloguing in Publication Data*
A CIP catalogue record for this book is available from the British Library

Typeset in 10 on 13 pt Sabon
by Graphicraft Typesetters, Hong Kong
Printed in Great Britain by T. J. Press Ltd, Padstow, Cornwall

This book is printed on acid-free paper

# Contents

# Preface

While numerous books exist that claim to offer their readers descriptions of English, very few attempt to do this in a way that offers beginning students much hope of understanding the essential characteristics of English that must be accounted for in such descriptions. They are either reference grammars, or descriptions written from a narrow theoretical perspective, or incomplete accounts that ignore major structural components of the language. This book attempts to present the essentials of English structure, i.e., information about English words, sentences, and sounds, in a way that should be comprehensible to beginning students.

The order of presentation is the one just mentioned. This order allows us to proceed from the relatively known to the relatively unknown. It is generally easier to discuss and understand what words are and how phrases and clauses are put together than it is to discuss and understand how we actually pronounce what we say. Obviously, some moving back and forth is necessary; the various parts of our language are not completely independent of one another. However, I have tried to keep such cross-cutting to the minimum but I have not avoided it completely because it is quite clearly unavoidable.

The book attempts to point out what appear to be certain essential facts about English. These facts are treated in a variety of ways: they are sometimes presented without comment; they are sometimes subjected to a certain amount of theoretical scrutiny; and, on occasion, their actual status as facts is questioned. In one sense all facts derive from theories of one kind or another; something is a fact because a particular theory gives it that status. I have employed various theoretical approaches in what follows but I espouse no particular theory to the exclusion of any other. This is not, for example, a "structural" approach to English, or a "functional" approach, or a "transformational-generative" approach, or a "government-binding" approach. It is deliberately eclectic and the emphasis deliberately shifts from chapter to chapter and sometimes within a single chapter in the belief that beginning students of the English language need to be informed about data, issues, and approaches. If at times the emphasis does seem to favor the kind of linguistic approach associated with Noam Chomsky, I offer no apology. Such an approach is at the heart of modern linguistics.

This is a "linguistics" book. Linguistic terms are used throughout but I have tried to keep them to a necessary minimum. They are also defined when they are first used. A previous exposure to linguistics will give a student using this book certain advantages, but such an exposure is not absolutely necessary. Indeed, a fundamental goal of this book is to bring to students' attention some of the basic concepts of modern linguistics.

The book is also deliberately pedagogical in its orientation. It is not a reference grammar. What it attempts to do is provide students with necessary information about English so that they can become familiar with some of its essential structural characteristics and how these might be described. Each chapter concludes with a number of exercises, some easily answerable, others more open-ended. For some of these exercises the text also provides examples of answers that are appropriate as a further guide to students. Instructors who use the book as a text should find plenty of opportunity to develop additional exercises that will lead students to apply and develop the knowledge they have gained from working through the chapters. They should also find plenty of opportunity to pursue their own theoretical concerns. The final chapter contains a list of books that students might profitably be encouraged to examine so as to further their knowledge about English structure. The concluding indexed glossary can be used for quick reference to matters covered at greater length in the text.

The material presented in the following chapters should also prove useful to anyone who wants to learn more – or even just something – about the structure of English. The book should be particularly useful to those who specialize in some way in "English" – students of the language and of the literature, teachers of English as either a native or second or foreign language, and teachers of reading and the language arts. It should also be particularly useful to beginning students of linguistics who want to see how some of the concepts they are acquiring apply to English. Students who are trying to learn English as a second or foreign language may also find in the following pages much that is helpful to them in overcoming some of the difficulties they face in such a task. Finally, the book should be of interest to native speakers of English who just want to know more about the language they use so easily.

An Instructor's Manual, which includes answers to all the exercises, is available to adopters of this textbook.

# 1

# Preliminaries

---

This is a book about the English language and how we might try to describe how it works. In the pages that follow we will attempt to discover how we can come to some understanding of the language if we go about that task using insights from modern linguistics. One consequence is that we may be forced to revise, perhaps even discard, some of the ideas we already have about English. However, we should find in the pages that follow a great wealth of ideas that will usefully replace them. It seems best then to begin our study of the language by making explicit certain concepts which underlie all that will follow.

## 1.1  Descriptivism and Prescriptivism

We will be focusing our attention on standard spoken English, the variety of the language we associate with people who speak the language natively and unselfconsciously, people who are also likely to be educated at least to high-school level and be without any kind of strong regional accent.

We will also concentrate on the spoken language rather than on the written language. (As we will see too, the actual spoken variety to be discussed in the chapters that follow is a **rhotic** variety, i.e., one that pronounces the rs in words such as *car* and *cart*; it is also one that distinguishes between the vowel sounds in *cot* and *caught*.) What is important to remember is that when we turn our attention to how we speak the language we must try to listen to how English is actually spoken and not let any assumptions about how it should be spoken get in the way. Such assumptions may derive from the idea that spelling should be used as an infallible guide in the pronunciation of certain words, or from certain kinds of instruction that we may have had, e.g., attempts to make us pronounce *what* differently from *Watt*, or from a belief that there exists somewhere a fixed, unchanged, and unchangeable entity called the English language whose characteristics are well known.

In the pages that follow we will adopt a descriptive approach to language study rather than a prescriptive approach. A **descriptive** approach is one that attempts to describe actual language use, in our case the use of the language by the kind of speakers described above. A **prescriptive** approach is one that expresses a certain dissatisfaction with language use in general and even the language of such speakers. Those who take such an approach believe that no one can be trusted to use the language "correctly." They believe that they know how the language works – usually like Greek or Latin; consequently, they constantly set out arbitrary rules and principles to make sure that "language standards" are upheld and that the language does not "decline." While there is no reason to believe that either their descriptions or their standards are appropriate or that the language is in fact declining, prescriptivists do have a number of **shibboleths** that they refer to constantly and you should be aware of these. For many people the avoidance of these shibboleths comprises the whole purpose of the study of English grammar.

Prescriptivism is a fact about attitudes toward English; it cannot be ignored. Most highly edited formal prose actually conforms to the demands of prescriptivists. However, carrying over the same prescriptive usages into speech is likely to make a person sound either pompous or pretentious, or both. It is important, therefore, to understand the difference between descriptivism and prescriptivism. Our concern will not be with the kinds of matters mentioned in the exercises that follow except in so far as what we say in the pages that follow sheds light on various issues contained there. Our concern will be with trying to describe the language in all its complexity so that we can achieve some understanding of how it actually works. We will find that we need a variety of approaches and techniques and that the more we find out the more intriguing the problems associated with understanding become.

## 1.2   Exercises

1   Much attention is given in teaching grammar to discussions of sentences such as the following. This book is really not concerned with the issues they raise. However, since it is important to know how prescriptivists feel about them, you should examine each sentence closely in order to try to understand just what it is that prescriptivists say about it. You might also consider what descriptivists have to say about the same grammatical issues. The first three are done for you.

(a)   The mission of the USS *Enterprise* is to boldly go where no man has ever been before.
      (Prescriptivists say that *to boldly go* is a "split infinitive," i.e., the adverb *boldly* should not be placed between *to* and *go*, the marked infinitive in English. Change to *to go boldly*. Descriptivists point out that speakers of English often place adverbs in this position and that the prescriptivists' rule

comes from applying a rule of Latin to English: you cannot "split" Latin infinitives because they are single words, e.g., *ire* "to go.")

(b)     I'm right, ain't I?
        (Prescriptivists say that *ain't* is not an English word no matter how frequently it is used. Change to *aren't I?* or *am I not?* Descriptivists point out that *ain't* has a long history in the language, is phonetically justified, has just as much validity as *aren't I?*, and *I aren't* is not possible.)

(c)     Hopefully, the weather will clear up tomorrow.
        (Prescriptivists say that *hopefully* cannot be used in this way as a sentence adverb (or disjunct) like *certainly* and *possibly*. Descriptivists point out that many native speakers do indeed use *hopefully* in this way.)

(d)     It's me who gets the blame for everything.
(e)     John and Sally love one another.
(f)     It was the most unique event in the history of the town.
(g)     You are taller than me.
(h)     Nobody said nothing.
(i)     Those kind of people get on my nerves.
(j)     If I was you, I would resign.
(k)     Everyone should bring their own lunch.
(l)     None of the guests have arrived yet.
(m)     He only had it for two days.
(n)     Who did you speak to at the time?
(o)     Finding the door unlocked, an opportunity to escape appeared at last.
(p)     Don't do it like he does it.
(q)     This one is different than that one.
(r)     Between you and I, he's crazy.
(s)     Try and do it soon.
(t)     When boarding, we remind you to move to the back of the vehicle.
(u)     This is a marker to our four friends whom are no longer with us.
(v)     He's going irregardless.
(w)     They interviewed the boy whom they thought had found it.
(x)     We open our meetings with a prayer because it helps us to make less stupid mistakes.
(y)     I suddenly felt very badly about it.
(z)     He seems to be quite disinterested these days.

2   Is there a "correct" pronunciation of each of the following words? If there is, why? Some of the issues related to the first three examples are indicated.

mischievous (Does the penultimate syllable have the vowel of *bit* or of *beet* and does the word rhyme with *devious*?), either (Does the first syllable have the vowel of *beet* or of *bite*?), asphalt (Does the word begin like *ass* or like *ash*?), diphthong, tomato, film, secretary, bath, clerk, shone, Arctic, comely, often, herb, athlete, ate, defence, dance, butter, soot, news

3   When a native speaker of English is said not to know his or her grammar, what actually does such a statement mean?

# 2
# Word Classes

The English language contains a very large number of words and when we speak or write in English we combine these words in various ways. As we will see in chapter 11, there is no easy definition of what a word is in English, but for the moment we will assume that words are the kinds of entities that find their way into the dictionaries we use. Furthermore, there seems to be good reason to believe that English words may be grouped into various categories traditionally called parts of speech, and that we make use of our knowledge of these categories when we combine them into larger units such as those we traditionally call phrases and clauses. In this chapter we will look at this kind of categorization to see what possibilities it offers us in our attempt to understand how the language works.

## 2.1 Parts of Speech

There is a longstanding tradition which says that there are eight **parts of speech** in English: nouns, pronouns, verbs, adjectives, adverbs, prepositions, conjunctions, and interjections. In one variation of this tradition **nouns** are said to be the names of persons, places, or things, e.g., *man, city, tree, courage, nothingness*; **pronouns** are said to be words that can replace nouns or be used instead of them, e.g., *he, someone, who*; **verbs** make predications or denote actions or states of being, e.g., *sell, leave, become, appear, be*; **adjectives** modify nouns (and sometimes pronouns), e.g., *big, alive, principal*; **adverbs** modify verbs, adjectives, or other adverbs, e.g., *very, not, quickly*; **prepositions** indicate relationships between the nouns or pronouns that they are said to govern and some other part of speech, and are words like *at, in, under*; **conjunctions** join clauses together, e.g., *and, until, when, because*; and **interjections** express some kind of emotion, e.g., *Oh!, Ouch!, Alas!*

There are many difficulties with this kind of classification. First, for the most part it is meaning-based: what exactly are "names," "actions," and "states of being"? Second, it combines statements about meaning (e.g., "nouns are names") with statements about distribution (e.g., "adjectives modify nouns") and when these conflict offers no guidance as to whether meaning takes precedence over distribution or distribution over meaning. For example, is *brick* a noun in *a brick* because it names something and an adjective in *a brick house* because of its distribution as a modifier of *house*? Third, it groups words which have very different characteristics into the same class, particularly into the class of adverbs. If *very*, *not*, and *quickly* do have certain similarities, what exactly are they? Finally, it ignores the many structural features of the language that might be useful for classificatory purposes, e.g., characteristic word endings, how phrases are built up, and how clauses are formed.

Some examples will be useful in further showing the inadequacies of many traditional definitions of the parts of speech. What does *emptiness* name in *Its vast emptiness amazed him*? What noun does *nobody* replace in *Nobody succeeded in solving the problem*? Why exactly is *swim* a noun in the sentence *He had a good swim* and a verb in the sentence *It's good to swim in*? In *I found John's hat outside*, what is *John's*, a noun or an adjective? If *old* and *stone* are said to be adjectives in *an old wall* and *a stone wall*, why is it possible to say *a very old wall* but not *\*a very stone wall*? (The \*indicates that what follows is **ungrammatical** in English.) Is it because certain adjectives must follow other adjectives when they are combined in phrases, or is it because *stone* is not really an adjective at all but is a noun that modifies another noun and therefore must follow an adjective that modifies that same noun? Note that in a sentence like *When the young girl entered, I gave her the parcel*, the pronoun *her* does not replace a noun (*girl*) but rather a noun phrase (*the young girl*). *Not*, *quite*, and *there* are all said to be adverbs in *It's not quite there*, but what other possible uniting feature do they have except that they do not fit into any of the other categories? To say that something is an adverb is really to say little more than it is not an adjective, conjunction, preposition, etc.

In a structural classification of the parts of speech in English there are two basic approaches to the categorization of words. One is to look at the **forms** of the words themselves in order to find out what structural characteristics they have and what kinds of changes occur as they are used in phrases, clauses, and sentences. In this approach we look at words in isolation in order to see what their formal characteristics might tell us about them: *cat* has another form *cats*, *bite* has the forms *bit* and *bitten*, and *big* has both *bigger* and *biggest*. (Of course, if words have no special formal characteristics, as *the*, *very*, *must*, *in*, etc. do not, such an approach is inherently limited.) The other approach, therefore, is to look at the **distributions** of words in the belief that words that regularly fill the same slots in basic recurring patterns in the language, e.g., as subjects, objects, complements, etc., may be said to belong to the same general category. In this way we will find that *cat* distributes like *plate*, *bite* like *take*, *big* like *old*, and so on. We will also find with words that show no changes in their forms that *the* distributes like *a*, *very* like *rather*, *must* like *can*, *in* like *under*, and so on. Let us now look at these two approaches in some detail.

By formal characteristics, we mean the characteristic **inflectional** changes or the characteristic word endings (**derivational** endings) that we observe in sets such as the following:

| Inflections | Derivations |
|---|---|
| *cat, cats, cat's, cats'* | *judgment, kingdom, baker* |
| *I, you, he, she, it, we, they* | *himself* |
| *bake, bakes, baking, baked* | *synthesize, pacify* |
| *long, longer, longest* | *topical, smallish, hopeful* |

We can then use the terms **noun, pronoun, verb,** and **adjective** respectively for typical members of each of the above rows. (We will continue to use traditional labels whenever they are useful.) As we will see, many English words are without inflectional or derivational marking. Consequently, the part-of-speech categorization of such words must require the use of some other criterion or characteristic.

By using distributional criteria, we mean the single words that can be inserted into slots such as those marked by $X$ in each of the following sentences:

| | |
|---|---|
| *He bought the X.* | X: *man, dog, butter, paper* |
| *He wants to X.* | X: *dance, leave, sing, cook* |
| *The boy is very X.* | X: *tired, young, pleasant, bright* |
| *He went X.* | X: *out, in, quietly, there* |

In this case single words that typically occupy the four slots can also be named **noun, verb, adjective,** and **adverb** respectively. However, there are many other possible distributions in the language and it is quite easy to show that when the distributional possibilities of words are taken into account, we must recognize a great many different parts of speech in English. We will also need to acknowledge that some words move easily from one grammatical category to another and that some are even unique in how they are used in the language.

Let us compare the different distributional characteristics of the bold-faced words in each of the following pairs of sentences. Within each pair the boldfaced words are sometimes said to be in the same part-of-speech category.

*The* **old** *man is here.*
*He is* **alive.**

We can note that *\*The alive man is here* is not possible but *He is old* is. *Old* and *alive* are both usually described as adjectives; however, *alive* has a much more limited distribution than *old* because it can appear only after a verb like *is* in the above sentences whereas *old* can occur both before a noun like *man* and after a verb like *is*.

We might want to say that *old* is therefore a more typical adjective than *alive*. We will find this concept of "typical" to be useful when applied to our study of language. Some items are more typical of a particular grammatical category or use than others. We will also see that some items are "fuzzy" in that they seem to belong to two or more categories at the same time.

In the next pair of sentences all the boldfaced words are usually said to be adverbs:

*It disappeared* **rather quickly.**
*He waited* **patiently outside.**

However, combinations like *\*rather outside, \*quickly patiently*, and *\*quickly rather* are not possible so some further categorization seems to be called for. A simple solution would be to put *rather* into another category again, one we will call **intensifier,** and to provide subcategories for the adverb class, perhaps "place" for *outside* and "manner" for *quickly* and *patiently*, with the proviso that one manner adverb cannot modify another manner adverb.

Finally, all the following boldfaced words are said to be pronouns:

*I know* **someone** *told* **him.**
**Who** *said* **that?**

However, only *who* can begin an information-seeking question, *him* and *someone* are not interchangeable (*\*I know* **him** *told* **someone**), and *that* contrasts with *this* in a way that is unique in the language.

The issue in the above examples is just how many different parts of speech there are. Are *old* and *alive* the same part of speech, sub-varieties of the same part of speech, or different parts of speech entirely? The same questions can be asked of each of the other examples.

In some cases individual words may be unique items so far as part-of-speech classification is concerned, e.g., *not, even, for,* and *to*. In the following sentences, for example, it is impossible to find any other words that have exactly the same distributional possibilities as those in boldface:

*He did* **not** *want the coffee.*
**Even** *Fred knows that.*

*She waited **for** she had no choice in the matter.*
*They want **to** eat.*

It so happens that the two approaches mentioned above, the formal and the distributional, produce conflicting results for some words, e.g., *dancing* in *The dancing ceased* where *dancing* has the *-ing* ending characteristic of a verb but the distribution of a noun. However, an approach which is based on both formal and distributional criteria appears to offer us a much better starting point for our work than one which uses the aforementioned traditional notions. At least we avoid needless confusion and do not arbitrarily give form preference in one set of circumstances and distribution preference in another. We recognize instead that both may be important at the same time in trying to understand what is actually happening in the language. We will also find that we need to consider many more categories than the traditional eight or so. As we continue to look closely at the structure of English, we will also become increasingly aware that we must consider matters of linguistic form and distribution in all kinds of circumstances. It is impossible to ignore one or the other, and we will have to move constantly between the two, between statements about form and statements about distribution.

## 2.2   Nouns

A typical **noun** is a word that is marked inflectionally (i.e., by a change in form) for **plural** or **genitive** or both. The regular spelling endings of the plural, the genitive, and the combined plural and genitive are the *-s*, *-'s*, and *-s'* endings. A **regular** ending is one that not only occurs frequently but also can be accounted for by a simple general statement (e.g., a spelling rule which says "add *-s* to form the plural of a singular noun"). (See chapter 11 for a discussion of the various pronunciations of these endings, which differ among the nouns that follow. Regular is also defined there in terms of pronunciation rather than spelling.) What follows are the regular plural, genitive, and combined plural and genitive forms for *cat*, *dog*, and *church* (with the *-es* and *-es'* forms being predictable spelling variants of *-s* and *-s'*). The uninflected *cat*, *dog*, and *church* – sometimes referred to as the "singular" forms – are regarded as the basic forms of the nouns and appear, for example, as the standard entries in dictionaries:

*cat, cats, cat's, cats'*
*dog, dogs, dog's, dogs'*
*church, churches, church's, churches'*

The regular plural for these **countable** nouns is found in words like *cap, sack, tub, bed, dish, judge, moon, sea, car*, etc. However, each of the following singular nouns has – or, in some cases, may have because usage varies – an irregular plural, i.e., one that is formed on some other principle than the one just explained. The plural for the first word in each row is indicated.

> *foot (**feet**), mouse, tooth, goose, woman*
> *calf (**calves**), knife, scarf, truth, wreath, leaf, wolf, life, house*
> *ox (**oxen**), child*
> *fish (**fish**), sheep, deer, salmon, trout, antelope, reindeer*
> *alumnus (**alumni**), stimulus, fungus, cactus, radius, syllabus*
> *alumna (**alumnae**), formula, antenna*
> *curriculum (**curricula**), stadium, auditorium, memorandum, symposium,*
>    *datum*
> *thesis (**theses**), axis, diagnosis, synopsis, oasis*
> *criterion (**criteria**), automaton, phenomenon*
> *stigma (**stigmata**)*
> *graffito (**graffiti**), concerto*
> *index (**indices**), appendix, matrix*
> *cherub (**cherubim**)*

Still other plurals are:

> *passers-by, menservants, governors general*

Some nouns end in an *-s* that might appear to be a plural inflection but this turns out not to be the case:

> *news, phonetics, billiards, linguistics, mathematics, the United Nations, the United States, rabies, measles*

Note that each of the above words would be followed by *is* rather than by *are* in a sentence, *The news is bad, The United States is ready*, etc. Other nouns that end in *-s* may not have a singular variant at all or, if there is a form without *-s*, it may have a somewhat different meaning:

> *pincers, tweezers, tongs, trousers, scissors, tights, spectacles, pajamas, binoculars, jeans, shorts, scales, premises, arms, spirits, surroundings, troops, earnings, means, funds, looks, minutes*

A few nouns do not take the *-s* plural inflection but are always found with plural verbs like *are* and never with singular verbs like *is*:

*cattle, people, police*

Some nouns do not have a plural when they are used as **mass nouns** but may take a plural when they are used as **countable** nouns:

*cheese, wood, air, wine, hope, love, devotion, happiness, courage, snow, equipment, weather, growth*

We can see the difference in use in examples like *I want **some cheese*** and ***These three cheeses** are from Holland* and ***Hope** springs eternal from the human breast* and *Their **hopes** were quickly dashed.*

Mass nouns also occur after words like *much* and *little*, whereas countable nouns occur after *many* and *few*. *There isn't **much** wine left* and *She shows **little** devotion to her work* contrast with ***Many** books were lost in the fire* and *They experienced **few** difficulties.*

A special group of nouns are sometimes called **proper nouns**. Proper nouns are the names of specific entities:

*John, London, Monday, Christmas, March, Ohio*

Proper nouns are part of a larger set of **proper names**. Many are phrasal units composed of two or more words:

*the Mississippi, Lake Ontario, New Year's Day, New York, the Alps, the Straits of Gibraltar, the Pyramids*

It is a spelling convention in English to write proper names with an initial capital letter. A proper name may be used just like a **common noun,** the name given to all the other nouns, in certain circumstances and indeed becomes distributionally identical with a common noun when it is so used. It does, however, retain its original capitalization in the English writing system.

*He was not the **John Smith** I saw.*
*There are several **Newcastles** in the world.*
*He is a regular **Don Juan**.*

Note the use of *the* in the first case, *several* and the plural in the second, and *a regular* in the third.

The *-'s* or *-s'* genitive is always regular when it occurs, being suffixed to either the singular or plural form of the noun: *cat's, cats'; judge's, judges'; man's, men's, child's, children's; phenomenon's, phenomena's*. The inflected genitive is sometimes called the **marked genitive**. In spelling there is generally only a simple difference in the placement of the apostrophe in the two genitive forms when the plural of the noun is regularly formed: singular *cat's* but plural *cats'*; however, irregularly formed plurals show a further difference of one kind or another:

> *woman's, women's*
> *foot's, feet's*
> *child's, children's*
> *attorney general's, attorneys general's*

The marked genitive contrasts with the **periphrastic genitive**, which requires the use of *of*, as in *friends of my mother* (*my mother's friends*), *the enemies of Napoleon* (*Napoleon's enemies*), and *the end of the play* (*the play's end*). However, the marked genitive is much more limited in use than the *of* genitive, for, whereas it is possible to say or write *the top of the mountain*, it seems decidedly awkward (although not completely unacceptable) to say or write *the mountain's top*. Human nouns and many animal nouns are much more likely to employ the marked genitive than non-human nouns, especially **mass nouns**, e.g., *in John's absence, the cat's food, *in hope's absence* (*in the absence of hope*).

The genitive can encompass a variety of meaning relationships, some of which are indicated below. It is because these relationships vary so much that we prefer to use the term **genitive** rather than the term **possessive** for this use of -*'s*, -*s'*, and *of*.

| | |
|---|---|
| possession | *Edward's hat* (Edward possesses the hat) |
| origin | *Sally's cable* (Sally sent the cable) |
| appositive | *the city of New York* (the city is New York) |
| partitive | *a few of the men* (several, not all, of the men) |
| subjective | *John's arrival* (John arrived) |
| objective | *the army's defeat* (someone defeated the army) |
| descriptive | *a ship's bell* (a bell made for a ship) |
| measure | *a month's delay* (a delay lasting a month) |

There are still further variants of the genitive: **group genitives** like *the captain of the ship's lawyer, the Queen of England's son, a man I know's nephew, Tom and Sarah's house, my son and his friend's wishes*; **double genitives** like *a friend of my mother's, a play of Shakespeare's*; **location genitives** like *at the doctor's*; and **elliptical genitives** like *This book sells better than John's*.

Certain derivational suffixes are also characteristic of nouns, i.e., words with such endings are usually nouns:

> *gangster, hunter, handful, trainee, hostess, realism, normalcy, kindness, motherhood, friendship, amusement, nation, pamphlet, growth, mutant, physician, cigarette, sadist, boredom, usage*

(Note that the *-er* in *hunter* – meaning "one who" – is different from the *-er* in *bigger* – meaning "more" – and that *handful* is a noun but *plentiful* with the same ending is an adjective. We therefore must be alert to both the meanings of such endings – they may have the same form but different meanings – and the kinds of words to which each is affixed or which result from the process of affixation.)

Some English nouns also show gender, i.e., sex-linking, either through suffixation or by having some other kind of gender differentiation:

> *waiter, waitress*
> *hero, heroine*
> *widow, widower* (note the unusual "male" suffix in this case)
> *usher, usherette*
> *goose, gander*
> *bull, cow*
> *cock, hen*
> *king, queen*
> *man, woman*
> *brother, sister*
> *boyfriend, girlfriend*
> *bride, bridegroom* (another "male" suffix)
> *he-goat, she-goat*
> *man-child, girl-child*

(We should note that some parts of this system are currently under attack because it is said to be "sexist," e.g., *actress, waitress, foreman,* **lady** *doctor,* etc.)

Nouns also have certain typical distributional uses. Words that can fill one or more of the places marked by *X* in the following sentences are almost certain to be nouns. They are typical noun positions.

> *The X is here.*      *X: man, sugar, house, mail*
> *Give me some X*      *X: money, eggs, paper, encouragement*
> *Show me a X*         *X: poem, tree, spoon, sailor*
> *X is good*           *X: snow, faith, John, courage*

## 2.3   Pronouns

There are various kinds of **pronouns**, some of which can be inflected for plural and genitive. The **personal pronouns** and the **relative pronouns** may also be inflected for **object case**, i.e., they are specifically marked as occurring as the objects of verbs or prepositions, e.g., *We introduced **her** to **them***; *the boy to **whom** you sent **her***.

The personal pronouns show inflectional marking for singular and plural and for subject and object uses. They also have two genitive forms, sometimes referred to as a **first possessive** (1 Poss.) or **attributive** form, e.g., *It is **my** book*, and a **second possessive** (2 Poss.) or **absolute** form, e.g., *It is **mine***. There is also a gender distinction in the third person singular: masculine (m.), feminine (f.), and neuter (n.). The inflectional system of personal pronouns is so irregular that it usually seems best to present the relevant data as follows rather than to attempt a detailed analysis. (Just as *cat, dog, church*, and so on are regarded as the base forms of the nouns so in this case *I, you, he, she*, etc. – the forms found in the subject position of a clause, e.g., *I left* – are regarded as the base forms of the pronouns.)

Singular

| Person | Subject | Object | 1 Poss. | 2 Poss. |
|--------|---------|--------|---------|---------|
| 1 | *I* | *me* | *my* | *mine* |
| 2 | *you* | *you* | *your* | *yours* |
| 3m. | *he* | *him* | *his* | *his* |
| 3f. | *she* | *her* | *her* | *hers* |
| 3n. | *it* | *it* | *its* | *its* |

Plural

| Person | Subject | Object | 1 Poss. | 2 Poss. |
|--------|---------|--------|---------|---------|
| 1 | *we* | *us* | *our* | *ours* |
| 2 | *you* | *you* | *your* | *yours* |
| 3 | *they* | *them* | *their* | *theirs* |

We should note that in the above system **plural** has a rather special meaning when applied to *I* and *we*: *we* is obviously not more than one *I* in the way that the plural *you* is more than one singular *you* and *they* is more than one *he, she*, or *it*. *We* is also ambiguous: it may or may not include the person or persons who are addressed. If it includes an addressee or addressees, it is said to be **inclusive**, e.g., *We* ("you and I") *should see him about it*; if it does not, it is said to be **exclusive**, e.g., *We* ("some one or ones including I but not you") *intend to stop you*.

*You, we*, and *they* may also be somewhat vague in their reference, meaning something like "people in general," as in *You know what people are like*, *We don't do things that way here*, and *They don't do it that way anymore*. *He*, *she*, and *it* are closely linked to gender, but babies may be referred to as *he*, *she*, or *it*, as may household pets; cars and ships are also often referred to as *she*.

The object forms of the personal pronouns are required after verbs and prepositions when a clear subject–object distinction exists in the pronoun system: *I followed him, He preceded me, to her, between you and me* (*you* and *it* have no subject–object distinction). The first possessive form is used before nouns, although not necessarily directly before, e.g., *her house*, *his old friend*, and in this use is sometimes also referred to as a **determiner** or **possessive pronoun**. In contrast, the second possessive form is used in absolute positions, i.e., by itself: *It's hers, Mine is ready*. (An expression like *mine eyes* is archaic. The old second person singular forms *thou, thee, thy*, and *thine* are also rarely found in use today.)

The **reflexive** (*I hurt myself*) and **intensifying** or **emphatic** (*He himself said so*) forms of the personal pronouns are composed of the first possessive forms plus -*self* (singular) and -*selves* (plural) in the first and second persons and the object form plus those same endings in the third person, e.g., *myself, ourselves, yourself, yourselves, himself, herself, itself, themselves*. (Nonstandard forms like *\*hisself* and *theirselves* are formed by analogy to the first and second persons.)

The **demonstrative pronouns** are *this* and *that*, each of which can be pluralized: *these* and *those*. These pronouns can be used alone as in *This is the book I want, He said that*, and *He wants these not those*, or they can be used as determiners, as in *He asked for that book you had mentioned* and *This new cake is good*. (It is useful to note that the demonstrative pronoun *this* is often used somewhat vaguely, its actual referent being unclear, e.g., *This resulted in a complaint being lodged* when the precise referent for *this* is some involved account.)

The **relative pronouns** are either the personal *who* or one of its forms or the impersonal *which*. *Who* has an object form *whom* and a genitive form *whose*. (Many users of English either avoid *whom* or are unsure of its use, particularly in speech.) Some typical standard uses are as follows:

> *The man **who** came in was Tim's father.*
> *The person **whom** you saw gave permission.*
> *The girl with **whom** she studies is my daughter.*
> *The boy **whose** book you have is outside.*
> *He wants the picture **which** you took of him.*

(Many users of English would use *who* rather than *whom* in the second sentence, would recast the third sentence as *The girl she studies with is my daughter*, and would omit *which* in the final sentence.) *Whose* may also be used impersonally, i.e., to refer to something non-human, on occasion as in *It's a new drug **whose** potential is as yet unknown.*

The **interrogative pronouns** are the same as the relative pronouns. We can also add *what* to the list. *Whose, which,* and *what* may also be used as determiners. Some typical uses are as follows:

> *Who came in?*
> *Who(m) do you want?*
> *Whose (pens) are these?*
> *Which (books) do you want?*
> *What (books) do you want?*

In the last two examples *which* seems to offer the listener a choice from among a predetermined set, whereas *what* seems to offer a completely free choice.

Other pronouns include **reciprocals** like *each other* and *one another*. *Each other* is usually used when there are two referents; reference to more than two requires *one another*: **John and Mary** *like* **each other**, **The triplets** *strongly resemble* **one another**. Reciprocal pronouns also have genitive forms: *Sally and Mary wear* **each other**'s *clothes*. The **indefinite pronouns** are *some, any,* or *none,* or combinations of *some, any* and *no* with *thing, body,* and *one*:

> *Some handed in their work on time.*
> *I don't have any.*
> *None survived the trip.*
> *Everything is fine today.*
> *Nothing happened to her.*
> *Don't tell anybody.*
> *Someone will have to do it.*

The combinations are occasionally found in plural and genitive forms. As plurals and genitives they distribute very much like nouns:

> *What a lot of silly* **nobodies**!
> *It must be* **someone**'s *property.*

*It, there,* and *one* are also pronouns when they are used as follows:

> *It's raining.*
> *It's five o'clock.*
> *It's good to know that.*
> *It happened that he knew.*
> *I thought it silly of him to do that.*
> *There's a time for everything.*

*There* *happens* *to* *be* *a* *war* *on.*
*Sue* *bought* *a* *red* *dress* *and* *Brenda* *bought* *a* *green* **one.**
*He* *wants* *a* *book* *and* *I* *want* **one** *too.*

Note that *it* in the above sentences makes little or no reference to anything in the real world but is required in certain kinds of grammatical constructions to do with weather and time. *There* acts as a "dummy" subject in certain sentence types. *One*, on the other hand, is a pronoun that actually does "replace" a noun in the penultimate sentence (*dress*) but a noun phrase (*a book*) in the final sentence.

Pronouns distribute much like nouns in sentences:

*John left.*
*He left.*
*Someone left.*
*Who left?*

*The* *boy* *asked* *the* *girl.*
*He* *asked* *her.*

Actually, as the final example shows quite clearly, it is more accurate to say that pronouns distribute like **noun phrases** (see chapter 3) rather than like nouns because it is noun phrases that they usually replace rather than nouns when they do serve as replacements:

*The boy spoke to his mother and she* (his mother) *listened to him* (the boy) *carefully.*
*Those boys climbing the tree will hurt themselves* (those boys climbing the tree).

## 2.4   Verbs

A typical **verb**, e.g., *bake* or *play*, is marked inflectionally for **third person singular** present tense subject agreement (*-s*), as in *he bakes* and *she plays*, the **present participle** (*-ing*), as in *we are baking* and *they are playing*, the **past tense** (*-ed*), as in *I baked* and *they played*, and the **past participle** (*-ed*), as in *she has baked* and *they had played*. (See chapter 11 for a description of the actual pronunciations of these endings.) The following verbs show the regular forms of these inflections:

*bake, bakes, baking, baked, baked*
*beg, begs, begging, begged, begged*
*wash, washes, washing, washed, washed*

Other verbs showing such regular inflections are *treat, wish, save, purr, try,*
*open, please, walk,* and *trip.* Sometimes the base forms of verbs are cited with
a preceding *to,* e.g., **to bake, to play,** etc. This *to* is not a preposition; rather
it is part of what is sometimes referred to as the **marked infinitive.** We can
therefore describe *to know* in *I want* **to know** as a marked infinitive and
*know* in *I don't* **know** as a **bare infinitive.**

Irregular inflections may occur in the past tense and past participle forms.
They involve such matters as changes in the base forms of the verbs, whether
or not an inflectional suffix occurs, what the exact form of that suffix is, and
whether or not the past tense and past participle forms remain identical. In
a few verbs there is also an additional change in the third person singular
form of the verb, and *be* has its own special peculiarities. In the following list
the past tense and past participle forms are given in that order for the first
verb in each row:

*bet* (**bet, bet**), *hit, cut, put, shut*
*burn* (**burnt, burnt**), *learn, spill* (in those varieties of English which
    favor the *-t* ending rather than the *-ed* ending)
*bend* (**bent, bent**), *lend, spend, build*
*feed* (**fed, fed**), *hold, read* (where the sound changes but the spelling
    does not), *lead*
*creep* (**crept, crept**), *feel, sweep, leap, sleep, meet, keep* (also *leave* with
    an additional change to *left*)
*dig* (**dug, dug**), *stick, strike, spin, win*
*bring* (**brought, brought**), *fight, catch, buy, seek, teach, think*
*bind* (**bound, bound**), *find, wind*
*get* (**got, got**), *shine, shoot*
*sell* (**sold, sold**), *tell*
*become* (**became, become**), *come, run*
*break* (**broke, broken**), *swear, know, bite, shake, rise, eat, write*
*drink* (**drank, drunk**), *sing, swim, ring*
*go* (**went, gone**)

(The change from *go* to *went* is called a **suppletive** change because there is
no phonological resemblance between the two forms, i.e., they are completely
different in their sounds.)

Three very important verbs in English *be, have,* and *do* are also quite
irregular, particularly the first with its suppletive forms.

*be*

| singular | *am, are, is* |
| past tense | *was, were* |
| present participle | *being* |
| past participle | *been* |

*have*

| 3 pers sglr | *has* |
| past tense | *had* |
| present participle | *having* |
| past participle | *had* |

*do*

| 3 pers sglr | *does* |
| past tense | *did* |
| present participle | *doing* |
| past participle | *done* |

Except for the present participle each inflected form of the above verbs is irregular. *Be* is also unique in that it has a special form *am* for the first person singular subject in the present tense and a special form *are* for all other non-third person singular subjects in that tense. Moreover, is has two forms *was* and *were* for the past tense instead of the usual one.

These three verbs are widely used in English. Each of them can be used as either a full verb, i.e., a **lexical verb**, or as an **auxiliary verb**. In the first sentence of each of the following pairs the verb is a lexical verb, i.e., the main or principal and sometimes only verb in its clause; in the second it is an auxiliary verb. When it is an auxiliary verb, the main (i.e., lexical) verb in the sentence is shown in plain boldface.

*John is happy.*
*John is* **going**.

*Fred does his work well.*
*Fred doesn't* **work** *well*.

*She had a good time.*
*She has* **taken** *her time.*

Still another important set of verbs, the **modal verbs**, are also irregular. In this case they are **defective** in that they lack inflections for the third person singular and the participles and cannot appear after *to* in marked infinitives:

*to must, *to can. (We can compare these verbs with to be, to sing, to open, etc. and note that the can and will of to can and to will are quite different verbs, in this case lexical verbs, in She's going **to can** the vegetables and He tried **to will** it to happen.) The forms given in the following parentheses are generally considered to be the past tense forms of the verbs that precede them, but must has no such past tense form.

can (**could**), will (**would**), shall (**should**), may (**might**), must

Like the auxiliary verbs above, modal verbs are used along with lexical verbs:

He **can** go.
We **should** do that.
You **must** go.

Auxiliary and modal verbs, therefore, differ from lexical verbs both in their inflectional and distributional characteristics.

When it does occur the **subjunctive** form of the verb in English is noticeable through the absence of the form of the verb that might otherwise be expected (given here in parentheses) as in the following examples.

I insist she **go** (goes).
I demand that they **be** (are) told.
It is necessary that he **see** (sees) her immediately.
If I **were** (was) to go, what then?
He wished he **were** (was) dead.
I move that Sally **ask** (asks) them to come.
The condition is that he **report** (reports) to the authorities daily.
I insist she **not** (doesn't) **go**.

Except with the verb be this kind of subjunctive can occur only with third person singular subjects since there is no possible distinction elsewhere:

I insist **you go**.
It is necessary that **they leave** immediately.
I move that **we ask** him to come.

(Many users of English seem to get by quite nicely without using this kind of subjunctive.) Another kind of subjunctive is found in certain fixed expressions:

God **save** the Queen!
God **help** him!

*The devil **take** him!*
*Come what may, we are going.*
*Be that as it may, I'll have none of it.*
*Come August, we'll be in France.*
*So be it!*

Verbs may also be recognized by certain characteristic derivational suffixes:

*indemnify, widen, hyphenate, synthesize, sparkle*

Words that can fill one or more of the places marked by *X* in the following sentences are almost certain to be verbs. These are typical verb positions.

*Birds X.*                    *X: sing, fly, exist, die*
*He will X.*                   *X: go, complain, eat, retire*
*Fred X happy.*               *X: became, is, appears, seems*
*People X such things.*        *X: eat, say, find, take*

## 2.5   Adjectives

**Adjective** is another inflected word class. A typical adjective can be inflected with the *-er* for **comparative** and the *-est* for **superlative**, e.g., *big, bigger, biggest*. There are also some irregularities in these inflections, as in *good* and *bad*, which like *go* and *be* in the verbs are **suppletive**: *good, better, best; bad, worse, worst*. Adjectives like *long* and *strong* also show the irregularity of having the final *g* pronounced in the comparative and superlative forms in contrast to the base forms in which the *g* is not pronounced (except in some very localized varieties of English).

Most inflectable adjectives are monosyllabic but certain disyllabic adjectives may also be inflected:

*simple (simpler, simplest), gentle, clever, narrow, common, happy, quiet, polite, able, feeble*

Certain adjectives derived mainly from nouns, i.e., *noisy* derives from *noise*, may also be inflected:

*noisy (noisier, noisiest), funny, friendly, manly, worldly, deadly*

Many uninflectable adjectives show the same possibilities for "comparative" and "superlative" by occurring after *more* or *most*, as in *more beautiful* and *most alarming.* However, for an adjective to do this, it must be a **gradable adjective**, i.e., the characteristic it describes must be subject to comparison, e.g., degrees of beauty, of alarmingness, etc. Adjective that are not gradable usually cannot occur after *more* or *most* or after *very*, *rather*, or *quite*, e.g., *\*very main*, *\*rather principal*, etc. The following adjectives are therefore not gradable adjectives:

> *main, principal, atomic, square, electric, French, comic, open, dead, male, female, pregnant, true, false, unique, daily, right, moral*

Occasionally, however, a nongradable adjective may be used as though it were gradable:

> *He is **more open** about it than she is.*
> *It's a **quite comic** situation.*
> *She's **very French**, you know.*
> *He's a **very moral** person.*
> *She's **very pregnant**.*
> *They were **quite dead**.*

Within gradable adjectives there are sometimes pairs of opposites like *good* and *bad*, *rich* and *poor*, *big* and *little*, and *high* and *low*. In many of these pairs one member is "unmarked" in relation to the other in that it somehow subsumes the other in certain contexts. For example, one asks *How **high** is it?* rather than *How **low** is it?* The latter would be used only in very marked, i.e., special, circumstances in which the actual lowness of something is an issue. A general query about height requires *How **high** is it?* Likewise, one answers *It's two feet **high*** but not *\*It's two feet **low*** in giving a "measure" answer. Here are some further examples:

> *How **deep**/shallow **wide**/narrow **strong**/weak **long**/short **thick**/thin **heavy**/*
> *   light is it?*
> *How **old**/young **big**/little is she?*
> *It's a yard **long**. (It's a yard **short** has an entirely different meaning.)*

Since not all speakers make the same gradable–nongradable distinctions, usages such as the following may generate a certain amount of controversy as to whether or not they are entirely "acceptable":

> *It was a **most unique** occasion.*
> *Juan is **very alive** today.*
> *He's **quite dead**.*
> *This is the **squarer** of the two. (But **rounder** seems to be fine.)*

Certain derivational suffixes are characteristic of adjectives.

> *wooden, active, helpful, hopeless, manly, picturesque, weepy, mulish, approachable, passionate, rational, poisonous, Wilsonian, revolutionary, praiseworthy, handsome, Japanese, declaratory, manlike, manic, economical, fertile*

Adjectives differ from one another in their distributional possibilities; in this respect they are just like members of any other word class, e.g., nouns, pronouns, and verbs. Some adjectives occur after **intensifiers** like *very* (**very** old), *rather* (**rather** sweet), *quite* (**quite** sound), *more* (**more** beautiful), and *most* (**most** anxious), but others do not (**\*very** main, **\*rather** principal, **\*most** pregnant). They also occur after words like *this, so,* and *too,* as in *It was* **this** big, *I'm so happy,* and *It's* **too** small. Another preferred position is between a word such as *a, the, my,* or *some* and a noun:

> *a* **big** *meal, the* **main** *reason, some* **atomic** *particles, my* **old** *friend*

This position before a noun is called the **attributive** position; indeed some adjectives can be used only attributively or will have rather different meanings if used **predicatively**, i.e., after a verb:

> *my* **former** *colleague,* **criminal** *law,* **atomic** *physics,* **medical** *science, the* **main** *reason, the* **same** *day,* **outer** *space, the* **upper** *teeth, an* **occasional** *meal,* **sheer** *luck, a* **belated** *excuse, the* **lone** *ranger, an* **east** *wind, the* **maximum** *amount, the* **western** *extension*

> *a* **big** *talker, the talker was* **big**
> *a* **perfect** *idiot, the idiot was* **perfect**
> *a* **real** *hero, the hero was* **real**
> *the* **late** *Fred Jones, Fred Jones was* **late**

Some adjectives cannot be used attributively and occur only predicatively, i.e., after certain verb forms, particularly parts of the verb *be,* as in the following examples:

> *Kim is* **awake/afraid/alive/ashamed**.
> *She is quite* **ill/well** *today.*
> *They looked* **alike**.

Some adjectives can occur predicatively after verbs such as *be, seems,* and *appears,* and sometimes before phrases introduced by words such as *to, on, of, about* and *with,* the choice of these words being highly constrained, i.e., **fond** *of* but not **\*fond** *about,* **due** *to* but not **\*due** *with,* etc.

*loath, flush, subject, afraid, intent, prepared, due, able, furious, apt, fond, averse, subject, capable, willing, upset, worried*

In some of these cases the following phrase is mandatory; in others it is optional. A clause introduced by *that* (or with *that* omitted) or by a phrase beginning with a marked infinitive is also possible after some such adjectives:

*He was **loath to** do it.*
*You are **subject to** the law.*
*He was **furious** (**with** the treatment he received).*
*I'm **upset** ((**that**) John has done it).*
*I am **afraid** (**of** her)/((**that**) he'll do it)/(**to go**).*
*He was **worried** (**about** it)/((**that**) she would say something).*

In certain fixed expressions the adjective always occurs after the noun with which it occurs:

*attorney **general**, court **martial**, letters **patent**, president **elect**, notary **public**, postmaster **general**, governor **general***

Standard English therefore requires the plural *governors general* rather than *governor generals*; nonstandard English usage often favors the second form, treating the whole phrase as a noun and pluralizing it.


## 2.6  Adverbs


A typical **adverb** may be recognized by the *-ly* suffix that has been attached to an adjective:

*beautifully, quickly, slowly, nicely, humbly, mortally*

This *-ly* suffix is not an inflectional suffix, as for example were the *-s* plural ending on nouns and the *-ed* past tense ending on verbs; it is a derivational suffix. (See chapter 11 for further information on these two types of ending.) We should also note that the following words which end in *-ly* are adjectives not adverbs, the *-ly* in this case deriving adjectives from nouns.

*friendly, kingly, cowardly, manly, fatherly, worldly*

Just like some adjectives some adverbs have comparative and superlative forms:

*badly, **worse, worst***
*well, **better, best***

The above adverbs have **suppletive** forms in their comparative and super-
latives. The comparative and superlative in most adverbs require use of *more*
and *most* as in **more** *commonly* and **most** *successfully*. Some adverbs like *here,
there*, and *then* cannot be compared at all. In each of the following sentences
the boldfaced word is an adverb.

*They get on **well** together.*
*He left **earlier** than expected.*
*They drive much **slower** now.*
*Aim **higher** next time.*
*He behaved **better** this time.*
*He fared **worst** on the last question.*

Certain derivational suffixes may also mark members of the adverb class:

*onward, backwards, sideways, province-**wide**, business-**wise**, head**long**,
southern-**style***

Most adverbs have no derivational marking at all and are adverbs because of
the places they fill in clauses and sentences. Some typical slots for adverbs are
marked by **X** in the following sentences:

*He did it **X**.*          **X:** *quietly, then, outside, backwards*
*She sings **X**.*          **X:** *beautifully, upstairs, loudly, here*
***X**, she eats there.*    **X:** *usually, sometimes, however, now*

Many adverbs can also occur after intensifiers such as *very, rather*, and *quite*,
as in **very** *quickly*, **rather** *well*, and **quite** *slowly*.
   It may be useful to contrast the adjectives and adverbs in the following
pairs of sentences. The adjective is in the first member of each pair.

*I caught an **early** train.*
*I arrived home **early**.*

*He aimed at the **higher** target.*
*He aimed **higher** next time.*

*He walked a **straight** line.*
*He went **straight** to his friend.*

*It's a **hard** job we have to do.*
*We tried **hard** to convince them.*

*Have a **long** rest!*
*Don't stay **long!***

*She caught the **late** train.*
*He stayed **late**.*

*They are too **short**.*
*They fell **short** of their target.*

*He's feeling **low** today.*
*Swing **low**, sweet chariot!*

In each case the deciding factor is how the word in question distributes in relation to other words in the sentence, e.g., *early* between *an* and *train* versus *early* following *arrived home*.

Sometimes certain constructions appear to offer a choice between adjective and adverb forms, but, when they do, opinions may differ as to which choice should be exercised:

*She bought them **cheap**.*
*She bought them **cheaply**.*

*Do it up **tight!***
*Do it up **tightly!***

*Drive **slow** and live!*
*Drive **slowly** and live!*

*Hold it **close** to you.*
*Hold it **closely** to you.*

Although the above forms without -*ly* look like adjectives, they clearly distribute like adverbs. Many English adverbs lack the -*ly* ending for historical reason (they are **flat adverbs**) but that ending is sometimes extended to them. Consequently, some adverbs can exist in two forms, one with the -*ly* ending and one without, as in *cheap* and *cheaply* and *slow* and *slowly*, which are merely alternate adverb forms. (However, some users of English may resist using words like *cheap* and *slow* as adverbs when alternates such as *cheaply* and *slowly* exist.)

# 2.7  Class Boundaries

Words ending in -ing or -ed (or some variant of the latter) may or may not be verbs; they may also be nouns or adjectives. They may also be used as verbs, in positions generally occupied by adverbs. In other words many of these words are not really typical members of the classes they find themselves in.

The -ing ending is a simple derivational suffix that marks nouns in words (usually denoting concrete objects) like *building, railing, painting, ceiling, opening,* and *closing.* Such -ing words are freely inflectable for the plural: *buildings, railings, paintings, ceilings, openings,* and *closings.* In addition in the following uses the -ing ending is usually regarded as marking a variety of noun, sometimes referred to as a **gerund** or **verbal noun**:

> *Singing is fun.*
> *The dancing went on all night.*
> *He likes fishing.*
> *His drinking is excessive.*
> *There was no chance of winning.*

Note that such nouns have no possibility of taking the plural inflection: *Singings are fun.* It is obvious too that either the verb or noun aspect of a gerund can be emphasized by adding further elements:

> *He likes the good fishing.* (with noun-like emphasis)
> *He likes fishing that stream.* (with verb-like emphasis)

In the following examples the -ing is usually regarded as marking a variety of adjective because of the resulting gradability:

> *an interesting example*
> *an amusing character*
> *her fascinating account*
> *a trying time*

In these cases we can easily insert *very, rather,* or *quite* before the -ing form, e.g., *a very interesting example.*

However, in the following cases the -ing forms are clearly not gradable and are therefore perhaps best regarded as verb forms:

> *her dying wish*
> *an ailing friend*

*a falling star*
*the skidding vehicle*

A sentence like *He was entertaining* is ambiguous out of context. Its meaning depends on whether *entertaining* is treated as an adjective or as a verb. In *He was very entertaining* we have an adjective – note the presence of the intensifier *very* – and in *He was entertaining his friends* we have a verb – *was entertaining* is actually the full verb form taking a grammatical object *his friends*.

The following -*ing* forms are the **present participles** of verbs:

**Weeping**, *the girl left the room.*
*He died* **laughing**.
**Seeing** *him enter, we stood up.*

In each case there is a very clear grammatical relationship between the -*ing* word, i.e., the present participle, and a noun phrase in the sentence which serves as the subject of that verb: **The girl** *was weeping,* **He** *was laughing,* and **We** *saw him enter.* If this relationship is violated as in *\*Playing in the garden, the window got broken* (where the window was not playing in the garden but someone who broke the window was), we have a **dangling participle**.

The -*ing* is a genuine verb inflection in the following examples. Note that they do not have any of the possibilities outlined above for -*ing* nouns, gerunds, adjectives, or participles:

*He was* **going** *home.*
*They have been* **growing** *roses for years.*
*He was* **entertaining** *his friends.*

With the -*ed* the choice is between adjective and verb in most cases. The -*ed* ending is attached to a noun rather than a verb in the following examples: *a* **walled** *garden, a* **skilled** *worker, a* **salaried** *employee, a* **gifted** *student, a* **winged** *creature,* etc. The resulting forms behave like certain adjectives we have seen. The possibility of the occurrence of *very, rather,* or *quite* would also seem to indicate that the following -*ed* forms are adjectives:

*It was a (very)* **isolated** *place.*
*He's (very)* **tired** *now.*
*She is a (rather)* **worried** *woman these days.*
*They were (quite)* **bored** *by it all.*

In the following examples opinions may differ as to whether the -*ed* forms are adjectives or verbs:

*He has **fallen** arches.*
*It's an **unwarranted** intrusion.*
*She assisted an **injured** spectator.*
*He fixed the **broken** window.*
*The **engaged** couple left.*

However, the *-ed* ending is clearly a verbal inflection, a past participle, in the following examples:

*He has **picked** the apples.*
*They have **broken** out of jail.*
*His leg was **broken** in the accident.*

The *-ed* past participle form of the verb is also used as follows:

*Badly **wounded**, he surrendered.*
*The meal, **burned** to a cinder, had to be thrown out.*

Note once again the requirement that we be informed of the subject of the past participle somewhere in the sentence: ***He was badly wounded*** and ***The meal was burned to a cinder.***

# 2.8   Other Parts of Speech

There are many other parts of speech but each must be identified solely through distributional criteria because none is formally marked through inflection and derivation as were many of the members of the classes discussed above. For example, there are various "joining" words, words that join or combine with other words, phrases, or clauses. These are sometimes called **conjunctions** and **prepositions**.

There are three kinds of conjunction: **coordinating**, **subordinating**, and **correlating**. Coordinating conjunctions are words like *and* and *but*. They usually coordinate similar structural elements in the language, e.g., pairs (or multiples) or identical parts of speech, phrases, clauses, etc. Coordinated elements have the same "weight."

*Jack **and** Jill left.*
*He did it **but** she refused.*

Subordinating conjunctions are words like *because*, *if*, and *when*. In this case the element headed by the subordinating conjunction has less "weight" than the element to which it is attached.

*I took it **because** it belonged to me.*
*If you see him, tell him I'm coming.*
*Do it **when** you are ready.*

Correlating conjunctions are pairs of words like *either* and *or*, *not only* and *but also*, and *whether* and *or*. Correlated elements are equally "weighted."

**Either** *Sally* **or** *Fred should tell him.*
**Not only** *was he late* **but** *he was* **also** *quite insolent.*
*I am leaving* **whether** *you are finished* **or** *not.*

Another class of words is sometimes referred to as **conjunctive adverbs.** These words distribute in some ways like conjunctions and in some ways like adverbs. They are words like *however*, *moreover*, and *nevertheless*. There is an equal "weight" relationship between the elements that are joined but the conjunctive adverbs are moveable:

*John left; Mary stayed,* **however.**
*John left;* **however,** *Mary stayed.*
*He broke it;* **moreover,** *he intended to break it.*
*She was asked not to go, but she went* **nevertheless.**

**Prepositions** are usually single words used in phrases in which they are said to govern either a noun or pronoun (but more properly, as we will see in the following chapter, a noun phrase) which follows the preposition. They are words like *to*, *at*, *over*, and *between*:

**to** *Frieda*, **at** *home*, **over** *the top*, **between** *them*

Certain groups of two or more words also seem to function as **complex prepositions:**

**because of** *the war*, **on account of** *his illness*, **in spite of** *the danger*, **in case of** *fire*, **instead of** *me*, **aside from** *that*

It is probably impossible to say just how many parts of speech there are altogether in English. For example, it is quite easy to argue that each of the following is a separate part of speech because each is unique in its characteristics: each of the verbs *be*, *do*, and *have*; the articles (or determiners) *the* and *a*; the demonstratives *this* and *that*; the various quantifying words like *many*, *few*, *less*, *all*, *none*, and *any*; intensifiers like *very*, *rather*, and *quite*;

the numerals, both the **cardinals** such as *one*, *two*, etc. and the ordinals such as *first*, *second*, etc.; the conjunction *for*; the modal verbs *shall*, *will*, *may*, *can*, and *must*; the conjunctive adverbs; and various individual words like *so*, *not*, *even*, *nor*, *and*, *such*, *one*, *well*, *anyway*, etc.

The preceding discussion shows that we gain only a very little understanding of how English works by placing words into the traditional eight parts-of-speech classes through use of the criteria that many grammar books employ. Such an exercise tells us next to nothing about English because it largely ignores the criteria that are significant. If we believe that words do fall into various classes and sub-classes – and that is a reasonable belief as we have seen – we must try to find the significant criteria in the language. As we have seen, these criteria are those of form, i.e., inflectional and derivational marking, and distribution, i.e., how words are used in relation to one another. Unfortunately, they do not produce the neat results of the eight parts-of-speech system but what results they do provide give us much more insight into how English works – at one level at least – than certain neat but essentially uninformative accounts.

As two final examples of just how difficult it is to come up with a brief, neat statement we have only to examine the five instances of *round* and the fifteen instances of *that* which occur in the following two sets of sentences. How many different "words" do we have here, i.e., how many different "meanings" are there for *round* and for *that*? How many different parts of speech are there and what should each be called? (Some tentative answers are suggested to this last question.)

*They began a new* **round** (noun) *of talks.*
*She pointed to a* **round** (adjective) *area in the middle.*
*Please* **round** (verb) *it off.*
*He went* **round** (preposition) *the corner for a while.*
*She'll come* **round** (adverb) *to our point of view.*


*Go and ask* **that** (determiner) *man.*
*I want* **that** (demonstrative pronoun).
*He's not* **that** (intensifying adverb) *fat.*
*They died* **that** (conjunction) *we might be free.*
*It was then* **that** (complementizer) *I noticed her.*
*He took the piece* **that** (complementizer) *I wanted.*
*She said* **that** (complementizer) *John could do it.*
*He said* **that** (complementizer) **that** (determiner) **that** (noun) **that** (complementizer) *you used should have been* **this.**
*He said* **that** (complementizer) **those** (determiner) **thats** (noun) **that** (complementizer) *you used should have been* **thises.**

# 2.9  Exercises

1   Assign every word in the following sentences to a part-of-speech category, trying both "traditional" criteria and those used in this chapter. The first one is done for you.

(a)   The little boy sat on the wall.
(Traditional: determiner/article/adjective; adjective; noun; verb; preposition; determiner/article/adjective; noun. Here: determiner/ article; adjective; noun; verb; preposition; determiner/article; noun)
(b)   They very quickly ate up the food.
(c)   What a horrible, decaying, old, red brick house!
(d)   I saw a couple of sparks and then heard a rather big bang.
(e)   'Twas brillig and the slithy toves
Did gyre and gimble in the wabe:
All mimsy were the borogoves,
And the mome raths outgrabe.

2   On what principle is each of the following noun plurals formed by those who use such plurals?

cherubs, auditoriums, court martials, lieutenant governors, Walkmans, syllabuses

3   What difficulties do you find, if any, in deciding just what part of speech each of the following italicized words is: noun or adjective? The first one is done for you.

(a)   She wore *black.*
(*Black* is in a position a noun would normally fill; however, it has no determiner and cannot be pluralized. In this way it resembles a mass noun like *hope* or *courage*. It is also the kind of word that can take the comparative -*er*, but not here, nor can it follow the intensifier *very* here. So it is neither a typical noun nor a typical adjective; it has characteristics of both.)
(b)   *Pink* is a color.
(c)   Give it to the woman in *red.*
(d)   The appeal of the *new* is sometimes very attractive.
(e)   These *reds* are brighter than those.
(f)   The *English* united with the *French* in Canada.
(g)   She's a leading *intellectual.*
(h)   They welcomed both *young* and *old.*
(i)   We have two *females* and one *male.*

4   Here is an English word coined for this exercise: *brug.* From the following sentences what can you say about both its form and its meaning? Why can you say this?

(a)   He learned a new brug.
(b)   Give me some more brugs.
(c)   He kept on brugging the crowd.

(d)   It's a rather bruggy thing to do.

(e)   She's quite a brugster.

(f)   No brugging allowed after dark.

5   *It* is a pronoun in each of the following sentences. But just what does *it* refer to in each sentence? The first one is done for you.

(a)   Play *it* again, Sam.
(*It* refers to something that both Sam and the person making the request know.)

(b)   I like *it* here.

(c)   I would hate *it* if she found out about the money.

(d)   I love *it* when they dress up.

(e)   *It's* good that you did *it* for him.

(f)   *It's* five o'clock.

(g)   Was *it* raining at the time?

6   How would you classify each of the following *-ing* words? The first two are done for you.

a *cunning* response (Since you can introduce *very* between *a* and *cunning* this suggests that *cunning* is behaving like an adjective here.), No *smoking* (The position is one typically filled by a noun, e.g., *No pets* and *No entry*; however, the *-ing* is a verb ending unlike the *-ing* of *No railings*. A typical verbal noun, i.e., gerund.), pleasure *boating*, a *promising meeting*, an *enterprising* individual, He stopped *laughing*, the *prevailing* wind, their *wedding*, an *exciting* incident, I enjoy *surfing*, She came in *laughing* to herself.

7   What part of speech is *ever* in each of the following sentences? If your answer is "adverb" how useful is it? That is, are there any other adverbs which have similar characteristics to *ever*?

(a)   He ate his biggest meal *ever*.

(b)   He's for *ever* doing it.

(c)   It's *ever* so good.

(d)   Will they *ever* learn?

(f)   He's been unhappy *ever* since.

(g)   Is she *ever* cute!

8   What meaning relationships appear to be expressed in the following inflectional and periphrastic genitives? The first three are done for you.

my brother's keeper (objective), Lady Chatterley's Lover (objective), Mozart's Requiem (origin), Krapp's Last Tape, The Emperor of Ice Cream, the Ides of March, Dante's Inferno, The Birth of a Nation, Portnoy's Complaint, the Dance of the Seven Veils, Whistler's Mother, the March of Dimes, Sally's illness, six weeks' pay, a glass of wine, John's picture

9   What is the structural difference between the following sentences? How does it affect the meanings of the sentences?

(a)   God helps those who help themselves.

(b)   God help those who help themselves!

# 3
# Constituents and Phrases

Only in a very narrow and uninformative sense are utterances and sentences constructed out of words. Whenever we put words together to form multi-word utterances or sentences, we must do so in a systematic fashion. There are only certain kinds of arrangements (or structures) that are possible and we use these over and over again. We will call such structures **syntactic structures**, and it is the purpose of this chapter to look at those we use to put together a variety of types of phrase in English. It is also necessary to know how phrases are constructed in English in order to gain a proper understanding of the structures of clauses and sentences. A **phrase** itself is the smallest syntactic arrangement in the language. However, we will also use the term to cover certain cases in which there is actually only one word because, as we will see, the entities which we will describe as phrases may be realized by single words.

## 3.1  Constituency

A phrase is a **construction** of some kind. By construction we mean a syntactic arrangement that consists of parts – usually two – called **constituents**. For example, the phrase *the man* consists of two constituents *the* and *man*:

Traveled slowly is also a construction with its constituents *traveled* and *slowly*:

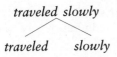

The sentence *The man traveled slowly* can be analyzed as a construction with two constituents *the man* and *traveled slowly* with each of these constituents also being a construction. There are therefore constructions within constructions.

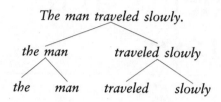

We can further increase the number of constructions in, and therefore the constructional "depth" of, the above sentence. For example, if we add *old* between *the* and *man*, *very* before *slowly*, and *unfortunately* at the very beginning of the sentence, we produce the following arrangement of constructions and constituents:

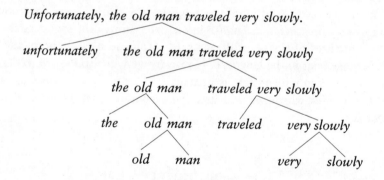

The above example illustrates how it is possible to show constructional relationships among the various parts of phrases, clauses, and sentences. We will shortly try to provide a little more evidence for justifying what we have just done here, i.e., claim that certain words, etc. are constituents of certain constructions. Such a claim denies other possible claims about constituency. For example, it denies the claim that in the final sentence given above there is any immediate constructional relationship between *man* and *traveled* or between *traveled* and *very*.

The constituents of a construction are likely to number just two and to be adjacent to each other. Analysis into constructions is not without its problems, however. For example, in the first of the following sentences there appear to be three constituents *sings*, *acts*, and *dances* plus the problem of *and*, and in the second sentence there is a definite discontinuity between *can* and *go* in the *can go* constituent.

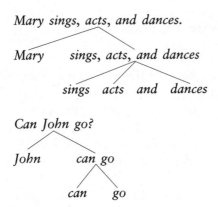

*Mary sings, acts, and dances.*

*Mary     sings, acts, and dances*

*sings    acts    and    dances*

*Can John go?*

*John      can go*

*can      go*

In the first case what has happened here is that *and* is one of those words (conjunctions) which can unite any number of constituents. In the second case it is the very characteristic of discontinuity which operates to signal a particular type of structure in English, in this case a question requiring either *yes* or *no* for an answer. Here is still another example of how the constituent structure of a sentence is built up hierarchically:

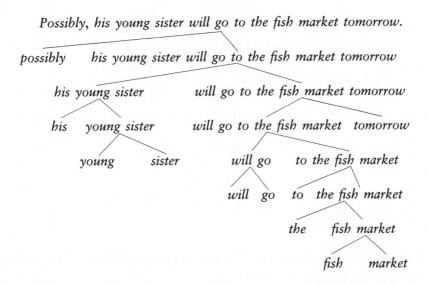

*Possibly, his young sister will go to the fish market tomorrow.*

*possibly     his young sister will go to the fish market tomorrow*

*his young sister          will go to the fish market tomorrow*

*his  young sister     will go to the fish market  tomorrow*

*young     sister     will go     to the fish market*

*will   go     to   the fish market*

*the      fish market*

*fish     market*

Phrases, clauses, and sentences are built up out of constructions even though the actual constructions involved may not always be easy to diagram. We will find more than one reason for such difficulties in later chapters, particularly in chapters 7 and 8. The immediate problem we should address though is just what kinds of constructions we have and how we should describe them.

## 3.2   Noun Phrases

A **noun phrase** (NP) is a construction that typically has either a noun (N) or a pronoun (Pro) as its central constituent, i.e., that noun or pronoun must be regarded as the "head" or most important element in the phrase. Any other constituent or constituents present in the noun phrase are usually said to be involved as **modifiers** of this constituent, i.e., they tell us something about it. Each of the following is a noun phrase with its head noun or pronoun given in boldface:

> *people*
> *he*
> *the* **man**
> *this French* **cheese**
> *all those other* **cheeses**
> **someone** *else*
> *a* **person** *your age*
> *a* **book** *that long*
> *the* **man** *to see*
> *the* **people** *at the back of the room*
> *the* **person** *who told me*
> *the* **place** *to be this year*

*The man* has the following constituents, a noun (N) and a determiner (Det):

We should observe too that the single word *people* can be labeled in this way because it is also a noun phrase:

Actually all nouns are NPs no matter where they occur, e.g., *man* in *the man* above, but we will refrain from such labeling.

As we will see later, we will also want to apply the term **noun phrase** to certain constructions that are not headed by nouns or pronouns, e.g., those indicated in the sentences that follow:

> *I knew **he could do it.***
> *To travel hopefully **is better than** to arrive.*
> *Marrying him **was a mistake.***

The reason for such an assignment is a distributional one. Such constructions occur in positions in sentences that the kinds of noun phrases given above usually fill.

> *I knew **the man.***
> *This French cheese **is better than** all those other cheeses.*
> *That reply **was a mistake.***

Whatever else such constructions may be they are also noun phrases. This is yet another instance of how we must take both form and distribution into account in describing the structure of English. Formally, we have an entity of one kind, e.g., a clause or a verb phrase, but, distributionally, it is an entity of another kind, in the above cases a noun phrase.

Our concern here is with noun phrases containing noun or pronoun heads, especially the former. Certain nouns can occur by themselves as complete noun phrases, e.g., **proper nouns** (*London, John, Canada*), plural **countable** nouns (*cats, books, pencils*), and **mass nouns** (*cheese, air, courage, love*).

> *London **is an** historic city.*
> *I like cats.*
> *Love makes the world go round.*

A very frequent initial constituent of a noun phrase is a **determiner** (Det) such as *the, a, my, this, some*, etc. Here are some noun phrases beginning with determiners:

> *the boy, a girl, my friends, their car, this apple, some money, any hope, each day, much effort, every moment, no time*

There are also certain **predeterminers** (Predet) which sometimes combine with determiners but, if they do, precede them, e.g., *all, both, half, double, once, twice, one-half, such*, etc.

> *all the books, once a week, such an effort, half the day*

Certain **quantifying** expressions, which themselves are noun phrases, also precede nouns, e.g., *a few, three dozen, ten million*, etc.

*a few friends*
*three dozen eggs*
*ten million dollars*

A group of **postdeterminers** (Postdet) can follow the determiners, e.g., *one,*
*two, three* (the **cardinal** numbers), *next, last, other, few, little, many, several,*
*more, less, only,* etc.

the **other** day, my **last** dollar, every **second** week, some **more** wine, the
**only** reason

Note that the predeterminers and postdeterminers may be regarded as sub-
classes of determiners and some may occur alone with nouns, e.g., *such*
*efforts,* **little** *hope,* etc.

We can now look at some of the various combinations that can occur:

He spent **such a lot** of money.
It rained **all the first** week.
He paid **twice the last** amount.

The presence or absence of determiners in noun phrases can either have
certain semantic implications or be a matter of common usage:

**Dogs** are **animals**. (all dogs, type of animal)
**A dog** is **a nice animal**. (all dogs, a nice type of animal)
**The mammoth** is extinct. (all mammoths)
I was looking for **a book**. (either any book or a specific book; therefore,
    Did you find **one**? or Did you find **it**?)
Love **God** and shun **the Devil**! (*the God, *Devil)
**The poor** are always with us. (a class of poor people)
Never let **a friend** down. (any friend)
Can you play **chess**? (*the chess: many games have no *the*)
Do you eat **pork**? (*the pork: many foods have no *the*)
She takes **the pill** every day. (a specific pill for birth control)
I visited **the Louvre**. (part of a proper noun)
Is **the train** on time? (a specific known train)
Please put **the kettle** on. (*kettle: some common implements or furnish-
    ings require *the*)
We went by **taxi**. (*the taxi: some forms of transportation have no *the*)
Have you had **lunch**? (*the lunch: no *the* with meals)
Did you eat **the lunch** I left? (a specific lunch)
He's at home in **bed**. (*the home, *the bed: fixed expressions)

Let us now look briefly at the constituent structure of some noun phrases.

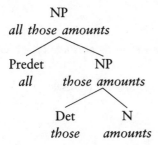

*Those amounts* is shown here as an NP within an NP; it is obviously a phrase and can only be a noun phrase.

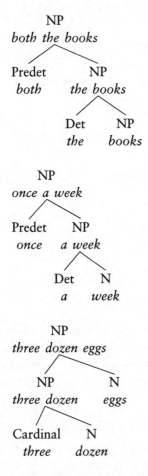

There are further possible components of the noun phrase. **Adjective phrases** (AdjP) often consisting of just **adjectives** (Adj) alone can be introduced between determiners and nouns. When more than one such adjective occurs, there is a fairly fixed ordering of the adjectives. One possible statement about such ordering is as follows:

general + size + shape + age + color + substance + nationality + NOUN

We can see how this ordering applies in the following phrases:

*a **good, new** coat*
*a **big, old** cat*
*the **small, red** card*
*a **black, plastic** spoon*
*an **old, Dutch** innkeeper*
*the **red, woolen** dress*
*a **lovely, big, square, wooden** table*
*an **expensive, old, white, French** tablecloth*

We can show the internal structure of *the small, red card* as follows:

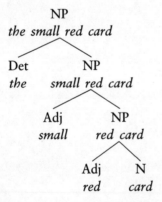

A close inspection of the above diagram shows that *red card* is described as an NP, as is *small red card*, and *the small red card*. *Card* itself is an N (and an NP too if completely labeled). One test that each of these constructions is itself a constituent is a substitution test using the word *one*, which substitutes for an NP constituent in English:

the small red card
the small red *one*
the small *one*
the *one*
*one*

This substitution test shows quite clearly how one construction can be embedded in another of the same kind.

When adjectives modify nouns they do not all do so in the same way. Note that *black insect* merely describes an insect that is black in color; however, *large insect* describes an insect that is large as insects go; there is an implied comparison with a norm. We can see this same kind of norm in the use of the adjectives in the following phrases:

> *a **tall** man, a **sharp** needle, a **little** elephant, a **big** meal*

We can compare the above with the following phrases in which no such norm seems to be implied:

> *a **young** man, a **sharp** ear, a **little** noise, a **big** tent*

Other adjectives do not so much describe the **agent nouns** with which they occur but appear to indicate how the referents of those nouns perform a certain activity:

> *a **good** writer* (writes well)
> *a **beautiful** dancer* (dances beautifully)
> *a **heavy** drinker* (drinks heavily)
> *a **light** sleeper* (sleeps lightly)

Notice that *beautiful dancer* is actually ambiguous: "she is a dancer and she is beautiful," or "she dances beautifully" but we do not know what she looks like. Consequently, we can have *She's a beautiful dancer but she's really quite ugly*.

A few adjectives follow the noun in a noun phrase:

> *inspector **general**, heir **apparent**, China **proper**, the amount **due**, the information **available**, the people **concerned***

Indefinite pronouns may also sometimes be modified in this way:

> *nothing **good**, something **interesting**, anything **worthwhile***

Other kinds of components may be inserted into noun phrases before the noun. Nouns and noun phrases may be used as modifiers:

> ***stone** wall, **business news** report, **language acquisition** device, **knife and fork** meal, **bacon, lettuce, and tomato** sandwich*

In *stone wall*, for example, while both words are nouns the head of the noun phrase is *wall* and *stone* is a modifier. We can see the difference between noun and adjective modification of a noun in the following pairs. In the first member of each pair we have noun modification of a noun and in the second member we have adjective modification of a noun:

> a **stone** wall      a **stony** silence
> a **gold** watch      a **golden** sunset
> a **blood** sample      a **bloody** scene

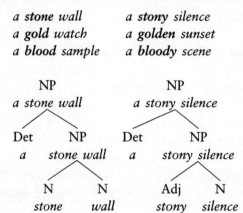

It is also possible to use the genitive form of a noun or a genitive noun phrase as a modifier of a noun: ***John's** hat*, ***the boy's** aunt*. Verbs (V) may also be used as modifiers of nouns: *a **failed** attempt*, *a **running** sore*. Adverbs (Adv) too can modify nouns: *the **upstairs** room*.

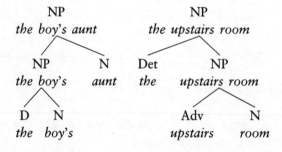

There is a fixed ordering in the various combinations of the above:

> *two new running sores*
> *a big old stone house*
> *Wednesday's business news report*
> *a leaking upstairs tank*

Each of the above also has a constituency structure. For example, the constituency structures of *a leaking upstairs tank* and *Wednesday's business news report* are as follows:

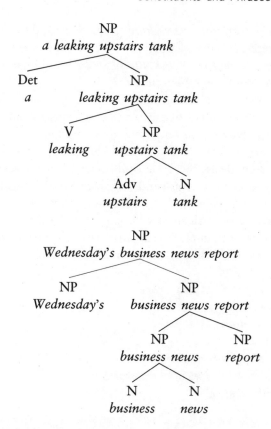

Noun phrases may also contain modifiers after the noun heads other than the adjectives noted above, i.e., *nothing **good**, inspector **general***. Adverbs may be used as modifiers: *the way **in**, the weather **outside***. So may prepositional phrases: *a piece **of cake**, the boy **at the back**, the girl **behind Peter***.

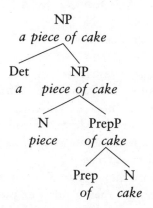

Clauses (S) beginning with words like *who, that, where, when*, etc. may be used as modifiers: *He **who hesitates** is lost, the place **where we are going**, the*

*time **when you spoke**, the **person you are seeking**.* Such clauses are called **relative clauses**. Certain verb-headed constructions may also be used: *the amount **owing to you**, a house **rented to him**, the place **to be***; as may appositives: *the fact **that you said it**, my husband **Fred**.*

An **appositive** is a restatement of a certain kind and it may be **restrictive** or **non-restrictive**. In the above examples *that you said it* is restrictive in *the fact **that you said it**,* whereas *Fred* is non-restrictive in *my husband **Fred**.* In the first case it is this important fact – that you said something – not any other that is at issue; in the second case the name *Fred* is merely an additional piece of information provided about the husband – he happens to be called Fred. (Of course there is just a possibility that *Fred* could be restrictive but then the speaker would have to be a bigamist who is naming Fred out of a set of husbands!) In the following examples the appositives in the first set are restrictive and the appositives in the second set are non-restrictive:

> *I am looking for the novel **War and Peace**.*
> *My cousin **Fred** sent it.*
> *The word **the** is a determiner.*

> *They are from Mali, **a country in Africa**.*
> *He borrowed a book, **a collection of short stories**.*
> *My cousin, **Fred Smith**, sent it.*

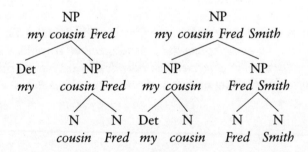

A fairly useful test of non-restrictiveness versus restrictiveness is to try to recast the phrase: if you can omit the appositive and supply the information it contains as "by the way" information, then it is non-restrictive, e.g., "They are from Mali and by the way Mali is a country in Africa." If you cannot do this, you have a restrictive appositive, e.g., it makes no sense to say "I am looking for a novel and by the way it is *War and Peace*."

We can also find phrases in clauses that are filling noun-phrase positions but which are headed by a part of speech other than a noun or pronoun: adjectives in *The **poor** are always with us*; ***Green** is my favorite color*; various verb forms in ***Seeing** him restored her confidence, **To do** is to be*; an adverb in ***Now** is the hour*; and a prepositional phrase in *from **under the bed**.* The typical noun-phrase position in clauses may be filled by almost anything: a letter (or sound) in *A is the first letter of the alphabet*; a word part in *Un- is a prefix*; a word in *Quietly is an adverb*; a phrase in *I said **at the back***; and a clause in *She noticed **what he did***. In the following diagrams Adj/(N), VP/(NP), and PrepP/(NP) are to be interpreted respectively as an adjective filling a typical noun position, a verb phrase filling a typical noun phrase position, and a prepositional phrase filling a typical noun phrase position.

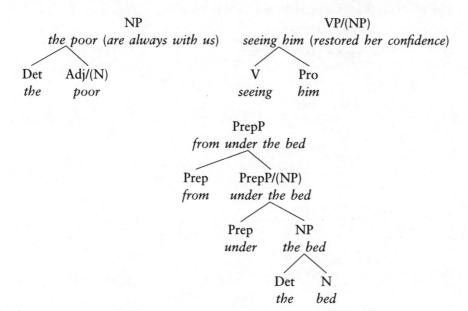

If we examine the noun phrases in the following sentences, we can see how they are different in structure.

*She's **a sex-movie star**.*
*She's **a sexy movie-star**.*

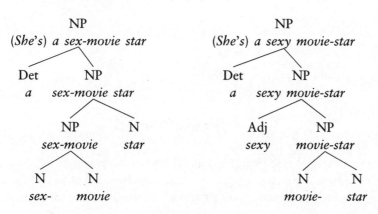

Now we can look at two further sentences which are identical so far as their words are concerned; however, the punctuation indicates that in one case she is a star in silent movies and in the other case that she is a movie star who is silent.

> *She's a silent-movie star.*
> *She's a silent, movie-star.*

The two constituent structures are as follows:

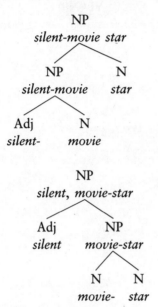

Noun phrases may also be conjoined and the conjoined noun phrases themselves form a new noun phrase: *Jack **and** Jill*; *the passengers **and** their luggage*; **both** *those who stayed **and** those who left*; *the ship **and** all who sail in her*; *Friends, Romans, **and** countrymen*

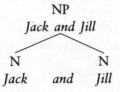

## 3.3  Adjective Phrases

A typical **adjective phrase** (AdjP) has an adjective constituent at its head. Just as single nouns are also noun phrases single adjectives are adjective phrases: *an **old** man, Sally is **clever***. Some adjectives are usually the sole realizations of the adjective phrases in which they occur:

*former, inner, outer, upper, mere, latter, main, principal, sheer, live*

Examples are *the **former** president, **inner** peace*, and *the **principal** cause*. The constituency structure of *an old man* is as follows:

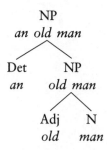

The adjective *old* is an AdjP just as the noun *man* is an NP.

Many adjectives take a premodifier: an **intensifier** (Int), such as *very, rather, quite*, etc. or an adverb (Adv) or even certain noun phrases:

**very** *cold*, **rather** *tired*, **extremely** *interesting*, **dark** *red*, **a yard** *long*, **a year** *old*, **a mile** *high*, **two inches** *thick*, **a little too** *big*.

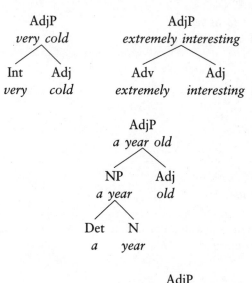

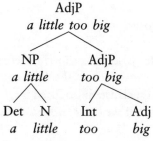

Adjective phrases often occur within noun phrases, i.e., they are used attributively, e.g., *a **very courageous** person.*

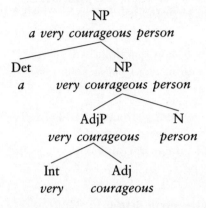

Adjective phrases that do not occur as parts of noun phrases, i.e., those that are used predicatively, show a considerable variety in their structures. Some require a **complement**, i.e., a further constituent to complete the whole construction, e.g., *apt, averse, fond, loath, subject, tantamount*:

> *He is **fond of chocolate**.*
> *The decision is **subject to appeal**.*
> *That's **tantamount to a confession**.*

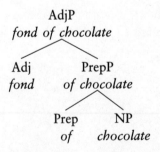

For others such a complement is possible but not obligatory, e.g., *successful, impatient, compatible, disappointed*:

> *John is **impatient**.*
> *John is **impatient to go**.*

There is also considerable variety possible in these complements. They may be prepositional phrases: *conscious **of the fact**, compatible **with the system**, amazed **at the consequences**;* clauses introduced by *that*, which may be omitted: *sure **that I knew**, amazed **that we came**, surprised **he spoke out**;* comparisons:

*happier **than he expected**, bigger **than the one he'd owned before***; and in-finitives: *certain **to do it**, wrong **to say so**, quick **to take offence**, difficult **to please***. Adjectives followed by infinitives may express a wide variety of mean-ings as we can see from the following examples, for each of which a para-phrase is provided:

> *John is **certain to please**.* (I am certain that John will please.)
> *John is **difficult to please**.* (It is difficult to please John.)
> *John is **eager to please**.* (John is eager to please someone.)

Still further variations and combinations in the structure of adjective phrases can be seen in the following examples: both premodification and post-modification in *so **very knowledgeable about it***, conjoining of postmodifiers in *faithful **to queen and to country***; and various kinds of discontinuity in *an easy **wall to paint*** (*the wall is **easy to paint***), *a most **difficult** sonata **to play*** (*the sonata is **most difficult to play***), *a **much larger** car **than ours*** (*a car **much larger than ours***), and *too **cold** a day **to go fishing*** (*a day **too cold to go fishing***).

It is now possible to show the constituent structure of an adjective phrase such as *so very knowledgeable about food* as follows:

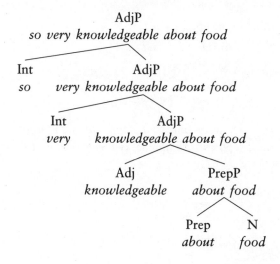

## 3.4   Prepositional Phrases

A **prepositional phrase** consists of a preposition, e.g. *in, to, at, over*, etc., as its head constituent and the **complement** or **object** of that preposition, typically a noun phrase: *in **China**, to **the back**, at **home**, over **the wooden bridge***. However, other kinds of complements may occupy this noun-phrase position, e.g., adverbs and various other phrases and clauses: *up **above**, near* *here, over **there**, to **what he said**, with **what you took**, by **saying those words**.* A prepositional phrase may also contain other such phrases within it:

> *at the back **of the house.***
> *at the top **of the stairs in the rear***

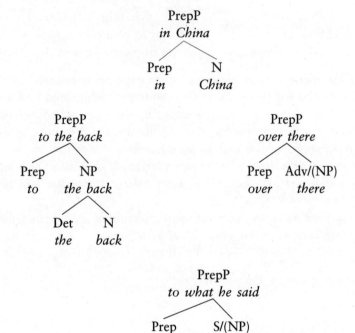

The constituent structure of the noun phrase *a young woman in the car*, which contains within it the prepositional phrase *in the car*, is as follows:

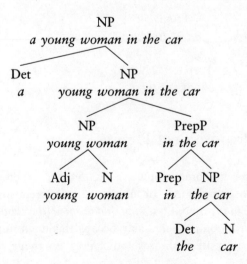

Some two- or three-word combinations, the complex prepositions, behave like single-word prepositions, e.g. *according to, away from, due to, by means of, in comparison with, in front of, in relation to, on top of* (in contrast to *on the top of*):

> *According to Sally, everything is taken care of.*
> *He's away today due to illness.*
> *On top of everything else that's too much.*

A prepositional phrase may also occasionally itself take a modifier: *right to the end, a mile behind the truck, a week before the trip, two years after the war.*

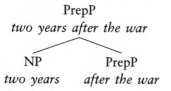

The justification for such an analysis resides in the interpretation of a sentence like *He stayed right to the end*: *right* can be omitted (*He stayed to the end*) but *to the end* cannot (\**He stayed right*).

The prepositions in prepositional phrases may become separated from their noun phrases as in the following examples, although some such uses may meet with disapproval from language "purists," i.e., prescriptivists.

> *The house I live in is over there.*
> *Who was the man you spoke to?*
> *Where did you leave from?*
> *What were you thinking about?*
> *He's easy to talk to.*
> *What did you do that for?*
> *It's going to be talked about for years to come.*

In such examples it is also difficult to show the constituent structure of the prepositional phrases because of the resulting discontinuities.

## 3.5 Verb Phrases

A **verb phrase** typically has a verb as its head. The phrase itself may be **finite** or **non-finite**, i.e., it may be marked for **tense** or not so marked. The verb phrases – in each case everything except the first word (which is an NP because the typical sentence itself has two constituents, an NP and a VP) – in the following sentences are finite and the verb actually marked for tense is given in boldface. However, those parts of the verb phrases included in the parentheses will not be of concern to us in this chapter but will be of concern in the chapter that follows when we look at **complements** and **predicate adjuncts** in some detail. From the following examples it is also apparent that the verb phrase in its entirety may contain within it a variety of other types of phrase.

> *She **likes** (Elvis).*
> *They **left** (yesterday).*
> *He **will** be going (there tomorrow).*
> *He **hasn't** done (it yet).*
> *We **couldn't** have known (that).*
> *He **has** been (very sick).*
> *I **don't** know (his address).*
> *I **may** have been told (about it).*

The boldfaced verb phrases contained in the following sentences are non-finite and fill positions in clauses usually filled by noun phrases; they there-fore distribute like noun phrases even though each is clearly a verb phrase so far as its form is concerned. The total finite verb phrase in each sentence is enclosed in parentheses.

> ***To know all** (is to forgive all).*
> *He (**likes to sing**).*
> ***Living dangerously** (has its own rewards).*
> *He (**likes playing the fool**).*

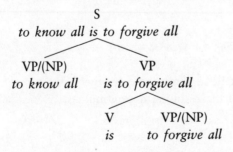

Restricting our concern therefore to the verbal part of finite verb phrases, we can observe that they contain an obligatory tense marking on the first verb of the phrase. That marking is for either **past tense** or **present tense**. Past tense indicates in some sense that an action or state has been "completed" relative to either the present moment or some past time. Sometimes the term **non-past** is used in preference to **present** for the other tense because of examples such as the following in which the verb indicates time extending beyond some kind of "present" moment, either "future" or "past, present, and future":

>   I *leave* for Rome tomorrow.
>   I always *like* to be informed in advance.
>   He *isn't* feeling well.

However, we will continue to use the traditional term **present tense** for this tense.

There are several additional optional elements in the verb phrase. One or more of the following elements may occur: modal verb, perfective aspect, progressive aspect, and passive voice. When more than one of these occurs, the order is as just stated. It is the first constituent of the resulting verb phrase that is marked for tense.

**Modality** refers to the possible worlds in which the state or event denoted by the verb is situated: the kinds of truth, possibility, necessity, etc. that must exist there. The modal verbs are *can, may, will, shall,* and *must*.

>   He *can* do it.
>   They *will* follow.
>   You *must* go.

The modal verbs are complicated in the kinds of meanings that they express. It is possible to try to make a distinction between their **epistemic** uses and their **deontic** uses; in practice, however, the distinction is not always clear. Epistemic uses are concerned with the speaker's knowledge or belief about the proposition that is being conveyed in the utterance. If it is a statement, the proposition in a sentence containing an epistemic modal may be true or false. If it is not a statement, the proposition it expresses may also be true or false.

>   He *may* go tomorrow. (or he may not – I'm not sure)
>   He *can* speak French. (I believe so from what I know of him)
>   He *must* have a wife. (because he said he was married)
>   John *will* sing at the party. (because he always does)
>   We *should* know tomorrow. (because the results are to be announced then)
>   *Can* he move it by himself? (because he seems strong enough)
>   *Would* he agree? (or not?)
>   She *must* know that. (because she's a physician and all physicians know that)

Deontic uses are concerned with the necessity, obligation, or possibility of acts which are to be performed by those responsible for them. They are also future-oriented.

> He *may leave.* (now that he's answered my question)
> He *can speak French.* (because he has my permission to do so)
> He *must do it.* (or we are lost)
> He *will go.* (or my name's not Captain Blood)
> *Truth will out.* (it always happens)
> *They should tell him.* (they have an obligation to do so)
> *May I sit down?* (Do I have your permission?)
> *Must you charge her?* (Are you obliged to do so?)
> She *must know that.* (because she cannot be left in ignorance)

Out of context – and sometimes even within context – a sentence with a modal may be ambiguous in that it may allow both epistemic and deontic interpretations.

> *She must know that.*
> *He may leave.*
> *John will eat the spinach.*

(Some users of English may insist that sentences like *Can I open the window?* (Do I have your permission?) are "incorrect" because *can* must be epistemic in this use (Do I have the ability?) not deontic; hence the response sometimes given to the question: *Yes, you can, but you may not.*)

A small group of verbs that appear in verb phrases are sometimes called **periphrastic modals**. They are given here following their normal modal equivalents:

| | |
|---|---|
| *can* | *be able to* |
| *will* | *be going to, be about to* |
| *must* | *have to, have got to* |
| *should* | *ought to, be to, be supposed to* |
| *would* | *used to* |
| *may* | *be allowed to* |

**Aspect** refers to the way in which a particular state or event expressed in the verb is viewed, e.g., its beginning, middle, or end, or its duration, continuation, or repetition. English has **perfective** and **progressive** aspects in its grammatical system. The perfective aspect covers a period of time stretching into the past beyond whatever time is indicated in the tense of the verb. It is realized by the **auxiliary verb** *have* and the past participle of the following verb, the *have+-en* combination. (Henceforth, we will use *-en* for the past participle form of the verb in order to contrast this form with *-ed*, the past tense form of the verb.)

> *I **have been** ready quite a while.*
> *She **had known** him for a year when he died.*

The progressive aspect is realized by the auxiliary verb *be* and the present participle of the following verb, the *be+-ing* combination:

> *John **is watching** a movie.*
> *They **were studying** Latin.*

Some verbs, called **stative verbs**, are not usually found marked for the progressive aspect: *be, see, hear, feel, taste, smell; know, believe, doubt, understand, remember; want, desire, like, love, dislike, hate; weigh, cost, measure, equal; have, own, contain, entail, belong*:

> *He **is** silly.*
> *I **see** what you mean.*
> *I **feel** good.*
> *The rabbit **tastes** good.*
> *The book **weighs** five pounds.*
> *They **like** spinach.*
> *They **have** a nice house.*

However, such verbs can be used with the progressive aspect when they are used for "actions," i.e., non-statively:

> *He **is being** silly.*
> *He **was seeing** her at the time.*
> *They **were feeling** the material for its quality.*
> *The rabbit **was tasting** the lettuce.*
> *The butcher **was weighing** the meat.*
> *They **are liking** spinach more and more each day.*
> *We **are having** some friends over this evening.*

(Aspectual-type characteristics are also conveyed in English through the use of certain verb sequences beginning with verbs such as *begin, continue, keep on,* and *finish,* e.g., *She **began** to sing, They **kept on** dancing.*)

With some verbs, called **transitive verbs**, i.e., verbs that can take one or more **objects**, the **passive voice** may be present in the verb phrase. It is realized by a combination of the auxiliary verb *be* and the past participle of the following transitive verb, the *be+-en* combination.

*The picture was taken at that moment.*
*John is accused of perjury.*
*He was asked to leave.*

(See chapter 6 for further discussion of **actives** and **passives**.)

As indicated above, the order of these possible constituents of the verb phrase is as follows, with the parentheses indicating optional components:

tense (modal) (*have+-en*) (*be+-ing*) (*be+-en*) VERB

We should observe once again that tense (present or past) and the *-en, -ing,* and *-en* of the optional two aspects and one voice constituents actually attach themselves to following verbal constituents. Here are some examples:

*present go → go+present*
**go** (or **goes**)

*past go → go+past*
**went**

*present will have+-en go → will+present have go+-en*
**will have gone**

*past may be+-ing speak → may+past be speak+-ing*
**might be speaking**

*past have+-en tell → have+past tell+-en*
**had told**

*past have+-en be+-ing run → have+past be+-en run+-ing*
**had been running**

*past can have+-en be+-en inform → can+past have be+-en inform+-en*
**could have been informed**

(It is of some interest to observe that we could also describe what happens above by saying that each verb moves to the left of any adjacent affix on its left and then the affix attaches to it. The final result would be exactly the same.)

There are two possible constituency structures for each of the above arrangements. We can use the last example to show the constituency structure (here given unlabeled) of the verb phrase that actually occurs in the language, i.e., of the verb phrase *could have been informed*:

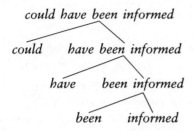

*could have been informed*

We can also show the constituency structure of the constituents of tense, modality, and aspect of *could have been informed* as follows:

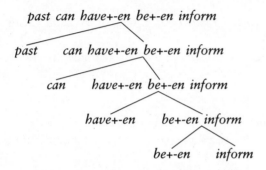

Combinations of tense, modality, and aspect can be used to express a variety of time and meaning relationships in the verb phrase, many of which can be shown as follows. Within single clauses the following combinations refer to present time:

*present*

*He **likes** cheese.* (a state)
*I **quit**.* (a unique event)
*I **work** hard.* (a habit)
*All men **are** mortal.* (a timeless truth)
*He **swings**. He **misses**.* (current action)

*present be+-ing*

*He's **getting** up.* (a temporary occurrence)
*She's **working** regularly these days.* (a temporary habit)

The following combinations refer to past time:

*past*

*He **lived** there at one time.* (a completed state)
*I **did** it.* (a completed event)
*I **liked** him a lot.* (a past habit)

*present have+-en*

*He's lived here ten years.* (a state existing to the present)
*I've worked hard all my life.* (a habit existing to the present)
*I've heard that before.* (the past is relevant to the present)
*You've burned the toast!* (the present result of a past event)

*present have+-en be+-ing*

*He's been standing outside for an hour.* (a temporary state existing to
   the present)
*He's been swimming since he was two.* (a temporary habit existing to
   the present)
*They've been drinking* (the present result of a temporary action)

*past have+-en*

*He had been there once before.* (the remote past)
*We had known her for ten years.* (a state existing to a point in the past)

*past be+-ing*

*They were reading the newspaper.* (the temporary past)

*past have+-en be+-ing*

*They had been waiting for him to pass.* (a temporary state relevant to
   some past time)

There are future time combinations:

*present*

*He goes tomorrow.* (a future known event)

*present be+-ing*

*They are leaving next week.* (a commitment for the future)

*present will/shall*

*John will come tomorrow.* (a future anticipated event)

*present will/shall have+-en*

*We **will have** finished it by then.* (the past viewed from the future)

*present will/shall be+-ing*

*You'll **be** hearing from us soon.* (a future intention)
*We **will be** doing that at noon.* (a future temporary event)

When verb phrases containing modal or auxiliary verbs are **negated**, the first verb in the verb phrase is followed by the negative, either *not* or its contracted form *n't*:

*You may do it.*        *You may **not** do it.*
*He will go.*           *He **won't** go.*
*I have seen him.*      *I **haven't** seen him.*
*They're going.*        *They're **not** going.*
*They're ready.*        *They **aren't** ready.*
*He was injured.*       *He **wasn't** injured.*

When there is neither a modal nor an auxiliary *have* or *be* in the verb phrase, the verb *do* is introduced along with the negative. It becomes the first verb in the verb phrase and consequently also carries the tense marking:

*He sings.*                       *He **doesn't** sing.*
*They played hard yesterday.*     *They **didn't** play hard yesterday.*

We also find that a non-finite, i.e., tense-less, verb phrase can be used in a clause in which it has a close relationship to a noun phrase in an accompanying clause containing a finite, i.e., tensed, verb:

***Being alerted**, he avoided the unlit street.*
***Badly burned**, the bread had to be thrown away.*
***To become proficient**, you must study hard.*
***By trying to avoid the dog**, he made things worse.*

(An adjective phrase may also be found in the same relationship: ***Angry with the results**, he stormed out.*) In these sentences *he had been alerted, the bread had been burned*, etc. We can call such a non-finite verb phrase a **phrasal adjunct**: it provides additional information about a noun phrase.

The complete verb phrase in a clause consists of the central verbal constituent, which has been our concern in this chapter, together with any **complement** or **predicate adjunct**. Various kinds of complements, i.e., obligatory constituents, are illustrated below. We will deal with them in some detail in the chapter that follows.

*John read the book.*
*Sally wrote her mother a letter.*
*We elected her treasurer.*
*They made her happy.*
*Juan is an engineer.*
*That flower is beautiful.*
*He is outside.*
*He put the book away.*
*He wants to go.*
*I said that he should do it.*
*We criticized Mike's reporting of the incident.*

Typical predicate adjuncts, i.e., optional constituents, are as follows:

*We played ball outside.*
*They left on Tuesday.*
*She did it because I asked her.*

# 3.6   Adverb Phrases

An **adverb phrase** (AdvP) typically has an adverb as its head and as its only
constituent, e.g., *silently* and *outside*, as follows:

*He did it silently.*
*He stood for a long time outside.*

The adverb may be modified in various ways, e.g., by an intensifier, **very
quietly**, by another adverb, **right outside**, by a prepositional phrase, **worst of
all**, or by a clause, **earlier than we expected**.

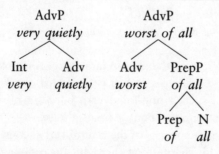

Adverb phrases are often found as internal constituents within other phrase
types. The following adverb phrases are all constituents of the indicated
phrase type:

noun phrase

*nearly all the books*
*such a mess*
*the man outside*
*that there book* (where such a phrase is used)
*the then president*
*quite a surprise*
*the biggest win ever*
*the day before*
*the above example*

adjective phrase

*extremely sorry*
*good enough*

prepositional phrase

*just outside London*
*right into the crowd*
*dead against it*

verb phrase

*was driving slowly*
*is living here*
*stood outside*

Semantically, adverb phrases tell us about the "how," "when," "where," "wherefore," etc. of "things," "actions," and "events." Such a semantic approach leads to attempts to classify any kind of phrase which performs such a semantic role as an adverb phrase. In that case an adverb phrase, as classified by distribution, may be comprised, in terms of form, of a noun or noun phrase as in *He works evenings* and *He died a rich man*, an adjective in *He died rich*, or an adverb in *He stood there*. It may be a noun phrase as in *He left, a book in each hand*, *He died a hero*, and *They resigned a long time ago*. It may be an adjective phrase as in *He believes in her, right or wrong*. It may be a prepositional phrase as in *John went to the movies* and *He was on time*. It may be a clause that contains a finite verb, as in *He did it when he was ready*, or an infinitive, as in *You'll have to be smart to outwit her*.

Adverb phrases are often classified **semantically**, i.e., by their meanings. One simple classification, undoubtedly not exhaustive, is as follows: **place** (or

**locatives**) like *there, in bed, at home*; **manner** like *thoroughly, quietly, with great care*; **time** (or **temporals**) like *yesterday, in June, during the war, for ten years*; **frequency** like *occasionally, every day*; and **purpose** or **reason** like *for the glory, because he was angry*.

Within clauses adverb phrases may have considerable freedom of movement but the resulting sentences rarely have exactly the same shade of meaning:

> *He left **very suddenly**.*
> *He **very suddenly** left.*

The adverb phrase *very suddenly* is in construction with *left* in each case and is a predicate adjunct. Compare these sentences with the following one:

> ***Very suddenly**, he left.*

In this sentence *very suddenly* is in construction with *he left* and is a **sentence adjunct**. An alternative way of writing this sentence might be:

> *He left, very suddenly.*

When more than one adverb phrase occurs within a verb phrase, there seems to be a preference for the following order: single words followed by prepositional phrases followed by clauses:

> *He went there by taxi because he was in a hurry.*
> *We went out in the rain when the party ended.*

There is also perhaps some preference for the following semantic ordering:

> place    manner    time    frequency    purpose/reason

> *He stood there quietly.*
> *She spoke carefully yesterday.*
> *We went there frequently.*
> *He enlisted in June for the glory.*

As we will see, many adverb phrases are used as **predicate adjuncts**, i.e., optional elements in the verb phrases in which they occur:

> *He left (**quietly**).*
> *They did it (**without any fuss**).*

However, adverb phrases are sometimes necessary **complements** of the verb phrases in which they occur; they cannot be omitted:

*Put it there.* (\**Put it.*)
*John is at the back.* (\**John is.*)
*We were on time.* (\**We were.*)

One kind of adverb phrase performs a special connective function. The particular words that occur in this kind of phrase are sometimes called **conjunctive adverbs**: *however, moreover, nevertheless, furthermore.* They not only join clauses but also can occur in different positions in the conjoined clause.

*He did it; he didn't have to do it, **however**.*
*He did it; **however**, he didn't have to do it.*

Finally, we sometimes find certain kinds of adverb phrases in constructions that produce a kind of "comment" on the utterance to which they find themselves attached, e.g., *naturally, fortunately, obviously, realistically,* etc. We should also note the freedom of movement that such adverb phrases have:

*__Obviously__, I think he's right.*
*I, **obviously**, think he's right.*
*I think he's right, **obviously**.*
*What, **realistically**, would you say it is worth?*
*__Naturally__, they did it.*
*They did it, **naturally**.*
*They, **naturally**, did it.*

We will call such sentence adverbs **disjuncts**. A disjunct is an adverb phrase that provides a kind of "frame" for the clause that it accompanies. Note that these last three sentences differ from the following sentence in which *naturally* is a predicate adjunct and part of the verb phrase, telling us how they did something:

*They did it **naturally**.*

Further examples of this kind of disjunction, not necessarily restricted to adverbs alone, may be found:

*__To be accurate__, there were twelve not eleven present.*
*__Funnily enough__, he doesn't know.*
*__Of course__, you'll get one.*
*__Seriously__, are you going?*
*He was out at the time, **fortunately**.*
*__Obviously__, you'll accept the offer.*
*It's a question of trust, **essentially**.*
*__Strictly speaking__, a tomato is a fruit.*

*Technically, he's not qualified for the position.*
*He comes in on Tuesdays, as a rule.*
*Anyway, why do it at all?*

We can see the difference between the disjunct *unfortunately* and the predicate adjunct *recklessly* in the following sentences if we try to switch their positions:

*Unfortunately, he drove home recklessly.*
*\*Recklessly, he drove home unfortunately.*

For many speakers of English *hopefully* is an adverb that belongs to the set of disjuncts; others accept it only in sentences like the first sentence that follows but reject it in the second and third:

*Hopefully, I can speak to her before she leaves.*
*Hopefully, the meeting will be over soon.*
*Hopefully, he won't come after all.*

## 3.7    Exercises

1   What are the component constituents of each of the following italicized verb phrases? The first three are done for you.

(a)   He *could do* it.
      (past can do)
(b)   She *had been* there.
      (past have+-en be)
(c)   He *has been visiting* her regularly.
      (present have+-en be+-ing visit)
(d)   They *might be coming* next week.
(e)   They *are* very good friends.
(f)   I *did* it yesterday.
(g)   He *has* a new car.
(h)   You *must have been told*.
(i)   *Have* you *seen* her?
(j)   He *went* there the other day.
(k)   She *has been going* out a lot recently.
(l)   We *had told* them about it.
(m)   They *could have left*.
(n)   The votes *are being counted*.
(o)   I *should be writing* to them soon.
(p)   They *must be* sad.
(q)   She *willed* it to happen.
(r)   It *should be* ready now.
(s)   John *has been informed* of our decision.

2  What is the constituent structure of each of the following labels found in a market selling fish and meat? The first two are done for you.

(a)  baby lobster tails

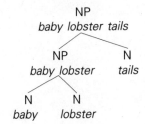

(b)  fresh deep sea scallops

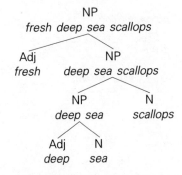

(c)  fresh red snapper fillets
(d)  fresh American white shrimp
(e)  extra lean fresh pork tender loin
(f)  fresh Ontario pork back spareribs
(g)  BBQ time boneless top sirloin steak
(h)  extra jumbo shrimps
(i)  fresh Atlantic salmon fillets
(j)  baby tiger shrimps

3  Diagram the constituent structure of each of the following italicized sentence parts. The first two are done for you.

(a)  It's *a very good idea.*

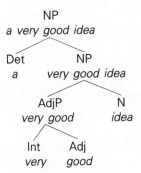

(b)   It's *an old iron fence.*

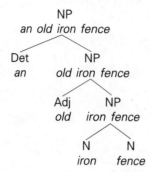

(c)   It's *a large, rambling, old house.*
(d)   It's *an ice-cold drink.*
(e)   *Lucille Ball, America's first lady of comedy,* died.
(f)   Look at *the boys at the back of the room.*
(g)   Please *seat the boys at the back of the room.*
(h)   It's *a rather sad story.*
(i)   I admired *his long but ultimately unsuccessful attempt.*
(j)   It's *his friend's cat.*
(k)   It's *his friend, the neighbor's boy.*
(l)   Enjoy *a free week of television.*
(m)  Store *in a cool and dry place.*
(n)   Go *to where they are standing.*
(o)   He took it *from behind his back.*
(p)   He read poetry *the night before the battle.*
(q)   She went *right up into the attic.*
(r)   He's *six feet tall.*
(s)   It was *a ten foot drop.*
(t)   He left *immediately after lunch.*
(u)   *At the top* is the only place to be.
(v)   She *threw out the rubbish.*
(w)  He ordered *a bagel with cheese and coffee.*

4   Diagram the constituent structure of each of the following phrases. The first one
    is done for you.

(a)   an inside the park home run

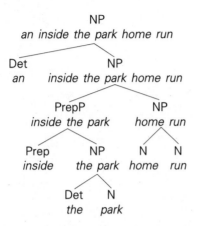

(b)   your lawyer friend's first court appearance
(c)   a fashion buyer for young contemporary women's wear
(d)   two dozen fire hardened floor tiles
(e)   my cousin Fred's restaurant business

5   Which bracketed words are also constituents in the following sentences? The
    first two are done for you.

(a)   [The boy] took a [very big] bite.
      (Both are constituents.)
(b)   The girl in [the red] suit [looks like] Sally.
      (Neither is a constituent, but *red suit, the red suit,* and *like Sally* are con-
      stituents.)
(c)   The [young man] has been [waiting there] [about ten] minutes.
(d)   [Go] and [get me] some three [inch nails].
(e)   He [picked out] the book [he] wanted to [give me].
(f)   His [friend's dogs] are [big and noisy].
(g)   [Her new] coat has [large leather] buttons.
(h)   My [wife's cousin] taught English [for years] at a [liberal arts] college.

6   The following sentences are ambiguous. For each diagram construct two differ-
    ent constituent trees, one for each meaning. The first one is done for you.

(a)   They have wounded people there.

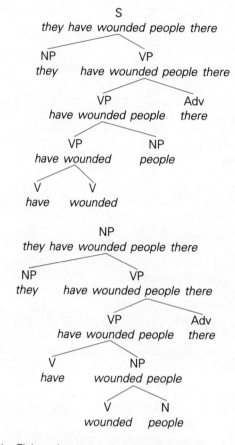

(b)   Flying planes can be dangerous.
(c)   Leslie is the son of Frank's daughter.
(d)   John took the book from the library.

7   Provide possible interpretations for each of the following uses of a modal verb.
    The first two are done for you.

(a)   He must know that.
      (1 Because of his background there is no way he does not know some-
      thing. 2 He does not know something so he must be told.)
(b)   She can't walk yet.
      (1 She lacks the ability to walk, e.g., she is only six months old. 2 She must
      wait a little while before she tries to walk again.)
(c)   You will tell lies!
(d)   He can deliver it tomorrow.
(e)   He must resign immediately.
(f)   There must have been an accident.
(g)   We could swim there at one time.
(h)   You must be John!

(i)   We shall overcome.
(j)   You may be right.
(k)   I must object to what you have just said.
(l)   I can see you.
(m)   She will tell him tomorrow.
(n)   You should explain yourself.
(o)   He'll be in Tokyo now.
(p)   That'll do!

8  Standard English has certain requirements that phrasal adjuncts must meet. Each of the following phrasal adjuncts "dangles," i.e., fails to meet a basic requirement. What is that requirement? How should the sentence be recast to meet it? The first one is done for you.

(a)   While reaching for the hammer, his hand was caught.
      (*Reaching* requires a subject somewhere in the sentence; rewrite as *While reaching for the hammer, he caught his hand.*)
(b)   By loosening the rope, the pain diminished.
(c)   Going into Paris, everything was quite recognizably unchanged.
(d)   Feeling thirsty, the glass of water tasted good to him.
(e)   To become a pilot, good vision is necessary.
(f)   Having been reprimanded by his boss, a pay raise seemed unlikely.
(g)   Ordered to leave, a look of contempt appeared on his face.
(h)   Angry at the accusation, a plan formed in her mind.
(i)   Approaching the crossroads, a collision seemed inevitable.

9  This sentence should probably never have appeared in this form in the *Toronto Star*. Why?

Our religion editor re-tells the story of Jesus' birth to a virgin in a stable in Bethlehem in his first article of a series.

# 4
# Basic Clauses

The **clause** is the smallest syntactic unit that is capable of being used completely independently in a language. The previous chapter dealt with various kinds of phrases as syntactic units because phrases are the smallest syntactic units. However, phrases do not usually occur independently. Whenever a phrase does occur by itself, we must rely on the context for full understanding. That is, a noun phrase such as *John Smith* requires some kind of question to elicit it (*What's your name?*), or is a social offer that John Smith himself is making (e.g., naming himself for some purpose), or, if said with a rising pitch (*John Smith?*) is a question. These are but some of the possibilities. *John Smith* is interpretable only from context. Each of the following also requires a context for full interpretation:

*At the back.*
*Really blue.*
*Will do.*
*Obviously.*

In this chapter we will consider a clause to be a construction that has a noun phrase, which we will call a **subject**, followed by a verb phrase, which we will call a **predicate**, with **subject-verb agreement** between that subject and predicate. This latter condition will restrict our concern to **finite** clauses, i.e., clauses that contain verbs with a tense marker. We will also be concerned only with single independent clauses.

## 4.1  Predicates and Roles

In one view the central components in any clause are the **predicate**, narrowly defined as the verb, of the clause and a number of **roles** (or **arguments**) associated with that predicate. For example, the predicate of the following clause is *strike* and there are three roles, *man, nail,* and *hammer*:

*The **man** strikes the **nail** with the **hammer**.*

Some of the same roles also occur in the following sentences:

*The **nail** is being struck with the **hammer**.*
*The **hammer** strikes the **nail**.*

We can give names to these three roles: *man* is an **agent** in the sentence in which it occurs and *nail* is a **patient** and *hammer* is an **instrument** in all three sentences.

There is a variety of roles that noun phrases can fill. These roles can be described as follows:

**agent**: an animate instigator of the action of the predicate

***John** took the apple.*

**patient**: an animate or object undergoing the action expressed in the predicate

*Fred washed the **dishes**.*

**experiencer**: an animate that experiences the action of the predicate

***John** thought hard about it.*

**instrument**: an object used in an action

*The **key** opened the door.*

**goal**: the end point toward which something moves

*We went to **New York**.*

**source**: the originating point from which something moves

*He took it from **Fred**.*

**location**: a place in which an action or state is located

*He lives in **Washington**.*

**benefactive**: an animate that is the beneficiary of the action expressed in the predicate

*They made the bed for **her**.*

**temporal**: a time at which some action occurs

*They left on **Thursday**.*

In this view clauses with different grammatical structures may have similar predicates and roles. For example, the following sentences

*The man took the money.*
*The money was taken by the man.*

are essentially identical in that each has the verb *take* as its predicate, *man* as an agent, and *money* as a patient. The sentence *The money was taken* differs from both of the above only in that the agent is unmentioned, i.e., we do not know who did the taking.

It is also possible to describe predicates, i.e., verbs, in terms of the roles that must accompany them. For example, *die, cry,* and *smile* seen to require only a single role, an experiencer. *Kill, catch, imitate, have,* and *believe* require at least two roles but not always the same two. The first three require an agent and a patient:

*The **man** killed the **mouse**.*
*I caught the **ball**.*
*John imitated Fred's **accent**.*

*Have* and *believe* do not take an agent; rather they take an experiencer as subject:

*She has a cold.*
*Sally believed the story.*

We can note that the agent need not actually occur in the first three cases but must be understood to occur:

*The mouse was killed* (by some agent).
*The ball was caught* (by some agent).
*Fred's accent was imitated* (by some agent).

In this way we can understand that verbs like *shave, wash, write, read, drink, eat,* etc. must be understood as having both agent and patient roles:

*John washed* (patient) *before leaving.*
*They drank* (patient) *heavily that night.*
*I was reading* (patient) *at the time.*

Verbs like *ask*, *buy*, and *give* require three roles although once again all three need not occur but, if they do not, must be understood to occur:

> *I* (agent) *gave her* (goal) ***something*** (patient).
> *He* (agent) *bought it* (patient) (from source).

Some verbs clearly have a patient as their subject and some other role left unexpressed; however, it may not be clear what that role is:

> *The door opened.*
> *The glass broke.*
> *The car started.*
> *The bell rang.*
> *The ice melted.*
>
> *This pen writes well.*
> *The plane flew smoothly.*
> *My car ran badly.*

The term **ergative** is sometimes used for predicate structures of this last kind.

Finally, the verb *be* is probably best not described as a predicate in the above sense:

> *John is here.*
> *Fred is happy.*
> *The dog is a spaniel.*

In the above clauses it is really *here*, *happy*, and *spaniel* that are in some kind of predicate relationship with *John*, *Fred*, and *dog* respectively rather than with the verb *is*. We can compare such sentences with those that follow:

> *Fred seems happy.*
> *The dog appears to be a spaniel.*

Once again "happiness" is being predicated of "John" in the first case and *seems* is a genuine predicate; however, the role that this predicate relates to is "John's happiness." Likewise, in the second sentence "the dog's spanielness" is one predication and the "appearance" of that another. We will return to this issue in chapter 8 in a discussion of **raising**.

## 4.2  Subjects

As indicated in the introductory remarks to this chapter, a clause is often said to be most easily described as a grammatical construction consisting of a subject and a predicate in that order. As we will see, the **subject** of a clause is not necessarily what the clause is "about," nor is it necessarily the noun phrase which one may consider to be the "theme" or the "topic" of the clause, nor is it always the first noun phrase in the clause:

> *Everybody loves John.*
> *The details we left to Paul to clear up.*

The first clause seems to be about John, and the topic of the second seems to be certain details, with *details* itself in the first position in the clause and the grammatical object of *clear up*. However, the actual grammatical subjects of the clauses are given in boldface.

Subjects also have various role relationships to verbs in the predicates of the clauses in which they occur. The subject may be an agent:

> *John took the apple.*
> *John opened the door.*
> *The boy read very badly.*

The subject may be a patient:

> *John was injured.*
> *The door opened easily.*
> *This house shows well.*
> *The paragraph read badly.*

The subject may be an experiencer:

> *She sighed.*
> *They considered the evidence.*

The subject may be an instrument:

> *The key opened the door.*
> *The flood destroyed the house.*

The subject may be a benefactive:

> *John won the prize.*
> *Sally received a standing ovation.*

Other roles are possible too. The subject may also be "empty" and filled by a special filler like *it* or *there*:

*It's decent of you to say that.*
*There's a man outside to see you.*

The verb *be* must also have a subject; there is no particular role relationship in such cases between that subject and *be*. (Any relationship that exists is between the subject and the complement, i.e., whatever follows *be*.)

**John** is **outside**.
*Those* **students** *are* **brilliant**.
**Nancy** *is a* **surgeon**.

Whatever its semantic relationship to the verb, the subject (here parenthesized) is the noun phrase that determines **agreement** with the verb that carries the tense-marking in the predicate:

*(May)* **likes** *\*like John.*
*(They)* **eat** *\*eats out quite often.*
*(Over the fence)* **is** *\*are out.*
*(They)* **are** *\*is outside.*
*(John)* **is** *\*are here.*
*(Swimming there)* **was** *\*were a favorite activity of theirs.*
*(To be)* **is** *\*are to do.*
*(That you know who took it)* **is** *\*are quite apparent.*
*(John)* **has** *\*have left.*
*(They)* **were** *\*was eating pizza.*

Subjects have certain other characteristics. The subject position is usually the first noun phrase in a clause. Phrases of other types than noun phrases may fill noun-phrase positions. In the above examples *over the fence* is a prepositional phrase filling a subject noun-phrase position and *swimming there* is a verb phrase similarly filling a noun-phrase position. It is possible to substitute a personal pronoun for the noun phrase that is subject. In the above cases that pronoun is *it*:

**Over the fence** *is out.*
*It is out.*

**Swimming there** *was a favorite activity of theirs.*
*It was a favorite activity of theirs.*

That pronoun will assume either the *he*, *she*, or *they* form rather than the *him*, *her*, or *them* form when such substitution is possible.

*John* did it.
*He* did it.
*\*Him* did it.

In *That you know who took it is quite apparent* the subject noun-phrase position is actually filled by a clause (*that you know who took it*). In most cases such a sentence is usually recast as *It is quite apparent that you know who took it* by moving the original subject to the end of the sentence and filling the vacant subject place with *it*.

In certain kinds of questions the subject – here given in parentheses – **inverts** with the first verb of the verb phrase or with a tensed form of *do* if there is only a single verb other than *be* (and sometimes *have*) in the corresponding non-inverted verb phrase:

(*The boy*) **will** go.
**Will** (*the boy*) go?

(*John*) **is** here.
**Is** (*John*) here?
(*The football team*) **played** well.
**Did** (*the football team*) play well?

(*You*) **have** the size I need?
**Do** (*you*) have the size I need?
**Have** (*you*) the size I need?

*Where* **are** (*the girls*) *going?*
*Why* **does** (*your friend*) *say such things?*

(However, in questions of this last kind when the question word is itself the subject there is no inversion: **Who** is going?)

In **tag questions** such as *John's going, isn't he?* the pronoun in the tag – the *he* in this case – is determined by the subject of the clause on which the tag is formed, in this case *John*. In the following questions both the pronoun in the tag and the subject to which it is related are indicated:

**All the children** have gone, haven't **they**?
**The play** is over, isn't **it**?
**Over the fence** is out, isn't **it**?
**Telling lies** is bad, isn't **it**?
**There**'s a book missing, isn't **there**?

Subject noun phrases do not occur only in special cases, e.g., in commands:

*Stand up!*
*Work quickly and do a good job!*

In neither of these commands is there a subject before the verb, i.e., before *stand, work,* or *do.* (Sometimes a *you* subject is said to be "understood" in such cases.) The verb is the uninflected base form.

   If we use some of the characteristics just stated for subjects as tests in clauses beginning with **expletive *it*,** we will see that we must consider this *it* to be the subject of those clauses:

   *It's good to know that.*
   *\*It are good to know that.*
   *Is it good to know that?*
   *It's good to know that, isn't it?*
   *\*Is good to know that.*

In clauses beginning with unstressed **expletive *there*** the above characteristics again point to *there* being a subject, particularly if we describe *there* as a pronoun because of its use in tag questions:

   **There**'s a pencil in the box.
   *\*There* are a pencil in the box.
   Is **there** a pencil in the box?
   **There**'s a pencil in the box, isn't **there**?
   *\*Is a pencil in the box.*

We should note that when the noun phrase that follows the verb in such a clause is plural, the determination of the subject is not always so clear. In the first example below the subject-verb agreement is between *boys* and *are*, but the inversion and the tag characteristics suggest that *there* has also certain characteristics of a subject:

   There **are two boys** outside to see you.
   **Are there** two boys outside to see you?
   There **are** two **boys** outside to see you, **aren't there**?

It should not surprise us then that we often find examples such as the following:

   **There's two boys** outside to see you.

It appears that those who use utterances of this kind regard *there* as the subject of the verb for the purpose of subject-verb agreement.

# 4.3  Subject-Verb Agreement

**Subject-verb agreement** is usually a fairly clearcut matter in English. If the first verb of the verb phrase is in the **present tense**, it agrees with the noun phrase that is the subject. In all verbs except *be* if the subject is **third person singular** and the verb has a third person singular ending – and nearly all verbs have such an ending – that verb ending must be used. Otherwise the uninflected base form of the verb is used.

> *He eats cheese.*
> *They eat cheese.*
> *I eat cheese.*

In addition to the *is* form for third person singular, *be* has a special form of agreement *am* for the **first person singular** and it uses *are* rather than *be* elsewhere in the present:

> *Sally is happy.*
> *I am ready.*
> *We are students.*

In the **past** there is no overt subject-verb agreement of the same kind except to a limited extent with *be*, which has a special form *was* for the first person singular and the third person singular.

> *I took it.*
> *She took it.*
> *They took it.*

> *I was happy.*
> *She was present at the meeting.*
> *They were merchants.*

From time to time certain issues do arise in subject-verb agreement. If the subject is somewhat distant from the verb, some speakers may use another noun phrase than the subject noun phrase to determine agreement, specifically one closer to the verb:

> *The purpose of **these sessions are** to introduce and familiarize staff with the new manual.*

In this clause *the purpose* is the subject, but the agreement – the verb *are* – is made with *these sessions* in the prepositional phrase. This kind of agreement is usually edited out of careful speech and writing. Here are some further examples with both the ignored subjects and the verbs given in boldface:

> *They pointed out that **public perception** of the universities and the arts **are** changing.*
> ***Our client**, an expanding and go-ahead company, **are** looking for a new chief executive.*
> ***Any ship or aircraft** which penetrates the specified zone **will** be regarded as hostile and **are** liable to be attacked.*
> ***This kind** of apples **are** good to eat.*

If the head noun of the subject is a **group noun,** there may be uncertainty as to whether or not the agreement should be singular or plural, i.e., whether there should be grammatical (singular) or semantic (plural) agreement:

> *The **class has** voted to go.*
> *The **class have** voted to go.*

If the subject contains coordinated noun phrases, the agreement is usually with the second noun phrase when the two noun phrases differ in number:

> *Either Fred or **his cousins are** going.*
> *Either my aunts or **my mother is** going.*

We can see various kinds of agreement in the following sentences.

> *Pink and white **is** my choice for that room.*
> *The news **is** good.*
> **Between Friends** *is a coffee table book.*
> *The committee **are** agreed on the matter.*
> *The committee **is** in session.*
> *A number of mistakes **were** made.*
> *A number **was** drawn out of the hat.*
> *Three-quarters of the liquid **is** red.*
> *Three-quarters of the cookies **are** ready.*
> *Neither **is** ready yet.*
> *More than one piece **was** broken in the move.*
> *Her courage and fortitude **was/were** impressive.*
> *The public **is/are** tired of that.*
> *She is one of the lawyers who **own/owns** property near here.*
> *My friend and mentor, John Smith, lives there.*
> *Either my nose or my teeth **are** broken.*
> *Either my teeth or my nose **is** broken.*
> *Bread and butter **is** quite nourishing.*

# 4.4   Complements

The predicate of a clause contains a lexical verb and often one or more complements. **Complements** are constituents of constructions in which one constituent always **governs**, i.e., requires and controls, another constituent. In prepositional phrases such as *to John* or *for the money* the prepositions *to* and *for* govern the noun phrases *John* and *the money* respectively. In verb phrases such as *are outside, took the bicycle*, and *made him an offer* the verbs *are, took*, and *made* govern the complements *outside, the bicycle*, and *him an offer* respectively. Complements are obligatory constituents of such constructions.

We can classify English verbs into the following five typical categories so far as the complements they take are concerned: **intransitive verbs**, i.e., verbs that do not take a complement at all; **monotransitive verbs**, i.e., verbs that take one object as a complement; **ditransitive verbs**, i.e., verbs that take two objects as complements; **linking verbs**, i.e., verbs that take either a noun phrase or an adjective phrase as a **subject complement** or take an obligatory adverb phrase following *be*; and **object complement verbs**, i.e., verbs that take one object and either a noun phrase or an adjective phrase in a complementary relationship to that object.

Except for the adverb phrase mentioned in connection with *be* in the above case with linking verbs, all the complements we are considering are noun phrases or adjective phrases. When some other type of construction is used as a complement, it assumes some of the characteristics of the noun-phrase or adjective-phrase position it occupies. For example, in *He wants her to sing* the constituent *her to sing* assumes the characteristics of a noun phrase as we can see from the following examples:

> *He wants **her to sing***
> *He wants **it***
> *He wants **what?***
> ***What** does he want?*

> *He wants **the book**.*
> *He wants **it**.*
> *He wants **what?***
> ***What** does he want?*

That is, in each of the above clauses we can substitute a noun phrase, i.e., *the book, it*, or *what*, for *her to sing*.

We should also note that many English verbs can be found to occur in more than one of the above categories. For example, we can find *make* used as follows:

*She made **them**.* (monotransitive)
*She made **them some hot soup**.* (ditransitive)
*She made **them happy**.* (object complement)

Note that in the monotransitive sentence *them* is a patient. In the ditransitive sentence *hot soup* is a patient and *them* is a benefactive. In the object-complement sentence *them* is in a relationship with *happy* (which is the predicate in what can be called a **small clause**, i.e., a clause without a verb at all) and not with *made*: *She made [them happy]*.

Verbs that do not take complements are called **intransitive verbs**. Typical examples are as follows:

*Mary **left**.*
*They **advanced**.*
*They **are dancing**.*

Such verbs may be followed by **predicate adjuncts** of various kinds:

*Mary left **quietly**.*
*He left **the house**.*
*He died **laughing**.*

Many intransitive verbs seem almost to require an adjunct:

*He went **out**.*
*Sally came **on Monday**.*
*They worked **hard**.*
*He stayed **at home**.*
*Julius Caesar lived **a long time ago**.*

Note that in some of the above cases, particularly the last, it may not be possible to make a clear distinction between an adjunct and a complement.

Some intransitive verbs like *die, laugh, sleep,* and *breathe* may be found occasionally with **cognate objects**, i.e., objects that restate the verb in some way:

*He died **a good death**.*
*She slept **a sound sleep** that night.*
*He breathed **a loud sigh**.*

It is not possible to form **passives** from such uses:

**A loud sigh **was breathed** by him.*

Such verbs are therefore very like intransitive verbs, with the noun phrase that is the cognate object functioning like an adjunct.

Some intransitive verbs are followed by particles. Together the verb and particle form a **phrasal verb**:

> *The plane **took off**.*
> *They **got up** late.*

Verbs that take one object, called a **direct object**, as a complement are called **monotransitive verbs**. Typically they can also be used in the **passive voice**, i.e., the subject and the direct object can be reordered as follows:

> *The girl **read** the book.*
> *The book **was read** by the girl.*

> *The committee **fired** John.*
> *John **was fired** by the committee.*

> *The cat **has caught** the mouse.*
> *The mouse **has been caught** by the cat.*

In the passive the *by* phrase is often omitted to avoid mention of the **agent** subject of the corresponding **active**, i.e., non-passive, form:

> *John was fired.*
> *The mouse has been caught.*

These are called **agentless passives**. Some verbs that take direct objects cannot be passivized:

> *He **has** two good friends.*
> \**Two good friends **are had** by him.*

> *It **cost** five dollars.*
> \**Five dollars **were cost** by it.*

> *She **resembles** her mother.*
> \**Her mother **is resembled** by her.*

> *She **grew** six inches that year.*
> \**Six inches **were grown** by her that year.*

> *The bucket **contained** water.*
> \**Water **was contained** by the bucket.*

*This tent **sleeps** five people.*
*\*Five people **are slept** by this tent.*

Consequently, these verbs are sometimes called **pseudo-transitive verbs**.

After certain verbs the direct object is "understood" rather than mentioned, i.e., one of the accompanying roles is missing:

*They **are drinking.***
*Fred **is studying.***
*I **was shaving.***
*She **was dressing.***
*Sally **was reading.***

In such circumstances what is usually understood is a "typical" activity associated with each verb so that each of the following sentences seems peculiar if it is meant to convey the meaning indicated in the parenthesized part:

*He **was reading** (the label on a can).*
*He **was shaving** (a customer).*
*She **was drinking** (tea) heavily at the time.*

Some transitive verbs may have a following **particle**, which forms a **phrasal verb** in conjunction with the verb, e.g., *blow up* in:

*They **will blow up** the dam.*
*The dam **will be blown up** (by them).*

Some transitive verbs may be followed by a preposition and then the object of the combination of verb and preposition, e.g., *comment on* in:

*They **commented on** the photos*
*The photos **were commented on** (by them).*

Such verbs are called **prepositional verbs**. Some transitive verbs, **phrasal-prepositional verbs**, may also be followed by a combination of the above, a particle and a prepositional phrase, e.g., *do away with* in:

*They **should do way with** that rule.*
*That rule **should be done away with** (by them).*

We will have more to say about these three varieties of verb in the section that follows on **verb-particle constructions**.

In certain fixed expressions, which allow for little internal variation, a verb may be followed by a noun, which can be modified, and a prepositional phrase:

> I *caught* (*brief*) *sight of* him.
> John *got* *hold of* the broker.
> We *keep* (*careful*) *track of* all our expenses.
> They *took* (*tearful*) *leave of* their friends.
> I *lost touch with* Peter.
> They *took* (*considerable*) *advantage of* their position.
> *Take* (*a lot of*) *care of* it!
> Please *Pay* (*close*) *attention to* what I'm about to say.

Passivization is either awkward (*Advantage was taken by them of their position*) or impossible (\**Touch was lost with Peter by me*) with the above.

Passivization is not possible with the following types of complement. Many monotransitive verbs may be followed by a verb phrase headed by the **marked infinitive**, i.e., the infinitive with the *to* marker, as a complement:

> I *expect* **to see** him.
> He *wanted* **to go**.
> She *tried* **to swim**.
> He *remembered* **to buy one**.

A verb phrase headed by the *-ing* form of the verb is still another possible kind of complement:

> He *finished* **eating**.
> He *enjoys* **writing poetry**.
> She *avoided* **doing it**.

Some verbs take only this *-ing* construction, e.g., *avoid, enjoy, risk, admit, finish, deny, defend*; some take only the marked infinitive construction, e.g., *want, expect, hope, decide, refuse, plan, choose*; some take both, e.g., *like, begin, start, continue, try, regret, remember*:

> He *began* **to sing**.
> He *began* **singing**.
>
> We'll *try* **to do it**.
> We'll *try* **doing it**.

In both of the above constructions the subject of the clause is also understood to be the subject of either the marked infinitive or the *-ing* form:

*I* expect [*I* to see *him*].
*He* finished [*he* eating].
*He* began [*he* to sing].

The complements may also be finite clauses beginning with *that* (often omissible) or some other clause (finite or non-finite) introduced by *if*, *where*, etc. Sometimes *so* or *not* may be **substituted** for the clause:

*I* said (**that**) *he should go*.
*We* felt (**that**) *he could do it*.
*He* doubted **if they knew**.
*He* guessed **why they had gone**.
*He* knew **where to put it**.
*I* decided **who to ask**.
*I* believe **she's ready**.
*I* believe **so**.
*I* trust **he won't do it**.
*I* trust **not**.

It is also possible for a non-finite clause that follows a finite verb to include what appears to be the direct object of that finite verb. In such cases the relationship of that object to the non-finite verb within the complement is a subject-verb relationship:

*I* expect **her to see him**. (She sees him)
*He* let **her go**. (She goes)
*I* wanted **John to do it**. (John does it)
*They* wanted **us to stay**. (We stay)
*We* kept **them waiting**. (They wait)
*I* advise **you to leave**. (You leave)
*He* had **the roof fixed**. (The roof was fixed)
*They* made **John do it**. (John did it)

Note that passive equivalents do occur for some of the above, e.g., *She was let go* (*by him*) and *You are advised* (*by me*) *to leave*.

Verbs that take two objects as a complement are called **ditransitive verbs**. The first object is called the **indirect object** and the second object is called the **direct object**. With some verbs the indirect object, which is either the goal or the benefactive of the object, may be omitted but not the direct object:

*The woman gave* (**the man**) *a dollar*.
*He left* (**her**) *a lot of money*.
*She made* (**him**) *a sweater*.
*He poured* (**her**) *a drink*.

With certain verbs either object is omissible:

> *They asked (her) (a lot of questions).*
> *The girl told (me) (a story).*

The direct object cannot be a pronoun when both kinds of object occur:

> **I gave the boy it.*
> **She made him it yesterday.*

Another arrangement of the object noun phrases is usually also possible. The indirect object may be incorporated into a prepositional phrase introduced usually by *to* or *for*; in this case the prepositional phrase follows the direct object:

> *The woman gave a dollar to the man.*
> *He left the money to her.*
> *The girl told a story to me.*
> *She made a sweater for him.*

This rearrangement is mandatory when the direct object is a pronoun.

> *I gave it to the boy.*
> *I made it for you yesterday.*

Two passives are usually possible for ditransitive verbs, i.e., either object of the active verb can become the subject of the passive verb, and the *to* and *by* phrases are optional:

> *He left her a lot of money.*
> *A lot of money was left (to her) (by him).*
> *She was left a lot of money (by him).*
>
> *The girl told me a story.*
> *A story was told (to me) (by the girl).*
> *I was told a story (by the girl).*

The second object may be a finite clause introduced by *that* (which is omissible) or it may be either a finite or a non-finite clause introduced by a *wh-* word, or a non-finite clause alone:

> *I told him (that) we were going.*
> *I asked him who was coming.*

*I advised them **where to go**.*
*He told **me to go**.*

Only one passive is possible in such cases:

*He **was told** (by me) (that) we were going.*
*\*(That) we were going **was told** (to him) (by me).*
*He **was asked** (by me) who was coming.*
*\*Who was coming **was asked** (to him) (by me).*
*I **was told** to go (by him).*

Still other ditransitive verbs with no movement possible for the indirect object and with only a single passive possible in some cases are verbs like *fine, bet, forgive, charge, envy, refuse, spare, cost,* etc.

*The fined him ten dollars.*
*He was fined ten dollars (by them).*
*\*They fined ten dollars to him.*
*\*Ten dollars were fined (to him) (by them).*

*He bet me a dollar.*
*\*He bet a dollar to me.*
*\*I was bet a dollar (by him).*
*\*A dollar was bet (to me) (by him).*

*Forgive us our trespasses.*
*I envy you your choice.*
*They charged us a fortune.*

We can now see that a verb like *leave* may take a variety of complements:

*He left **the money**.*
*He left **her**.*
*He left **her the money**.*
*He left **the money to her**.*
*He left **her to sing**.* (which is ambiguous as to who sang)

**Linking verbs** are those verbs that take either a noun phrase or an adjective phrase as a **subject complement** or take an obligatory adverb phrase. When the complements of linking verbs are either noun phrases or adjective phrases, they give us further information about the subjects of those verbs. It is for this reason that they are called subject complements. When the complement is an obligatory prepositional phrase or adverb phrase with *be*, it gives us another kind of information about the subject, e.g., location, etc.

Noun phrases occur as subject complements in the following:

> *The teacher was **an old friend**.*
> *That was **the information he sought**.*
> *He seems **a good sort**.*
> *It's **mine**.*
> *They are **a fine couple**.*
> *His goal was **more weapons**.*

From the last two examples we can also observe that there is no necessary **number agreement** between the subject and the subject complement. Adjective phrases occur as complements in the following:

> *You are **very sensible**.*
> *Bill appears **uncertain**.*
> *The coffee tastes **good**.*
> *How do you stay **so young**?*
> *Keep **quiet**!*
> *Are you **afraid of flying**?*
> *It seems **certain to happen**.*
> *The picture looks **good**.*
> *He looks **well**.*
> *The milk turned **sour**.*
> *It tastes **bad**.*

With verbs like *seems* and *appears* it is also possible to introduce the *to be* infinitive in certain cases before the noun phrase or adjective phrase:

> *He seems **to be** a good sort.*
> *Sally appears **to be** uncertain.*

We also find non-finite clauses containing subject-less marked infinitives as complements after verbs like *be*, *seems*, and *appears*. In these cases there is a definite subject-verb relationship between the subject of the clause and the non-finite verb:

> *He is **to speak**.* (He speaks)
> *She seemed **to tire**.* (She tired)
> *They appear **to know**.* (They know)

Prepositional phrases or adverb phrases are the obligatory complements of *be* in the following clauses:

*They are **outside**.*
*He is **at the races**.*
*John and Mary were **in London**.*
*The water is **off**.*

Verbs that take an object and an object complement are called **object complement verbs**. The object complement can be either a noun phrase or an adjective phrase. This noun phrase or adjective phrase provides additional information about the object, again in another **small clause** arrangement. There is only one possible passive and there is no possible rearrangement of the noun phrases with *to* or *for*.

The object complement is a noun phrase in the following:

*We elected him **president**.* (He is president)
*He was elected **president** (by us).*
*\*President was elected (to him) (by us).*
*\*We elected **president** to him.*

*They considered the job **a success**.* (The job is a success)
*The club made him **secretary**.*
*We appointed her **treasurer**.*
*The news made me **very angry**.*

It is sometimes possible to insert *to be* between the object and the object complement:

*We elected him **to be** president.*
*They considered the job **to be** a success.*
*We appointed her **to be** treasurer.*

The object complement is an adjective phrase in the following sentences:

*You make me **very happy**.* (I am very happy)
*Please paint this room **pale yellow**.*
*She takes her coffee **black**.*
*I considered the excuse **quite unacceptable**.*

Passives are possible:

*Her coffee was taken black.*
*The excuse was considered quite unacceptable.*

Again, it is sometimes possible to insert *to be* between the object and the object complement:

*I considered the excuse **to be** quite unacceptable.*
*The excuse was considered **to be** quite unacceptable.*

## 4.5   Verb-Particle Constructions

As indicated in the previous section, there are various verb-particle combinations: **phrasal verbs**, **prepositional verbs**, and **phrasal-prepositional verbs**.

A **phrasal verb** consists of a verb and a particle. These particles look like adverbs but unlike adverbs they have little semantic content. We can note, for example, that *Slow down!* and *Slow up!* are alike in meaning so that *down* and *up* here do not have the kinds of meanings they have in *Hands up!* and *Hands down!* The verb-particle combinations may be either **intransitive** or **transitive**. Some intransitive examples are as follows:

> *The plane **took off** on time.*
> *They didn't **catch on**.*
> *We'll never **give in**.*
> ***Drink up!***
> *We'll never **give up**.*

Some transitive examples are as follows:

> *They **turned out** the light.*
> *We **blew up** the bridge.*
> *They **called out** the guard.*
> *They **brought up** the children.*
> *The court **handed down** its decision.*
> *Please **hand over** the money.*

We should note that the corresponding information-seeking questions include the particle:

> *When did the plane **take off**?*
> *What did they **turn out**?*
> *What did they **blow up**?*

When the phrasal verb is transitive, the particle may follow the object noun phrase:

> *They **turned** the light **out**.*
> *We **blew** the bridge **up**.*

*They **called** the guard **out**.*
*They **brought** the children **up**.*
*The court **handed** its decision **down**.*
*Please **hand** the money **over**.*

This arrangement is obligatory if the object noun phrase is a personal pronoun:

*They **turned** it **out**.*
*\*They **turned** out it.*

*We **blew** it **up**.*
*\*We **blew** up it.*

With phrasal verbs it is not possible to introduce an adverb phrase between the verb and the particle:

*\*The plane **took** slowly **off**.*
*\*They **called** quickly **out** the guard*

When the noun phrase is quite long, the particle is unlikely to be moved so that the first of the following constructions is likely to be preferred to the second:

*They **turned** on the new light in the outside hallway.*
*They **turned** the new light in the outside hallway **on**.*

Passivization is possible with transitive phrasal verbs:

*The light was turned out (by him).*
*It was blown up (by us).*

The particles in phrasal verbs are almost invariably stressed in speaking, particularly when they occur finally, i.e., separated from the verb.
  The following two sentences look alike in their structures:

*He **looked** over the plan.* (He examined the plan)
*He **looked** over the parapet.* (He looked down over the parapet)

However, the first contains a phrasal verb and the second a prepositional phrase used as a predicate adjunct. We can see the differences if we try various rearrangements:

*He **looked** the plan over.* (He examined it)
*He **looked** it (the plan) over.* (He examined it)

*He **looked** quickly **over** the plan.
He **looked** quickly **over** the parapet.
*He **looked over** it (the plan). (It cannot be that he examined it)
*He **looked** the parapet **over**. (It cannot be that he looked down over it; he examined it)
*He **looked** it (the parapet) **over**. (It cannot be that he looked down over it; he examined it)
He **looked over** it (the parapet). (He looked down over it)

A **prepositional verb** consists of a verb followed by a prepositional phrase, with the particular preposition that occurs determined by the verb in each case:

They **commented on** his appearance.
We will **attend to** the matter.
They **lived on** next to nothing.
We won't **laugh at** you.
It **consists of** three parts.
Carlos **listened to** the recording.
We are **looking for** a solution.
They **insisted on** going.
You can't **live on** nothing.

Prepositional verbs should be intransitive. However, it is possible in many cases to make a passive-like change:

His appearance **was commented on** by them.
You won't **be laughed at** by us.

Furthermore, we should note that the corresponding questions beginning with *wh-* words are *What did they comment on?*, *What will we attend to?*, etc. not *How did they comment?*, *Where will they attend?*, etc. That is, *comment on*, *attend to*, etc. behave as semantic wholes and the objects are the objects of these semantic wholes not just of the prepositions alone.

  If the noun phrase within the prepositional phrase is a pronoun, that pronoun follows the preposition:

They **commented on it**.
We will **attend to it**.
They **insisted on it**.
How do you **account for it**?

This kind of construction clearly contrasts with constructions involving phrasal verbs, which allow – indeed require – arrangements like *They **tried** it **on*** and forbid *They **tried on** it*.

An adverb phrase may be introduced between the verb and the preposition or at the end of the whole construction:

> *We commented (**immediately**) on his appearance (**immediately**).*
> *They lived (**quite well**) on next to nothing (**quite well**).*

A **phrasal-prepositional verb** contains both a particle and a prepositional phrase:

> *He **got away with** murder.*
> *She **walked out on** him.*
> *They **did away with** protocol.*
> *They **cut down on** their sugar.*
> *They don't **get along with** each other.*
> *I don't know how you **put up with** it.*
> ***Stand up for** your rights!*
> *You should **keep away from** those people.*
> *I'll **catch up on** work later.*
> *They'll have to **face up to** the facts sooner or later.*
> *Are you **looking forward to** the party?*

Once again the corresponding questions beginning with *wh-* words are *What did he get away with?* and *Who did she walk out on?* and not *How did he get away?* and *Where did she walk out?* Passivization is also sometimes possible, as in *Protocol was done away with* and *The facts will have to be faced up to sooner or later.*

An adverb phrase may be introduced between the particle and the prepositional phrase:

> *She walked out (**straightaway**) on him.*
> *I don't know how you've put up (**so long**) with it.*

## 4.6  Exercises

1   Try to specify the role of each of the italicized nouns in the clause in which it occurs. The first two are done for you.

    (a)    The *man* ate the *cake* with his *fingers*.
           (agent; patient; instrument)
    (b)    *Fred* liked *Toronto*.
           (experiencer; location)
    (c)    *John* left the *house* to his *sister*.

(d)   The *car* struck the *wall*.
(e)   *Roses* grow nicely in *Nice*.
(f)   *Nancy* burned the *papers* for her *aunt*.
(g)   *John* burned on the *beach* last *weekend*.
(h)   The *plane* flew to *Chicago*.
(i)   *Mary* flew the *plane* to *Chicago*.
(j)   *Sally* grows *roses*.
(k)   The *explosion* released deadly *gas* into the *atmosphere*.
(l)   The new *car* parked easily.
(m)   The *leaves* dried in the *sun*.
(n)   *Sally* grew a *foot* in just over a *year*.

2   Explain the agreement principle that was used in each of the following sen-
    tences. The first two are done for you.

(a)   The last round of talks are not going well.
      (*Are* agrees with the nearest preceding noun *talks* rather than with the
      grammatical subject *round*.)
(b)   The differences between the territories, for example between Jamaica, St
      Lucia and Barbados, necessitates in most cases different techniques in
      each territory.
      (*Necessitates* agrees with the preceding noun *Barbados* rather than with
      the grammatical subject *differences*.)
(c)   The literary and biographical richness of the many works on ethnicity have
      not played as large a role as they should.
(d)   The last days of classes for this term are Dec. 16 and Dec. 17.
(e)   A growing percentage of revenues are going to pay for debt, and that's not
      healthy for Canada.
(f)   The act requires shareholders' consent when a major chunk of company
      assets are sold.
(g)   The social and economic implications of confraternal development is touched
      upon.

3   Classify each lexical verb in the following sentences using such terms as *intran-
    sitive, linking, phrasal*, etc. You may have to use more than one label for a
    particular verb. The first three are done for you.

(a)   Where was it delivered?
      (*deliver*: transitive [used here in its passive form])
(b)   They ran up a long incline.
      (*run*: intransitive [followed here by a prepositional phrase])
(c)   They have all sorts of money.
      (*have*: pseudo-transitive)
(d)   They were looking out for him at the time.
(e)   He ran up a very large bill.
(f)   Make it hot and thick.
(g)   Are they inside the room?
(h)   She was disturbed by the allegation.
(i)   She felt great after the competition.
(j)   They have just named Sally Jones, Graduate Registrar, to the position.

(k)     She felt carefully along the edge of the door.

(l)     Do you find it at all interesting?

(m)    They have just named Sally Jones Graduate Registrar.

(n)     He was amused by the news that John had escaped.

(o)     Was it really so obvious?

(p)     They gave Sally Jones, Graduate Registrar, an award, Best Administrator of the Year.

(q)     How do you get on with her now?

(r)     We were just talking about you.

4    Are the following pairs of sentences the same or different in structure? The first one is done for you.

(a)     Mary left this book. Mary left this morning.
         (While *this book* and *this morning* are both noun phrases, *this book* is a direct object and we can have a passive *This book was left by Mary*. However, *this morning* is an adjunct and *\*This morning was left by Mary* is not possible. Furthermore, *Mary left this book this morning* is possible but *\*Mary left this morning this book* is not because the direct object must precede the adjunct. *This book* is also a patient and *this morning* is a temporal and they cannot be coordinated for that reason too. The two sentences have quite different structures.)

(b)     He waited for an hour. He waited for a taxi.

(c)     She appears every night. She appears angry.

(d)     We made him an offer. We made him an officer.

(e)     She looked up the word. She looked up the stairwell.

(f)     John grew several inches that year. John grew several orchids that year.

(g)     The driver looked hard. The driver looked carefully.

5    Explain the ambiguity of each of the following sentences. Draw on the grammatical terminology used so far in this book to do so. The first one is done for you.

(a)     John ran down the hall.
         (When this sentence tells us where John ran, i.e., down the hall *down* is a preposition and *down the hall* is a prepositional phrase following *ran*, an intransitive verb. When this sentence tells us that John was critical of the hall *down* is a particle and *ran down* is a phrasal verb, and we can also rearrange the parts of the sentence as follows: *John ran the hall down*.)

(b)     They took her money.

(c)     They have wounded men there.

(d)     They were holding up the bank.

(e)     The rabbit cooked beautifully.

(f)     John painted the wall in the house.

(g)     The idea that he proposed is preposterous.

(h)     He is a close friend and a loyal supporter of the Prime Minister.

(i)     Has anyone considered how violent women feel when they see such things?

(j)     She kissed the boy in the bus.

(k)     They disapproved of cheating students.

(l)   They commented on the paper.
(m)   She looked much harder than her sister.
(n)   He looked after dinner.

6   Explain why the first of the following sentences is ambiguous but the second and third are not.

(a)   She found him a good friend.
(b)   She found him a good wife.
(c)   She found him a good husband.

7   It is possible in English to recast certain verbs into verb phrases using *give, have, take,* or *make,* e.g., to recast *She looked carefully at it* into *She took/had a careful look at it.* What kinds of structural changes occur? Find other examples. Try these if you are at a loss: *She bit the apple, He is lecturing at noon, The prisoner attempted to escape, Please taste it!*

# 5
# Coordination and Embedding

A sentence consists of one or more clauses. In this chapter we will be concerned with how the basic clausal structures described in the previous chapter are joined in various ways to produce what are traditionally called **compound** and **complex** sentences. We will describe how finite clauses are combined through coordinating and embedding to form multi-clausal sentences. In the chapter that follows we will discuss such variations in structure as passives, different types of questions and negatives, and imperatives.

## 5.1  Coordination

Words, phrases, and clauses may be conjoined with various conjoining devices into **coordinate constructions**, which usually have the same function as their coordinated constituents. This characteristic of coordination is sometimes referred to as the **coordinate construction constraint**. In the sentence *Boys and girls like candy*, the noun phrase *boys and girls* has the same function as *boys* in *Boys like candy* and as *girls* in *Girls like candy*. The coordinate construction constraint provides a very useful test of "sameness" so far as structures are concerned. A few examples will show this:

*Sally is sorry.*
*Sally is a lawyer.*

*They made him an officer.*
*They made him an offer.*

*The boy struck the nail.*
*The hammer struck the nail.*

*John left the book.*
*John left the room.*

Each of the following conjoinings of these pairs of sentences is ungrammatical:

> *Sally is sorry and a lawyer.*
> *They made him an officer and an offer.*
> *The boy and the hammer struck the nail.*
> *John left the book and the room.*

*Sorry* and *a lawyer* are different types of phrase (adjective phrase and noun phrase respectively), *made him an officer* and *made him an offer* are different complement types (object complement and indirect object plus direct object respectively), *boy* and *hammer* have different roles in relation to the predicate *strike* (agent and instrument respectively), and *book* and *room* also have different roles in relation to the predicate *leave* (patient and location respectively).

Here is another example of coordination in the following set of sentences in which the final sentence is constructed from conjoining the two previous sentences with *either* and *or*:

> *John goes.*
> *The whole team will refuse to go.*
> **Either** *John goes* **or** *the whole team will refuse to go.*

We can therefore coordinate a wide variety of grammatical constituents: phrases, roles, clauses, etc.

Coordinated constituents are often also reversible with no change in meaning:

> *boys and girls*
> *girls and boys*
>
> *They play cards and sing songs.*
> *They sing songs and play cards.*
>
> *John is a sailor and Sally (is) a lawyer.*
> *Sally is a lawyer and John (is) a sailor.*
>
> *Do you want tea or coffee?*
> *Do you want coffee or tea?*
>
> *Fred is weak but Jean is strong.*
> *Jean is strong but Fred is weak.*

The following phrases and sentences illustrate the use of some of the common **coordinators** (either **coordinating conjunctions**, e.g., *and*, *but*, etc., or

**correlating conjunctions**, e.g., *not only . . . but also*, etc.). The coordinated constituents are bracketed.

> [*calmly*] **and** [*efficiently*]
> [*young*] **and** [*old*] *alike*
> *will* [*sing*] **and** [*dance*]
> *very* [*tired*] **and** [*discouraged*]
> [*very tired*] **and** [*discouraged*]
> *to* [*the bank*] **and** [*the office*]
> *He* [*sings*] **and** [*dances*].
> [*She went outside*] **but** [*I stayed in*].
> [*Put up*] **or** [*shut up*]!
> **Either** [*he goes*] **or** [*I do*].
> *It's* **neither** [*one thing*] **nor** [*another*].
> *He asked* **whether** *I was* [*coming*] **or** [*going*].
> *She* **not only** [*likes cheese*] **but also** [*likes wine*].

The most frequently used coordinator *and* may actually express a considerable variety of meaning relationships depending on how it is used and in many uses the coordinated constituents are not reversible:

> *boys* **and** *girls* (both boys and girls)
> *old men* **and** *women* (old men and women of any age/old men and old
>    women)
> *young* **and** *old men alike* (young men and old men)
> *people from England* **and** *France* (people from England and people
>    from France)
> *red* **and** *green flags* (red flags and green flags/two-colored flags)
> *She talked faster* **and** *faster.* (Her talk speeded up)
> *They danced* **and** *danced* **and** *danced.* (They danced for a long time)
> *She washed* **and** *ironed the shirt.* (She washed it first and then she
>    ironed it)
> *Do it* **and** *see what happens.* (If you do it, then you will find out what
>    will happen)
> *Go* **and** *do it.* (Go in order to do it)
> *Try* **and** *do it.* (Attempt to do it)
> *I took a pill* **and** *fell asleep.* (I took a pill and as a result fell asleep)
> *John went to the library* **and** *visited his friends.* (His friends were at the
>    library)
> *John went to the library* **and** *visited friends this morning.* (His friends
>    may or may not have been at the library)
> *There were cats* **and** *cats* **and** *cats.* (There were lots of cats, probably
>    too many)
> *There are friends* **and** *there are friends.* (Not all friends are alike)

(It has been said that the saying *Starve a cold and feed a fever* is ambiguous between an *if-then* reading and a strictly coordinate, i.e., reversible, one.)

The following phrases with *and* are sometimes called **irreversible binomials**:

| | |
|---|---|
| knife *and* fork | thick *and* thin |
| soap *and* water | ladies *and* gentlemen |
| fish *and* chips | down *and* out |
| bread *and* butter | back *and* forth |
| safe *and* sound | come *and* go |

Phrases like *\*fork and knife*, *\*gentlemen and ladies*, and *\*butter and bread* are not possible with the kinds of meanings and uses associated with the irreversible binomials.

There are no non-conjoined equivalents for coordinates such as the following:

*X and Y are parallel.*
*\*X is parallel.*
*Juan and Maria are a fine couple.*
*\*Juan is a fine couple.*
*Fred and Mary live together.*
*\*Fred lives together.*
*Alice and Sarah met in Lisbon.*
*\*Alice met in Lisbon.*

In the last two cases we do have roughly synonymous equivalent sentences in *Fred lives with Mary* and *Alice met Sarah in Lisbon*. What we have here are instances of a special kind of phrasal coordination. Other possible examples of such coordination occur as follows:

*Mike and Joan are brother and sister.*
*These animals are cats and dogs.*
*John and Fred married Sarah and Mary respectively.*

From the above examples we can see how it is possible to conjoin instances of the same grammatical type, e.g., noun phrase and noun phrase, verb phrase and verb phrase, or clause and clause. However, it is also possible on occasion to conjoin different types, but this is not a typical kind of coordination:

*He is a lawyer and wealthy.* (noun phrase and adjective phrase)
*Tell him and I'll see you get the contract.* (imperative and statement)
*I told him last week and when I saw him yesterday.* (noun phrase and
   clause but both are adjuncts)

We can note that in the first sentence above a reversal of *wealthy* and *a lawyer* to *He is wealthy and a lawyer* is at least peculiar because the original coordination appears to indicate his wealth is a consequence of his vocation, an interpretation that is not possible with the reversal. In the second example the interpretation is an *if . . . then* one, i.e., "If you tell him then I'll see you get the contract," and no reversal of the clauses is possible. Once again we can see that any violation of the coordinate construction constraint is highly **marked**, i.e., it produces a very special effect in the language.

When three or more constituents are conjoined with *and*, only the last *and* usually occurs, the others being omitted: *She is wise, kind, and generous.* The *and* is not omitted in structures like *She danced and danced and danced* where the repetition conveys the prolonged activity of dancing. The *and* may also be used for deliberate effect where it could have been omitted: *She is wise and kind and generous.* It is even possible to omit all occurrences of *and*, once again for deliberate effect: *She is wise, kind, generous.*

The coordinator *or* functions much like *and*:

> *John **or** Peter will do it.*
> *Give it to Sally, Juanita, **or** Mary.*
> *Do it **or** take the consequences.*
> *Would you like tea **or** coffee?*

This last *or* is actually found in an ambiguous sentence. Is the offer a choice of either tea or coffee when both are available, or is the offer one to provide either tea or coffee to the addressee if the addressee would like either?

The coordinator *but* occurs as follows:

> *He is rich **but** crazy.*
> *He did it slowly **but** carefully.*
> *He put it on the table **but** out of reach.*
> *She said that she'd go **but** I'm sure she didn't mean it.*

*But* contrasts with *and* in phrases such as the following:

> *tall **but** sad **and** stupid*
> *quickly **and** angrily **but** unwisely*

Note that the pair of phrases conjoined by *and* is contrasted with the phrase conjoined to that pair by *but*. The following bracketing shows the conjoining in the above phrases:

> *[tall] **but** [sad **and** stupid]*
> *[quickly **and** angrily] **but** [unwisely]*

As we can observe from some of the preceding examples, *and* and *but* may conjoin clauses. They appear between the clauses they conjoin.

> *John ate clams **and** Fred had salmon.*
> *I tried hard **but** I did not succeed.*

*For* has much the same meaning as *because*:

> *He did it **for** he had really no choice in the matter.*
> *He did it **because** he really had no choice in the matter.*

However, whereas it is possible to move a clause beginning with *because* to the front of the sentence in which it occurs, it is not possible to do this with a clause beginning with *for* just as it is impossible to move a clause with *and* or *but*:

> *He did it **because** he really had no choice in the matter.*
> ***Because** he really had no choice in the matter, he did it.*

> *He did it **for** he really had no choice in the matter.*
> ****For** he really had no choice in the matter, he did it.*

> *John ate clams **and** Fred had salmon.*
> ****And** Fred had salmon, John ate clams.*

It is for this reason that *for* is sometimes described as a coordinating conjunction along with *and* and *but*.

Other coordinators can also be used to join clauses:

> *Take it **or** leave it.*
> ***Not only** John came **but** Fred did **also**.*
> ***Either** you go **or** I'll tell your father.*
> ***The** more he spoke, **the** more confused he became.*
> ***The** less he knows about, **the** better I'll feel.*

Still another set of coordinators are the **conjunctive adverbs** *moreover, furthermore, however,* and *nevertheless*. Such words may be used to conjoin two clauses into one sentence in writing; however, in speech the clauses are separated by a distinct pause. The conjoining is largely a semantic matter rather than a grammatical one in that the second clause adds a further comment on some aspect of the content of the first clause. Conjunctive adverbs have a considerable freedom of movement in that they can appear at the beginning of the second clause, or at the end, or between certain constituents within the second clause:

*He did it; **however**, he shouldn't have done so.*
*He did it; he shouldn't have done so, **however**.*
*He did it; he shouldn't, **however**, have done so.*

The adverb function of these words is at least as important as their conjoining function.

Note that there is no theoretical limit to coordination:

*John, Fred, Mary, Peter, Mario, . . .*
*John drinks, Mary dances, Sally sews, . . .*
*She sings, but Mary dances, Peter cooks, . . .*
*I like apples, pears, cheese, oranges, . . .*

## 5.2  Embedded Clauses

One clause may be embedded within another, that is, it may be used as a constituent part of another clause. Such a clause is called an **embedded clause** (or a **subordinate clause**) and the clause within which it is embedded is called the **matrix clause**. The embedded clause becomes a constituent of the matrix clause. A clause that could occur on its own as a sentence is called a **main clause**. In the following examples the embedded clauses are given in boldface; each of the matrix clauses is also a main clause.

*The boy **who came** is his cousin.*
*I told him **that I would go**.*
*He left **when the bell rang**.*

The three kinds of embedded clauses illustrated here are a **relative clause** (*who came*), a **noun clause** (*that I would go*), and an **adverb clause** (*when the bell rang*).

Here are some further examples of each of these types of clause. Relative clauses are boldfaced in the following sentences:

*Here is the book **that you asked for**.*
*The room **we went into** was dark.*
*The car **in which they were riding** had been stolen.*
*He spoke quite coherently, **which surprised all of us**.*

Noun clauses are boldfaced in the following sentences:

*The idea **that he's happy in his present job** is ridiculous.*
*It's agreed then **that Mary will do it**.*

*I asked him **what he wanted**.*
*We don't know **whether they'll buy the house**.*

Adverb clauses are boldfaced in the following sentences:

*It's as much as **I expected**.*
*The room is really longer than **it appears to be**.*
*I'm afraid **he'll get hurt**.*

(In these last examples *as . . . as* and *than* may also be included as parts of the adverb clauses in the sentences in which they occur.)

It is also quite possible to embed one clause within another clause which is itself an embedded clause. In the following sentence the relative clause *he bought* is embedded in the adverb clause *because the house is huge*: *They live with him because the house **he bought** is huge*. We can also use brackets as follows to show this structure:

*[They live with him [because the house [he bought] is huge]]*

## 5.3  Relative Clauses

**Relative clauses** are usually constituents of noun phrases. They are introduced by either a **relative pronoun** (sometimes preceded by a preposition), e.g., *who, whom, whose, which*, etc., or by the **complementizer** *that*, or by nothing at all. This introductory word is itself a constituent of the embedded clause:

*The girl **who came** is his sister.*
*The book **which he read** belonged to John.*
*The bank **in which I keep my money** is sound.*
*The money **that you owe** is now due.*
*The book **you want** is out.*

The introducing word (*who, that*, etc.) is often said to be a **substitute** (or a replacement) within the embedded clause for a noun phrase that is identical to one in the matrix clause. Consequently, *who* in *who came* is said to substitute for (or replace) *the girl* in the first of the above sentences, and *which* is said to substitute for *the book* in the second:

*The girl [**who** came] is his sister.*
*The girl [**the girl** came] is his sister.*

*The book [which he read] belonged to John.*
*The book [he read **the book**] belonged to John.*

There are certain problems with such an analysis in sentences in which the noun phrase in the matrix sentence is a **quantifier:**

*Anybody who says such a thing is crazy.*
*Everybody who came brought one.*

Embedded clauses with *anybody* and *everybody* as subjects are not easily accounted for in such an analysis because of the very different meanings that are involved:

*Anybody [**anybody says such a thing**] is crazy.*
*Everybody [**everybody came**] brought one.*

This is but one of several instances of how quantifiers must receive special consideration in a comprehensive grammar of English. They behave very differently from other words to which they may have a superficial similarity. *Who* is used when the noun phrase substituted for is the **subject** noun phrase of the embedded clause and the reference is to a person:

*The editor **who** read the manuscript liked it.*
*The editor [**the editor** read the manuscript] liked it.*

*Whom* (sometimes *who* in informal use) is used when the noun phrase substituted for is an **object** noun phrase in the embedded clause and the reference is to a person:

*The man **who(m)** Mary insulted was very hurt.*
*The man [Mary insulted **the man**] was very hurt.*

The *who(m)* may also be omitted:

*The man Mary insulted was very hurt.*

*Whom* is required to refer to a person when the substitute is the **object of a preposition** and follows that preposition; it cannot be omitted:

*The boy **who(m)** Mary spoke to was very polite.*
*The boy **to whom** Mary spoke was very polite.*
*The boy [Mary spoke **to the boy**] was very polite.*
*\*The boy to Mary spoke was very polite.*

From these examples we can also see that the preposition may either precede *whom* in the relative clause or be left where it normally occurs.

*Which* is used in similar circumstances and similar ways for noun phrases that do not refer to persons:

> *The dog **which** barked belongs to them.*
> ***The dog** [**the dog** barked] belongs to them.*
> *The umbrella **which** she took is mine.*
> *The umbrella she took is mine.*
> ***The umbrella** [she took **the umbrella**] is mine.*

> *The place **to which** we are going is warm in winter.*
> *The place **which** we are going **to** is warm in winter.*
> ***The place** [we are going **to the place**] is warm in winter.*
> *The dress, the material **of which** was silk, pleased her.*

*Whose* is used when the noun phrase substituted for is a **genitive** noun:

> *The people **whose** books these are don't know about it.*
> ***The people** [these are **the people's** books] don't know about it.*

*Where, when,* and *why* are used as relative pronouns when the noun phrases substituted for are adverbs of place, time, and reason respectively. They are sometimes also omissible.

> *Show me the place (**where**) you found it.*
> *Show me **the place** [you found it **at the place**].*

> *It was raining the day (**when**) the accident happened.*
> *It was raining the day [the accident happened **on the day**].*

> *The reason (**why**) it happened was not hard to see.*
> *The reason [it happened **for the reason**] was not hard to see.*

*That* is not a relative pronoun although it appears in relative clauses. It is a **complementizer** which, in certain circumstances, appears where the relative pronoun would appear. It can occur instead of *who, who(m),* and *which* when these are subjects or objects in an embedded clause and instead of *where, when,* and *why*:

> *The boy **who** came brought it.*
> *The boy **that** came brought it.*

*The boy **who(m)** you saw did it.*
*The boy **that** you saw did it.*

*He planted the tree **which** grew there.*
*Her planted the tree **that** grew there.*

*It was raining the day **when** the accident happened.*
*It was raining the day **that** the accident happened.*

*That* cannot occur instead of a relative pronoun when that relative pronoun is the object of a preposition:

*The person **to whom** I spoke told me so.*
*\*The person **to that** I spoke told me so.*

*That* is required rather than a relative pronoun when the relative clause functions within a **superlative** noun phrase:

*the **best** time **that** I had*
*the **worst** thing **that** happened*
*the **finest that** we have*

In some varieties of English *that* is also required after *all* and after **indefinite pronouns** ending in *-thing*:

***all that** was done*
***something that** was said*
***nothing that** happened*
***anything that** I said*

The *that* is omissible in the last two cases when it is not the subject of the embedded clause:

*the **finest** we have*
***anything** I said*

If we return to an earlier sentence for which we provided the somewhat abstract structure as follows:

*The boy [Mary spoke to the boy] was very polite.*

We can now see that there are four possible ways of producing a relative clause:

*The boy **to whom Mary spoke** was very polite.*
*The boy **who(m) Mary spoke** to was very polite.*
*The boy **that Mary spoke** to was very polite.*
*The boy **Mary spoke** to was very polite.*

Relative clauses themselves may be restrictive or non-restrictive. A restrictive relative clause may not be omitted from a sentence without bringing about a drastic shift in the meaning of that sentence:

*The books **I want** are those.*
*The person **you are to ask for** is Peter.*
*He's someone **I've never met before**.*
*We'll share the food **they sent**.*

In contrast, a non-restrictive relative clause is omissible. If omitted, the result is no such drastic change of meaning because a non-restrictive relative clause merely provides additional non-essential (i.e., "by the way") information. Such information could have been supplied in another sentence:

*My television set, **which is portable**, is battery-operated.*
*My television set is battery operated. It is (also) portable.*

*The movie, **whose director is a Swede**, is really good.*
*The movie is really good. Its director is a Swede.*

*The chest, **in which I kept old clothes**, was destroyed.*
*The chest was destroyed. I kept old clothes in it.*

It is not possible to use *that* in non-restrictive relative clauses or to omit the relative pronoun when it substitutes for an object in the relative clause:

*\*My television set, **that** is portable, is battery-operated.*
*John Smith, **whom** I've known for ten years, told me.*
*\*John Smith, I've known for ten years, told me.*

If a noun phrase is followed by both restrictive and non-restrictive relative clauses, the restrictive clause must occur first:

*The television set (that) I bought last week, which is quite portable, wasn't expensive at all.*
*\*The television set, which is quite portable, (that) I bought last week wasn't expensive at all.*

Sometimes relative clauses are used in construction with full clauses rather than with noun phrases. Such relative clauses are called **sentential relative clauses**. These clauses begin with *which*:

> *He wanted out,* **which didn't surprise us at all.**
> *She told Bill about him,* **which turned out to be a good idea.**

In each of the above cases the antecedent of the sentential relative clause is the whole preceding clause. We can substitute *it* for *which* in each case and make two sentences with the *it* referring back to the whole preceding clause:

> *He wanted out.* **It** *didn't surprise us at all.*
> *She told Bill about him.* **It** *turned out to be a good idea.*

## 5.4   Noun Clauses

We will define a **noun clause** as a clause that fills a position that a noun phrase typically occupies in a matrix clause:

> **What he said** *disturbed us all.* (subject)
> **That he had done it** *was obvious.* (subject)
> *He said* **that he was hungry.** (object)
> *He asked* **where we were going.** (object)

> **The news** *disturbed us all.*
> **It** *was obvious.*
> *He said* **something.**
> *He asked* **a question.**

The embedded clauses in the following sentences beginning with *it* are also noun clauses. However, in these cases there are no corresponding sentences with noun phrases in the positions the noun clauses occupy:

> *It is possible* **that he has gone.**
> *It happens* **that we do know.**
> *It is possible* **the news.**
> *It happens* **the news.**

We will assume in such cases that the noun clause has actually been moved, sometimes obligatorily, after the verb and that *it* occurs in the position that the clause occupied before any movement occurred, i.e., whereas [*That he has gone] is possible* permits such movement, [*That we do know*] *happens* requires it. Such a noun clause is an **extraposed noun clause.**

Noun clauses show considerable variety in their internal composition. Many noun clauses are introduced by the **complementizer** *that*. *That* may be omitted except initially in sentences:

> *He told me (that) I could go.*
> *It is obvious (that) he knows all about it.*
> *It appears (that) they are ready.*
> *That he confessed so readily was shocking.*
> *That he knew about it we had no idea.*
> *We had no idea (that) he knew about it.*

For many speakers the verb of a noun clause must be the **subjunctive** (i.e., base) form when that clause follows certain verbs:

> *I insist that he be told.*
> *It is essential that he do it immediately.*
> *They require that I be there at noon.*

Noun clauses may be introduced by *wh-* words. Some such clauses have a strong resemblance to relative clauses – they are therefore sometimes referred to as **free relative clauses** – and, others, as we will see, to **embedded questions** and even **exclamations**:

> *Take what you want.*
> *Whoever did that acted rather foolishly.*
> *What was left over wasn't very much at all.*
> *Tell me how strong it is.*
> *I asked him who came.*
> *Give it to whoever comes for it.*
> *They told me where you live.*
> *She told him what a good job he had done.*
> *I wanted to know whether they were going.*

Unlike relative clauses, however, these noun clauses do not make reference in any way to a noun phrase in the matrix clause and it is possible to substitute a word like *something* or *someone* for the embedded clause in each case:

> *Take what you want.*
> *Take something.*
>
> *Whoever did that acted rather foolishly.*
> *Someone acted rather foolishly.*

As we have seen, noun clauses may occur as subjects and objects of matrix clauses and in *Give it to **whoever comes for it*** as the object of a preposition: ***to*** [*whoever came for it*]. They may also appear as **appositives** and be either **restrictive** or **non-restrictive**. Restrictive noun-clause appositives often follow words like *fact, knowledge, idea, possibility, proposal, statement*, etc.

> *The fact **that you did it readily** should help.*
> *The knowledge **that he was guilty** struck me at that moment.*
> *He originated the idea **that all men are equal.***

We can compare the above restrictive noun clauses with the non-restrictive noun clauses in:

> *That fact, **that you are willing to testify now**, means nothing.*
> *This knowledge, **that all was not yet lost**, consoled me.*
> *He had a good idea, **that we should all contribute.***

We can observe that this distinction between restrictive and non-restrictive uses parallels the one we find in appositives which are phrases rather than clauses. For example, the following appositives are restrictive:

> *the word **the***
> *my friend **Bill***
> *the novel **War and Peace***

However, the following appositives are non-restrictive:

> *I want you to meet my friend, **John Smith.***
> *I have a present for you, **a pair of gloves.***
> *Some professions, e.g., **medicine and the law**, are well regulated.*
> *I want a couple of things: **a pen and an eraser.***

Finally, we should note a number of similarities and differences between an appositive clause and a relative clause. The first sentence that follows contains an appositive clause and the second a relative clause:

> *The fact **that you mentioned it** is interesting.*
> *The fact **that you mentioned** is interesting.*

*That* may be omitted in both sentences:

> *The fact **you mentioned it** is interesting.*
> *The fact **you mentioned** is interesting.*

However, *which* may be used only in the relative clause:

> **The fact which** you mentioned it is interesting.
> The fact **which** you mentioned is interesting.

In addition, *the fact* may only be inserted into the relative clause:

> **The fact** [*you mentioned it **the fact**] is interesting.
> **The fact** [you mentioned **the fact**] is interesting.

Furthermore, *the fact* may be omitted only in the sentence containing the appositive:

> *That you mentioned it is interesting.*
> **That you mentioned is interesting.*

Finally, only the sentence containing the appositive clause may be recast to begin with *it* if the initial noun phrase, in this case *the fact*, is omitted:

> **It** is interesting that you mentioned it.
> **It** is interesting that you mentioned.*

# 5.5   Adverb Clauses

An **adverb clause** is usually either a **predicate adjunct**, i.e., is in a construction with a verb, or a **sentence adjunct**, i.e., is in construction with one or more clauses. Each of the following adverb clauses is a predicate adjunct:

> He resigned **after the takeover was completed.**
> He likes them **because they are sweet.**

Each of the following adverb clauses is a sentence adjunct:

> **After the takeover was completed,** he resigned.
> He resigned, **after the takeover was completed.**
> **Because they are sweet,** he likes them.
> He likes them, **because they are sweet.**

Many adverb clauses are introduced by **subordinating conjunctions**: these are words like *because, after, before, while, until, since, although, unless,* and *whereas*. Other words and phrases like *so* (*that*), *now* (*that*), *supposing* (*that*), seeing (that), provided (that), as far as, as soon as, so long as, as if, as though, in case (that), etc. also introduce adverb clauses.

> We stayed **until the concert ended.**
> She continued to play **although she was injured.**

Clauses introduced by words like *when, where, whenever,* etc. may also be used as adverb clauses and be predicate adjuncts:

> Play it **where I can't hear you.**
> Put it back **where you found it.**
> He'll leave **when(ever) he is ready.**

The complementizer *that,* or nothing at all, may introduce an adverb clause when it follows certain adjectives (which have some of the properties of predicates) such as *certain, angry, sad, disappointed, anxious, sure, shocked, irritated,* etc.

> I am certain **(that) he is angry.**
> He was happy **(that) they arrived safely.**
> We are grateful **(that) you remembered.**
> It was so big **(that) we couldn't carry it.**

Adverb clauses involving **comparison** are introduced by *than* or by *as . . . as*: She's taller *than I expected,* He ran *as quickly as he could.*
    Although many adverb clauses may be used as either predicate adjuncts or sentence adjuncts, some cannot perform this last function:

> Play it **where I can't hear you.**
> *__Where I can't hear you,__ play it.

> He acts **how he pleases.**
> *__How he pleases,__ he acts.

> *__(That) they arrived safely,__ he was happy.
> *__(That) you remembered,__ we are grateful.
> *__That I expected,__ she is taller.

As we noted earlier, a clause beginning with *for* also cannot be moved before another clause:

> He did it **for he really had no choice in the matter.**
> *__For he really had no choice in the matter,__ he did it.

However, clauses with *because*, *if*, and so on are not similarly restricted; hence we find the different conjunction categorizations of *for* (coordinating) and *because* (subordinating).


## 5.6  Simple, Compound, and Complex Sentences

An often-used system of sentence classification uses the terms **simple, compound,** and **complex** (along with **compound-complex** too) to describe sentence types. The system classifies sentences according to the number and types of clauses they contain. A clause must contain a subject and a finite verb, i.e., a verb marked for tense. Consequently, both *I want an apple* and *I want to go* are defined as having only a single verb since *to go* is not a finite verb but an infinitive. A sentence like *John and Sally sing* is also considered to have only a single clause, one with a **compound subject.** *Sally sings and dances* is also only a single clause, one with a **compound predicate.**

A sentence with one clause, therefore a main clause, is called a **simple sentence:**

> *John sings in the choir.*
> *Fred expects to go.*
> *Are Peter and John ready?*
> *The children ate their food and then left.*

In this system of classification the following sentences are simple sentences:

> *John and Mary sang all night.*
> *Mary sang and danced all night.*
> *John and Mary sang and danced all night.*

The first of the sentences above contains a compound subject *John and Mary*, the second a compound predicate *sang and danced all night*, and the third both a compound subject *John and Mary* and a compound predicate *sang and danced all night*.

A sentence with only coordinated main clauses is called a **compound sentence:**

> *Fred sings and Sally dances.*
> *I left but Peter stayed.*
> *Either you do it or I will get John to do it.*

A sentence with one main, i.e., matrix, clause and one or more subordinate, i.e., embedded, clauses is called a **complex sentence:**

*I went when I was sent for.*
*He asked what I wanted.*
*The idea that he did it is absurd.*
*It's sensible that you told her.*
*Did he bring the book you requested?*
*The plane he caught left shortly before they arrived.*
*Bill rants and raves when he's angry.*

A sentence with two or more main clauses and one or more subordinate clauses is called a **compound-complex sentence:**

*The boys who were in the field were playing soccer but there were no adults with them.*
*If you visit Mexico, you must come and see us and you must stay a while.*
*The plan you have sounds exciting and we must really give it serious thought.*

## 5.7 Exercises

1  Describe as fully as you can each subordinate clause in the following sentences, e.g., subject noun clause, restrictive relative clause, etc. The first four are done for you.

(a)   He knows what he wants.
       (*what he wants*: object noun clause)
(b)   The facts that you explained to me clarified the matter.
       (*that you explained to me*: restrictive relative clause)
(c)   People who live in glass houses shouldn't throw stones.
       (*who live in glass houses*: restrictive relative clause)
(d)   Who did it I don't know.
       (*who did it*: object noun clause)
(e)   The party was much livelier than we expected it to be.
(f)   He left when the party was over.
(g)   What did you see that time you went there?
(h)   The claim that he's brilliant amazes me.
(i)   Whose woods these are I do not know.
(j)   This is the very book I'm looking for.
(k)   He asked for a transfer, which surprised all who knew him.
(l)   What she wrote angered her sister.
(m)   I really want the book he's borrowed from you.
(n)   Don't believe a word he says.
(o)   It's easy to say that you'll do it.
(p)   He asked where we were going to spend our vacation.
(q)   I told her where I'd been.

(r)    My colleague, who is a fine pianist, got the job.
(s)    We stayed in the village we reached that night.
(t)    Go when you please.
(u)    London, where Sally lives now, is a fine place.
(v)    The dog whose tail was caught belongs to my neighbor.
(w)    That idea, that John is worthy of such an honor, disgusts me.
(x)    Nothing that occurred that day changed my mind.
(y)    I am grateful that you spoke up about it.
(z)    That she already knew about it came as a great surprise.

2   Describe as fully as you can each subordinate clause in the following sentences,
    e.g., subject noun clause, restrictive relative clause, etc. The first four are done
    for you.

(a)    I like the idea that we should all go together.
       (*that we should all go together*: restrictive noun clause)
(b)    He gave her all that she wanted.
       (*that she wanted*: restrictive relative clause)
(c)    He never knows what he wants to eat.
       (*what he wants to eat*: object noun clause)
(d)    Whoever said that told you a lie.
       (*whoever said that*: subject noun clause)
(e)    She's where she's always wanted to be.
(f)    He told me he would do it.
(g)    The idea that he's quite competent is absurd.
(h)    She's made him what he is today.
(i)    She made him what he's wearing today.
(j)    The book I was looking for is out.
(k)    Ask not what your country can do for you but what you can do for your
       country.
(l)    He left when it was all over.
(m)    Who will be chosen next no one knows.
(n)    The idea, which never came to anything, bothered me at the time.
(o)    He noticed which one was broken.
(p)    The play he's in folded last night.
(q)    The pictures, those you bought at the sale, appear to have been stolen.
(r)    He who hesitates is lost.
(s)    What I want to know is why you did it.
(t)    If you do that, you'll regret it.
(u)    Don't ever go where I've just been.
(v)    Don't ever ask where I've just been.
(w)    Profit was what mattered then.
(x)    That that that you wrote you misspelled.
(y)    It's sad that you should believe such a thing.

3   Use the classification described in this chapter to label each of the following
    sentences as simple, compound, complex, or compound-complex. The first two
    are done for you.

(a)    My cousin and his wife came and spent a week with us.
       (simple)

(b)   He is going to give them what they've always wanted, a trip to Bali. (complex)

(c)   He'll do it when he's ready.

(d)   The people who live down the road are leaving and going to Florida.

(e)   He said he would do it; however, he forgot.

(f)   It's not at all easy to find such a thing these days.

(g)   What you see is what you get.

(h)   Being caught out in the rain, we got quite wet and had to change.

(i)   My cousin plays hockey and flies a small plane but her mother doesn't approve because she says it's dangerous.

(j)   We were all very happy when John came because we hadn't seen him for years.

(k)   I came, I saw, I conquered.

(l)   Ask him what he wants.

(m)  Did you like the movie you saw last night?

(n)   Seeing is believing.

4   Is (c) formed from a combination of (a) and (b)? Your answer should make use of some of the grammatical terms found in the text.

(a)   The fact that he came is surprising.

(b)   The fact that he mentioned is surprising.

(c)   The fact that he mentioned that he came is surprising.

5   How might you try to show that in the following sentences the noun phrases that follow *left* are quite differently related to the verb?

(a)   Sally left the house.

(b)   Sally left this morning.

(c)   Sally left this painting.

6   The following sentence is ambiguous. Explain why it is so by reference to the different clausal structures of the two meanings.

John believed Mary and Fred trusted Sally.

7   Add clauses to the following sentences as indicated in the brackets:

(a)   *The meal* [restrictive relative clause] *wasn't very good* [adverb clause].

(b)   *Sally met John Smith* [non-restrictive relative clause] *and* [main clause].

(c)   *The order* [restrictive relative clause] *came too late* [adverb clause].

(d)   *It's unlikely* [extraposed noun clause] [adverb clause].

(e)   *It's unlikely* [extraposed noun clause [adverb clause]].

(f)   *He requested* [noun clause [restrictive relative clause]].

# 6
# Clausal Variation

In the last chapter we saw how we could coordinate clauses and embed one clause within another. In this chapter we will look at how we can vary clause structure. We will assume that the kind of simple clause discussed so far, one consisting of a subject and predicate in that order, is the basic type against which we can compare all other varieties. In the two chapters that follow we will develop this latter idea in a way which reveals some very interesting and unexpected characteristics of the language.

## 6.1 Passives

**Passive clauses** can be recognized by the presence of some form of the verb *be* immediately before the head verb of the verb phrase, which itself will be in the past participle form. As we saw in chapter 3, this is the *be+-en* constituent followed by a head verb with the *-en* actually attached to the following verb. The *be+-en* itself also follows the **tense marker** (**present** or **past**) and any **modal** and/or **auxiliary verb** that may be present in the verb phrase:

> *past have+-en* **be+-en** *eat*
> **had been eaten**
>
> *present will have+-en* **be+-en** *tell*
> **will have been told**
>
> *present* **be+-ing** **be+-en** *hold*
> **am/is/are being held**

We can use the above verb phrases in the following sentences:

> *The cake* **had been eaten** *by the dog.*
> *John* **will have been told** *about it.*
> *John* **is being held** *by the authorities.*

The head verb in the verb phrase must be a **transitive verb**, i.e., a verb capable of taking a **direct object** as its **complement**. Most sentences containing passive verbs may be related to corresponding sentences with active verbs. The direct object of the active pattern, i.e., the pattern that does not contain the *be+-en*, becomes the subject of the passive pattern and the subject of the active pattern, when there is such a subject, is moved to a position following the head verb into a prepositional phrase beginning with *by*:

> ***John** took **the book**.* (active)
> ***The book** was taken **by John**.* (passive)

Simple **monotransitive** verbs like *take* function in this way. So do other slightly more complicated verbs such as transitive **phrasal verbs**:

> *We **blew up** the bridge.*
> *The bridge **was blown up** by us.*

However, if the **particle** in a phrasal verb has been moved to follow the direct object, no passive is possible:

> *We **blew** the bridge **up**.*
> *\*The bridge **was blown** by us **up**.*

**Prepositional verbs** may also have passives:

> *We **will attend to** the matter.*
> *The matter **will be attended to** by us.*

**Phrasal-prepositional verbs** may also have passives:

> *They **should do away with** that rule.*
> *That rule **should be done away with** by them.*

Verbs with **object complements** may also have passives:

> *We **elected** him president.*
> *He **was elected** president by us.*

> *I **considered** it quite unacceptable.*
> *It **was considered** quite unacceptable by me.*

With many **ditransitive verbs**, i.e., verbs with two objects, either object of the active pattern may be made the subject of the passive pattern:

*I gave the man the money.*
*The money was given to the man by me.*
*The man was given the money by me.*
*The money was given by me to the man.*
**The man was given by me the money.*

In such cases if the direct object of the active pattern (*the money* in the above example) becomes the subject of the passive pattern, the indirect object (*the man*) appears in a prepositional phrase headed by *to* or sometimes *for*. Here is a further example:

*The tailor made **Bill** a suit.*
*A suit was made **for Bill** by the tailor.*

While the last sentence is somewhat awkward, a passive with *Bill* as the subject is ungrammatical:

**Bill was made a suit by the tailor.*

When verbs like *make* have two objects, one of which is in a **benefactive** role, only the direct object, in the **patient** role, may become the subject of a passive. Here are some further examples:

*My cousin baked Sally **a cake**.*
*A cake was baked for Sally by my cousin.*
**Sally was baked a cake by my cousin.*

*Juan wrote Peter **an essay in Spanish**.*
*An essay in Spanish was written by Juan for Peter.*
**Peter was written an essay in Spanish by Juan.*

*Our hosts called us **a cab**.*
*A cab was called for us by our hosts.*
**We were called a cab by our hosts.*

Passives without *by* phrases occur very frequently; there seems to be a preference for them in actual use because, unlike the active pattern, the passive pattern does not have to identify the subject of the verb. All of the above passives could have the *by* phrase omitted and several might appear to be more "natural" with such an omission. Here is one way of showing the relationship of active sentences to passive sentences when the passives lack the *by* phrase and are, therefore, **agent-less passives**:

(Unspecified agent) *took the book.*
*The book was taken.*

(Unspecified agent) *gave the man the money.*
*The money was given to the man.*
*The man was given the money.*

Although a verb like *have* takes a noun phrase as its object, it is not a transitive verb but a **pseudo-transitive verb** if we insist that one test of transitivity is that a verb must be able to occur in both the active and passive patterns:

*My cousin has a new car.*
**A new car is had by my cousin.*

It is a fact that *A good time was had by all* is a passive but the expression seems "**frozen.**" The same active-passive test may be applied to verbs such as *cost, weigh,* and *last*; it shows that these verbs too are pseudo-transitives:

*It costs five dollars.*
**Five dollars is costed by it.*
*The festival lasted a week.*
**A week was lasted by the festival.*

Even when another noun phrase intervenes between such a verb and the noun phrase the verb is still not a genuine transitive verb but rather a pseudo-transitive verb like *have*:

*It cost the man five dollars.*
**The man was costed five dollars by it.*
**Five dollars was costed to the man by it.*

There are also passives for structures of the following kinds:

*(We) are keeping track of all our expenses.*
*All our expenses are being kept track of (by us).*

*(We) kept them waiting.*
*They were kept waiting (by us).*

*(I) advised him what to do.*
*He was advised what to do (by me).*

However, the following passives are not possible:

*I expect to see him.*
*\*To see him is expected by me.*

*He finished eating.*
*\*Eating was finished by him.*

*He doubted if they knew*
*\*If they knew was doubted by him.*

*They wanted us to stay.*
*\*We were wanted to stay by them.*

There are also no passive equivalents of active sentences that contain **reflexive pronouns**:

*The girl hurt herself.*
*\*Herself was hurt by the girl.*

An idiom like *kicked the bucket* (i.e., "died") also cannot be passivized and retain its idiomatic meaning:

*He kicked the bucket last Tuesday.*
*\*The bucket was kicked by him last Tuesday.*

We also find the occasional passive with no active counterpart:

*He is said by historians to have been a wise king.*
*\*Historians say him to have been a wise king.*

Likewise, certain other passives may also lack easily recognizable active equivalents:

*Fred is rumored to be a spy.*
*I was born in England.*

In informal English there are frequent occurrences of what we will call the *get* **passive**:

*He got hurt.*
*They got vaccinated.*
*They'll get married tomorrow.*
*It will get laundered soon.*
*Don't get caught!*

Such sentences nearly always omit the noun phrase that could be the subject of the equivalent active sentence, i.e., they usually have no prepositional phrase headed by *by*. But such a phrase can be used on occasion: *Don't get caught by the police!*

This use of *get* should be distinguished from the use of *get* as a linking verb:

> *They got sick last week.*
> *They'll get dry in the sun.*

## 6.2   Imperatives

Certain **requests** and **commands** have a characteristic **imperative** form: they lack a subject and the verb is the uninflected base form:

> *Sit down!*
> *Tell me your name.*

They can be made more emphatic with an introductory *do*:

> *Do sit down!*
> *Do tell me your name.*

In the negative, as prohibitions of some kind, they are prefaced by *don't*:

> *Don't sit down!*
> *Don't tell me your name.*

Imperatives may be accompanied by certain other features either singly or in combination: some form of address (a **vocative**), e.g., a proper noun, the pronoun *you*, or one of the **indefinite pronouns** like *everybody* or *somebody*, or, in the negative, certain negative indefinite pronouns like *anybody* or *anyone*; an introductory *let's* or *let* followed by a noun phrase; a word like *please*; and either positive or negative question **tags** like *will you?* or *why don't you?* Less frequently we find tags like *can you?*, *can't you?*, and so on. (Another possible interpretation of these "tagged" commands is that they are reordered questions so that *Speak up, can't you?* derives from *Can't you speak up?* They therefore widen the range of structures used to "command" or "request" in the language.)

> *John, stand up!*
> *Wake up, Sally!*

*You, get up!*
*Please stop!*
*Please, George, don't do that!*
*Everybody rise!*
*Somebody say something!*
*Nobody move!*
*Get up, you!*
*You be the witch!*
*Don't you do that!*
*Don't anybody move!*
*Let's go!*
*Let him do it!*
*Let the dog have it!*
*George, don't let's go out tonight!*
*Sit down, will you?*
*Sit down, won't you?*
*Take the trash out, why don't you?*

If *let's* is the shortened form of *let us* ("allow us" or "permit us"), it is of the **inclusive** form that is used to refer to the addressee or addressees. We can have *Let's go, shall we?* However, *Let us go!* may or may not include the addressee(s), because you can say *You, let us go!*, and *Let us go, will you?* but not *\*You, let's go!* or *\*Let's go, will you?*

Requests and commands may be expressed with other syntactic forms than the imperative one just given. They may also lack a verb:

*You will sit down!* (statement)
*The company will parade at 0800 hours.* (statement)
*Will you please send me the application forms for the position you are seeking to fill?* (question)
*What's so funny?* (question)
*Everybody outside!* (verbless)
*Off with his head!* (verbless)

"Requesting" and "commanding" themselves are hardly the intent of imperative structures such as the following:

*Get well soon!*
*Mind your step!*
*Have a nice day!*
*Sleep well!*
*Do that again and you'll be sorry!*

# 6.3  Questions

There are two basic kinds of **question**: *yes-no* questions, which seek either *yes* or *no* for an answer, e.g., *Are you ready?*; and information-seeking questions, either echo questions, e.g., *You want what?* or *wh-* questions beginning with a *wh-* word, e.g., *What do you want?*

The ***yes-no* question** is found in three varieties: the inverted question, the typical examplar of this kind; the inverted question offering an alternative (which actually may require more than just a simple *yes* or *no* for an answer); and the tag question:

> *Are you going?* (inversion)
> *Are you staying or going?* (inversion with alternative)
> *You're going, aren't you?* (tag)

The **inverted question** merely inverts the subject and the first verb of the verb phrase of the corresponding statement pattern when that verb is either a modal or an auxiliary verb or the verb *be* and sometimes *have*. The question itself may be positive or negative:

> *She is leaving on Wednesday.*
> *Is she leaving on Wednesday?*
>
> *The jewelry was stolen.*
> *Was the jewelry stolen?*
>
> *You aren't going.*
> *Aren't you going?*

A positive question appears to be neutral as to the expected response – *yes* or *no*. However, a negative question seems to hold out the distinct possibility of a negative response:

> *Are you going? Yes/No.*
> *Aren't you going? No.*

In the event that there is only one verb, the **head verb** or **lexical verb**, in the verb phrase the verb *do* is introduced so that subject-verb inversion can occur. This *do* carries the tense marking, which shifts from the head verb. However, *do* is not introduced if the head verb is *be* and in some varieties of English if the head verb is *have*:

*He sang yesterday.*
*Did he sing yesterday?*

*Fred lives in Wales now.*
*Does Fred live in Wales now?*

*She's happy again.*
*Is she happy again?*

*They have a lot of friends.*
*Have they a lot of friends?*
*Do they have a lot of friends?*

The **inverted question** offering an **alternative** employs *or* in various ways. In
the following examples the bracketed questions (where given) appear to be
the "full" versions of the forms that are given. Only in the first example is
a simple *yes* or *no* the only possible answer. In the second example, depending on the **intonation** of the question, i.e., the way the voice rises or falls
during its actual utterance, any one of four answers seems possible, two
providing either *yes* or *no* answers and the other two providing information.
In the third example the answer must provide information.

*Are you ready **or** not?*
(Are you ready or aren't you ready?)
*Yes/No.*

*Are you going to London **or** Oxford?*
(Are you going to London or are you going to Oxford?)
*Yes/No/London/Oxford.*

*Are you going to do it **or** are you just kidding me?*
*I'm going to do it./I'm just kidding you.*

In **tag questions** the tags are formed by repeating the first verb of the verb
phrase (with the provision for the use of *do* that is stated above), changing
the positive-negative **polarity** of that verb, and inverting that verb with a
pronoun that matches, i.e., agrees with, the subject of the tagged clause:

*He is going.*
*He is going, **isn't he**?*

*She sings beautifully.*
*She sings beautifully, **doesn't she**?*

*It **wasn't** taken.*
*It **wasn't** taken, **was it**?*

*The **car** started.*
*The car started, **didn't it**?*

*His **mother** speaks Spanish.*
*His mother speaks Spanish, **doesn't she**?*

Note also what happens when two coordinated clauses are tagged in this way:

*John sings and Sally dances, **don't they**?*

The polarity shift applies to the verb in the clause that is tagged. There may be a negative word in that clause, as in the second example below. Such a negative word does not affect the required polarity change:

*He's kind, isn't he?*
*He's **unkind**, isn't he?*

However, because each of the following tags is positive, the verb or verb phrase in each of the tagged clauses must be considered to be "negative" so far as tag formation is concerned:

*She has **no** money at all, **has she**?*
*It's **hardly** worth doing, **is it**?*
*There seems to be **no** way out, **does there**?*

The last example also shows that *there* must appear in the tag when it is the subject of the tagged clause. When there is no polarity shift in the tag, the result is not a question but an affective statement, one that offers some kind of comment:

*He's satisfied, **is he**?* (Well, I'm not!)
*She isn't going to do it, **isn't she**?* (We'll see about that!)

There are two varieties of **information-seeking questions**, the echo question and the *wh-* question. The **echo question** is typically signaled in speech through a combination of extra heavy stress, or emphasis, on the echoed constituent and a rising pitch on the final word of the utterance, i.e., rising intonation, in contrast to the usual falling pitch of a statement, i.e., falling intonation. If such questions contain interrogative words in non-initial position, as in *He* *said **what?***, *It costs **how much?***, and *He wants **what?***, these words alone may come to mark the question and there may be no final pitch change in speaking. (In writing, we use a final question mark in all such questions.)

> *He left yesterday.*
> *He left **yesterday?***

> ***Going?***
> *He said **what?***
> *It costs **how much?***
> *Under the **table?***
> ***John?***
> *Get **up?***
> *You're **sure?***

We should note that a question like *Who said that?* with an initial question word and final rising intonation is an echo question, one that seeks some kind of repetition of the identity of the person referred to as *who*. Since echo questions often seem to seek confirmation or repetition of some part of a preceding utterance – sometimes even for just a *yes* or *no* answer – they are also virtually unlimited in their possible structures.

**Wh- questions** begin with *wh-* words such as *who, who(m), whose, which, what, where, when,* and *how*. Some of these words may also occur following an introductory preposition. Such questions will usually be spoken with normal stress on the *wh-* word and final falling intonation.

> ***Who** did it?*
> ***Who**(m) do you want to see?*
> ***Whose** socks are these?*
> ***Which** house does he live in?*
> ***What** is happening?*
> ***Where** are they going?*
> ***When** did you last see them?*
> ***How** big is it?*
> *To **what** do I owe this pleasure?*

We should note that questions with multiple *wh-* words are almost certainly echo questions:

> ***Who** said **what where?***
> *He wants **what when?***
> ***Who's** going **where?***

When the *wh-* word or phrase headed by the *wh-* word is the subject of the question there is normal subject-predicate word order:

> **Who is coming** tonight?
> **What happened** then?
> **Which cup fell?**

In all other cases there is subject-verb inversion (and the necessity to supply *do* if there is only one verb in the verb phrase and it is not *be* and not *have* for those who do not invert *have*):

> What **can you** see?
> Where **have they** been sent?
> Whose assignment **is this?**
> What **did they** want?
> How much **did they** spend on it?
> Which edition **does he** have?
> Which edition **has he?**

*What* and *which* are often interchangeable in *wh-* questions. *What* seems to offer a wider range of choice to the listener than *which*, which seems to imply choice from a limited set:

> **What** do you want?
> **Which** do you want?

> **What pictures** do you like?
> **Which pictures** do you like?

In the following pairs of questions the first question is a *wh-* question (if spoken with the kind of stress and intonation we would expect to find in *I intend to go to France this year*) and the second question is an echo question:

> **What resort** do you intend going to this year?
> You intend going to **what resort** this year?

> **With whose help** will we succeed?
> We will succeed **with whose help?**

> **What hotel** did you hear it's rumored I'm alleged to have been seen
>     going into?
> You heard it's rumored I'm alleged to have been seen going into **what
>     hotel?**

Questions may be used for rhetorical effect:

> *Are we going to let them get away with it?*
> *Does anyone believe that these days?*
> *Who cares about that?*

Such **rhetorical questions** have entirely predictable answers and are therefore
equivalent to statements in their intent:

> *We are not going to let them get away with it.*
> *No one believes that these days.*
> *No one cares about that.*

## 6.4   Emphatics

**Emphatics** are sentences with extra heavy stress in the verb phrase. This stress
is placed on the first verb of the verb phrase unless that verb is the head verb.
The only exception to this rule is *be* as a head verb; it can carry emphatic
stress. (In some varieties of English the head verb *have* is also an exception.)

> *He **IS** going.*
> *They **COULD** be coming tomorrow.*
> *I **DO** like that.*
> *I **DO**n't like that.*
> *You **ARE** in a position of authority.*
> *I **HAVE** the money after all.*
> *I **DO** have the money after all.*
> *I **HAVE**n't the money after all.*
> *I **DO**n't have the money after all.*

## 6.5   Negatives

When sentences are **negated** with *n't* (or the full form *not*), the negative
follows the first verb in the verb phrase if it is a modal, *be*, or, in some
varieties of the language, the head verb *have*; otherwise, *do* is required in just
the same situations as those mentioned previously:

> *My son **is** at school today.*
> *My son **isn't** at school today.*
> *My son **is not** at school today.*

*He **can** read Greek.*
*He **can't** read Greek.*

*She **sings** in the choir.*
*She **doesn't** sing in the choir.*

*He **has** many friends.*
*He **hasn't** many friends.*
*He **doesn't** have many friends.*

The meaning of a sentence like *My son isn't at school today* may be para-
phrased as "It is not the case that my son is at school today," i.e., what is
negated is the total proposition "My son is at school today."

If the negative *not* is used in tags and questions, it distributes differently
from *n't* in that it follows the inverted subject:

*He's going, **isn't** he?*
*He's going, **is** he **not?***

*Which plants **didn't** you water?*
*Which plants **did** you **not** water?*

Further changes may be required in the predicate when there is negation:

*He owes us **some** money.*
*He doesn't owe us **any** money.*

*I saw **something** ahead of us in the road.*
*I didn't see **anything** ahead of us in the road.*

Certain "negative adverbs" such as *never, rarely, scarcely,* and *hardly* can
also produce the same effect in the predicate:

*They have **some** food.*
*They never/rarely/scarcely/hardly have **any** food.*

Such adverbs can also be used initially in sentences. When they are so used
they require subject-verb inversion:

*Never **have** I seen such a mess.*
*Rarely **does** he speak out about it.*
*Scarcely **were they** out of sight than the noise started up again.*
*Hardly **had he** begun to speak when the door opened.*

These adverbs also require positive tags:

> *It never happened,* **did it?**
> *It hardly matters,* **does it?**

It may also be possible to argue that pairs of sentences such as the following have some kind of positive-negative relationship:

> *They have some too.*
> *They* **don't** *have any either.*

> *I have just seen him.*
> *I* **haven't** *seen him yet.*

However, an alternative interpretation is that some negative sentences (including those above) have no corresponding positives (and perhaps that some positives have no corresponding negatives):

> *\*They haven't some too.*
> *\*They have any either.*
> *\*I haven't just seen him.*
> *\*I have seen him yet.*

We could then add still further examples:

> *He* **didn't** *do it at all.* *\*He* **did** *it at all.*
> *She* **didn't** *lift a finger to help.* *\*She* **lifted** *a finger to help.*
> *I* **can't** *help noticing such things.* *\*I* **can** *help noticing such things.*
> ***Don't*** *ever do that again.* *\****Ever** *do that again.*
> ***Don't*** *bother doing it then.* *\****Bother** *doing it then.*
> *You* **needn't** *do it.* *\*You* **need** *do it.*
> *He* **didn't** *budge.* *\*He* **budged.**

A negative in a sentence or in some smaller syntactic constituent negates whatever is within the **negative scope** of that negative. In each of the following sentences the part given in parentheses is in the scope of the boldfaced negative. A basic assumption here is that in many clauses the negative negates the proposition stated in the whole clause so that *John* **isn't** *a teacher* ("It is not the case that John is a teacher") is the negation of *John is a teacher* ("John is a teacher").

> *It was a* **non***(-event).*
> *John is* **un***(friendly).*

*(John is)n't (un(friendly)).*
*(He did)n't (speak clearly).*
*I want no (excuses).*
*Clearly, (he did)n't (speak).*
*Not (one student) passed.*
*It is too soon to dis(agree).*
*(It is)n't (too soon to dis(agree)).*
*(I have)n't (seen him working).*
*(It's) not (obviously true).*
*It's obviously not (true).*
*Not (all my friends) know, do they?*
*(He did)n't (do it) because he liked her.* (He liked her so he didn't do
  it)
*(He did)n't (do it because he liked her).* (He did it for some other
  reason)

## 6.6  Miscellaneous Patterns

There are certain **exclamatory** patterns in English containing a subject and a
verb. Many begin with a *wh-* word and perform a "comment" function:

*How kind you are!*
*How often we went there that spring!*
*How clever he is!*
*What a beautiful day it is!*

Unlike *wh-* questions there is no subject-verb inversion in the above. Other
exclamatory patterns occur:

*What a beautiful day!*
*What a woman!*
*Serves you right!*
*Pardon!*
*Excuse me!*
*Pardon!*

They perform a variety of functions: commenting, requesting a repetition,
apologizing, etc.

Certain **pseudo-imperatives** require *you* after the verb. They are not commands but insults, e.g., *Damn you!* However, *Bless you!* is not an insult but
a **frozen** expression uttered after someone sneezes or as an alternative to

*Thank you!* Expressions like *Cheers!* and *How do you do?* and sayings like *Waste not, want not* and *The more the merrier* are also frozen.

Finally, there is an assortment of **exclamations** like *Ouch!*, *Gosh!*, *Oops!*, *Ugh!*, *Wow!*, *Oh!*, and *Eh!* These can occur in isolation or with other constructions:

> *Ouch!*
> *Oh, what do you want?*
> *It's – ugh! – quite disgusting.*
> *He did it after all, wow!*

As we can see, these exclamations can occur in various positions in utterances although not all possibilities are allowed:

> *\*What do you want, oh?*
> *\*He did – wow! – it after all.*

# 6.7  Exercises

1   Form a *yes-no* question and a tag question from each of the following state-ments. What changes are necessary? The first one is done for you.

   (a)   They have been there already.
          (*Have they been there already?*: Inversion of *they* and *have*. *They have been there already, haven't they?*: inversion of *they* and *have* to form a tag together with the addition of *n't* to *have* in the tag.)
   (b)   John and his brother took it.
   (c)   The story she told turned out to be true.
   (d)   Yellow goes with green.
   (e)   They bought new shoes for their children.
   (f)   John hasn't any money with him.
   (g)   John doesn't have any money with him.
   (h)   He should be told about it.

2   Form a passive sentence from each of the following active sentences. What changes are necessary? The first one is done for you.

   (a)   The men took the paper from John.
          (*The paper was taken from John by the men*: The original direct object *the paper* becomes the new subject, *be+-en* is introduced into the verb phrase, and the original subject *John* is moved into a final prepositional phrase headed with *by*.)
   (b)   Peter gave Sally the brush.
   (c)   Government workers were building a house for him.
   (d)   A maid was making up his bed for him.

(e) Sally and her friend took me to the movies.
(f) The agency provided them with the necessary clothing.
(g) The invading army captured the port they needed to supply themselves.

3 Form a *wh-* question from each of the following echo questions. What changes are necessary? The first one is done for you.

(a) John wanted what?
   (*What did John want?*: *What* is moved to the front of the sentence, inversion is provided, *did John*, which in this case requires the addition of the verb *do* to carry the past tense that was part of *wanted* in the original sentence.)
(b) Sally went to which school last year?
(c) He is going where for his holidays this year?
(d) You borrowed which book last week?
(e) The fish you caught yesterday was how big?
(f) He plays which instrument quite well?
(g) You can lend me how much?
(h) He did it why?

4 How might you try to refine the rules for tag formation given in section 6.3 in light of the following examples?

(a) None of us can go, can we?
(b) Not everyone knows that, do they?
(c) Nobody should blame her, should they?
(d) Anyone can be wrong, can't they?
(e) Everyone has one, haven't they?

# 7

# Underlying
# Relationships

From what we have said in the preceding chapters, it is apparent that any thorough statement about the structure of English must include a recognition that there are different categories of word types in the language, that words combine into grammatical constructions of various kinds, and that certain structural relationships exist between various clause types, e.g., between actives and passives, statements and questions, etc.

In one widely current view of how facts such as the above should be incorporated into an account of English structure, these facts follow from conceiving a language to be a system of rules and principles which speakers of that language draw on when they produce and comprehend sentences in that language. The precise form that such rules and principles take owes much to a genetic component in the make-up of all human beings because, in this view, all languages share certain properties, sometimes called **language universals**, as a consequence of the particular way in which human minds are constructed. However, each language has its own local variations of these rules and principles. In this view a grammar of English is a set of rules and principles which is organized according to properties shared by all languages but with a local variation of those rules and principles that makes the particular result English rather than French, Swahili, or some other language. English sentences are therefore those sentences that this particular set of rules and principles produces or **generates**. This set itself may actually be referred to as an English grammar. Grammatical statements about English therefore should attempt to characterize this set of rules and principles that speakers of English draw on to construct English sentences.

One important caveat seems to be in order: we are talking about how a grammar of English might best be characterized. How that grammar might or might not be "wired" in people's heads, how it is learned, if indeed it is learned in the usual sense of that word, and how it should be taught, e.g., as a second or foreign language, are not our concern. In the sense used here an English grammar is the most economical principled account we can provide of the structure of English sentences – no more but no less either!

# 7.1  Sentence Generation

A grammar of a language is a set of explicit statements about how sentences are formed in that language, so an English grammar is a set of explicit statements about the construction of English sentences. Grammars of this kind are called **generative grammars**. One such statement might be about what an English sentence essentially consists of, i.e., what its basic constituent parts are. We might say that a **sentence (S)** consists of two constituents, a **noun phrase (NP)** and a **verb phrase (VP)**. One way of recasting this statement is as follows:

S → NP + VP

Each of these constituents could then in turn be described according to its own internal constituent structure as follows:

NP → (Det) + N
VP → Vt + NP

The parenthesized **(Det)** indicates that this constituent, a **determiner**, is an optional constituent in the structure of the noun phrase, which may consist of a **noun (N)** by itself or of a determiner and a noun. The constituents given here for the **VP** are an obligatory **transitive verb (Vt)** and an obligatory **noun phrase (NP)**. Further constituent structures may be assigned in this way until we reach a level of ultimate constituents which are usually filled with lexical items, i.e., words. In the above example if each of Det, Vt, and N is considered to be an ultimate constituent, it could be realized respectively as one of *the*, *my*, etc., *take*, *say*, *eat*, etc., and *sheep*, *people*, *grass*, etc. We now have a little **generative grammar**:

S → NP + VP
NP → (Det) + N
VP → Vt + NP

Det → *the, my,*...
Vt → *take, say, eat,*...
N → *sheep, people, grass,*...

Let us now examine some of the advantages of the above system. If all sentences are realizations of an initial S constituent, we have a way of explaining why a language is a set of sentences in that sentence (S) becomes the starting point for everything the grammar generates, i.e., accounts for. We have a grammar of sentences. If we can construct a single set of explicit rules that accounts for all the sentences of English, we can say that our rules comprise a grammar of all the sentences of English and that any sequence of words that does not conform to the rules is not an English sentence. For example, it may be an ungrammatical sequence or be a sentence of some other language. In addition, each sentence the set of rules accounts for will have a constituency structure. For example, the rules in the simple grammar given above also give us the following constituency structure for the sentence *The sheep eat grass*:

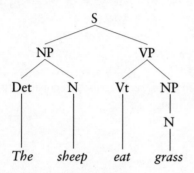

Furthermore, each of the ultimate constituents specifies a part-of-speech category so a complete statement of the rules tells us just exactly what parts-of-speech categories are necessary in English, in this case determiner, noun, and transitive verb. The rules therefore give us a complete structural description for each of the sentences they generate. All vocabulary items in the language would also be classified by category.

In an interesting current view of such issues one category of word, the verb, is particularly important. In this view clauses, for example, have verbs as their central components and each verb has associated with it a set of grammatical frames in which it can occur. It is these frames that essentially establish the grammatical structure for the clause in which a particular verb appears. For example, the verb *think* requires a grammatical frame which must contain an experiencer, and *bake* requires an agent and a patient together with the grammatical framework necessary to state some kind of proposition about baking. Such a view reduces considerably the necessity for supposing that humans have an inherent knowledge of constituent structure; instead it requires them to have an inherent knowledge of certain fundamental principles of what can possibly go with what in language. (This latter view is called the **government-binding** approach to language study and we will have occasion to refer to certain aspects of it in this chapter and the one that follows.)

Any set of rules or principles – no matter how long it is – must have still another property if it is to account for all the sentences of a language. We know that each language allows those who use it to create sentences that are completely new, e.g., *Did you see that boy in the green sweater and red scarf actually talking quite seriously with those two withered dandelions in my new neighbor's backyard last night?* A language is not only a set of sentences, it is also an unlimited set of sentences. However, the set of rules or principles which account for these sentences must be a limited one: it has been learned or acquired in a finite time by a finite being yet the possibilities it must allow for are not themselves finite. Such a set can capture this ability to account for a non-finite set of sentences if it is given the property of **recursion**, that is, if it allows for looping back through the set itself. For example, if the initial rule in a grammar that uses rules begins with S and some later rule – or various later rules – allows in its formulation the possibility of going back to that initial S, and so on, and so on, we have a possible solution to the dilemma of how a finite set of rules can allow for a non-finite set of possibilities. If the first rule of the grammar is something like:

S → NP + VP

and some later rule is:

NP → (Det) + N + (S)

we can produce structures in which one S is embedded within another S and even a further S within an embedded S:

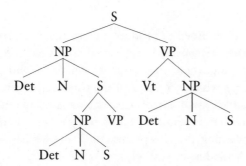

What we have just proposed is a view of accounting for sentences which claims that sentences are best described as resulting from the use of a finite set of rules or principles which contains a built-in recursive property. This set assigns each sentence a structural description by reason of its derivation and tells us what the various grammatical categories are in the language. It also tells us the category of each lexical item in the language. Finally, the recursive characteristic allows us to understand how certain multi-clausal sentences are constructed through the embedding process.

Any close examination of linguistic work using this generative approach to structure will show that in recent years less and less emphasis has been placed on trying to write elaborate systems of rules of this kind for English. There is no dispute that such rules must eventually be constructed. However, most linguists agree that it is still too early to seek the kinds of precision linguists once sought in rule writing. We will adopt such a view: sentence generation is rule-governed but the precise rules that apply are not always clear. In addition, as we will see, there is much to be gained if we are interested in trying to formulate principles of sentence organization and interpretation as well as rules of construction.

This last issue is directly connected to certain other issues that we have not resolved. Two are immediately obvious. The first is that when one clause is embedded in another, it often undergoes considerable structural change. How is such change to be accounted for? The second is that there are certain structural relationships among sentence types that a grammar should probably capture since they appear to be part of the user's "knowledge" of the language, e.g., the active-passive relationship, the various statement-question relationships, and so on. Should such relationships be captured in a grammar and, if so, how should they best be captured? To deal with such issues we require a set of principles of some kind. We will now turn our attention to this set of principles in order to examine some of its essential characteristics.


## 7.2   Relationships


We can use rules of the kind just described to produce a constituent structure for each sentence in the language. However, it appears that sentences have two kinds of structures that are important, one structure which we will call the d(eep) structure and the other which we will call the s(urface) structure. Both structures are necessary and a grammar of a particular language must include a set of principles for relating the two kinds of structure in that language. For example, in explaining the d(eep) structures of English sentences it may be necessary to show that in verb phrases tense markers occur before verbs and aspect markers have the forms *have+-en* and *be+-ing*. However, actually occurring English verb phrases place tense markers as suffixes on the verbs that follow them and the *-en* and *-ing* of the aspects also appear as suffixes of the verbs that follow them. Therefore, whereas in d(eep) structure we might seem to require such sequences as the following (with the internal + signs used in chapter 3 omitted from now on):

*past go*
*present have -en be -ing see*

in the s(urface) structure we require:

> *went*
> *has been seeing*

A grammar of English would have to state this relationship in some way. This particular relationship involves the movement of certain structural elements. The term **transformation** is sometimes used to describe a movement of this kind. What the above transformation does is rearrange the constituents of a construction into a new structural relationship.

A transformational relationship is only one of a number of relationships that must be accounted for between d(eep) and s(urface) structures. It is that relationship we will concentrate on in most of the discussion that follows. However, we will also discuss other kinds of relationships in order to show how these sometimes provide us with plausible alternatives to a transformational account.

Once again what we are emphasizing is that the current view of grammatical description holds that a grammar must account for the structure of any sentence at two simultaneous levels: d(eep) structure and s(urface) structure with the two levels explicitly related by means of principles of various kinds. Speakers and listeners "know" (though not consciously) all about these matters when they use the language since that is what we mean when we say they are native speakers of the language. The linguist's task is to try to make this knowledge explicit.

We will devote the rest of this chapter and the whole of the following chapter to sketching some of the structural relationships in English in a manner consistent with what we have just said. We will also indicate a few interesting issues that arise from looking at English structure in this way.


## 7.3   Passives

The active-passive relationship would seem to be almost ideally suited for an account that recognizes the kinds of relationships just mentioned, particularly a transformational relationship. Every genuinely transitive verb should appear in both an **active** sentence and a corresponding **passive** one, i.e., a passive sentence with the same meaning as the active sentence:

> *John ate the candies.*
> *The candies were eaten by John.*

All that seems to be necessary is to allow the rules that account for the structures of sentences to choose a passive constituent, i.e., *be -en*, in the verb phrase if the verb is categorized as a transitive verb. The presence of this *be -en* would bring about the **passive transformation**, which moves the object in the d(eep) structure to become the subject in the s(urface) structure and moves the agent subject of the d(eep) structure into a prepositional phrase with *by* as its head.

Let us propose then that any transitive verb (Vt) must co-occur with a subject NP ([X] in the following statement), a direct object NP ([Y] in the following statement), and a following PrepP (*by* [Z] – where [Z] is also an NP – in the following statement). The transitive verb itself may or may not be passive, i.e., may or may not have a preceding *be -en* (here given in parentheses to show its optionality).

[X]   tense   (*be -en*)   Vt   [Y]   *by*   [Z]

If no *be -en* constituent is present, then the *by* [Z] constituent remains un-filled, i.e., no NP can fill the [Z] position. We eventually derive sentences of the following kind:

| [X] | tense | Vt | [Y] | *by* [Z] |
|---|---|---|---|---|
| [*John*] | past | eat | [*the candies*] | *by* [  ] |
| [*Peter*] | past | follow | [*the wolf*] | *by* [  ] |

**John** *ate the candies.*
**Peter** *followed the wolf.*

The *by* [Z] constituent is deleted because there is nothing in the [Z] slot and all unfilled slots must be deleted, including one with *by* in this case, because the total PrepP *by* [Z] falls within this deletion principle.

If the *be -en* constituent is present the [X] slot may or may not be filled:

| [X] | tense | *be -en* | Vt | [Y] | *by* [Z] |
|---|---|---|---|---|---|
| [*John*] | past | *be -en* | eat | [*the candy*] | *by* [  ] |
| [     ] | past | *be -en* | eat | [*the candy*] | *by* [  ] |

Whatever is in the [X] position, the agent subject position, moves to fill the [Z] position and whatever is in the [Y] position moves to fill the [X] position:

[*the candy*] *past be -en eat   by* [*John*]
[*the candy*] *past be -en eat   by* [     ]

If the [Z] position remains empty then the whole *by* phrase is deleted:

*the candy    past be -en eat   by John*
*the candy    past be -en eat*

We now have the two sentences:

*The candy was eaten by John.*
*The candy was eaten.*

What we have just done is produce a general statement for transitive verbs which allows us to show the active-passive relationship in a very simple way. We have also produced a d(eep) structure configuration which resembles an actual s(urface) structure configuration:

NP  Vt  NP  PrepP

All other things being equal, a grammatical model in which the d(eep) structures of sentences closely resemble the s(urface) structures seems more desirable than one in which there is little or no such resemblance.

The above examples also show why it is that active sentences and their corresponding passives have the same meaning: they merely redistribute the noun phrases. They also show why certain passives are agentless. The agent has not been deleted; it never existed and, when it does not exist, the form of the surface sentence is rather rigidly prescribed.

One further observation can be made. The [X] and the [Y] positions in the above examples comprise everything that fills the final [X] and [Y] positions. For example, in the following sentence the [Y] position is filled by *the books and the money* not just by *the books*:

*John took **the books and the money**.*

The only possible passive is:

***The books and the money** were taken by John.*

It is not possible to have:

****The books** were taken by John **and the money**.*

We should note that both *the books* and *the books and the money* are object noun phrases that directly follow the transitive verb. However, the passive transformation operates on the larger of these phrases, i.e., on *the books and the money* rather than on just the first one alone *the books*. In the same way it moves both *Sally and Peter* in the following sentence from the subject position and not just either *Sally* or *Peter* alone:

> *Sally and Peter ate the pizza.*
> *The pizza was eaten by Sally and Peter.*
> *\*And Peter the pizza was eaten by Sally.*
> *\*Sally and the pizza were eaten by Peter.*

Should this last sentence occur it would obviously derive from an entirely different source, one whose corresponding active sentence is as follows:

> *Peter ate Sally and the pizza.*

Any discussion of the passive transformation brings up the issue of **subject-verb agreement** in English. Finite verbs in English agree with their subjects but these subjects are their final, i.e., s(urface), subjects not their d(eep) subjects. Sentences with passives show that this agreement process, or the **agreement transformation** if we wish to call it that, must occur after any movement of NPs required by passivization has taken place:

> *Mary was watering the plants.*
> **The plants were** *being watered by Mary.*

There are other ways of dealing with passives transformationally. For example, in an alternative approach the *by* phrase is filled with the d(eep) subject and only the d(eep) object is moved. The d(eep) structure is then something like this for our sentence *The candy was eaten by John*:

> [NP] *past be -en eat the candy by John*

There is only one movement of a constituent, the movement of *the candy* into the initial NP position:

> [ ] *was eaten* **the candy** *by John*
> **The candy** *was eaten by John.*

While such a procedure reduces by one the movements required in a transformational account of the passive, this saving is at the expense of an interpretative rule which must be added to the grammar. We require such a rule to tell us that the noun phrase after *by* is in some sense the "subject" of the verb and is taking an agent role in relationship to it. Moreover, if the *by* phrase is empty then the rule must also tell us that there is no such subject or agent in the sentence.

## 7.4  Imperatives

One possible interpretation of **imperatives** is that they have d(eep) structures containing certain constituents (an *imperative*, a *you* pronoun as subject, and the presence of *pres* and *will* in the verb phrase) which do not occur in the s(urface) structures:

> *imperative you pres will get up*
> *imperative you pres will pour you a drink*
> *imperative you pres will put your own shoes on*

Such a process would account for the following sentences if an **imperative transformation** deletes the above boldfaced constituents (and *you* in the second example is reflexivized to *yourself*):

> *Get up!*
> *Pour yourself a drink!*
> *Put your own shoes on!*

It would also account for sentences like:

> *You, get up!*
> *Get up, **you**!*
> *Pour **yourself** a drink, **won't** you?*

Therefore, the following would not be genuine imperatives:

> \**He, get up!*
> \**Pour **himself** a drink!*
> \**Put **our** own shoes on!*

Sentences like the following (here marked with an initial?) would also be atypical imperatives:

> ? *Pour yourself a drink, would you?*
> ? *Do it yourself, can't you?*

Such facts as the occurrences of the address form *you*, of the reflexive *yourself*, of *non-past* plus *will* and *you* in the tag (*won't you?*), and of *your* in *your own shoes*, the impossibility of the address form *he* or of the reflexive pronoun *himself* (and of any pronoun except *you* or *yourself* or *yourselves* in these positions), and the somewhat unusual sentences with *would* and *can't* – hence the use of the question marks above – might be used to argue for a d(eep) structure-s(urface) structure account of imperatives like the one proposed above.

   If this view is correct, then some other interpretation than the imperative origin given above is required for utterances such as:

> *Let's go!*
> *Bless you!*
> *Damn you!*

particularly as the following forms do not seem to be possible:

> \**You, let's go!*
> \**Bless **yourself**!*
> \**Damn you, **won't you**!*

However, that result is not at all surprising. Such utterances have a very different import from the imperatives given above: *Let's go!* is a suggestion or request involving at least one other participant in the execution of the proposed action, and expressions like *Bless you!* and *Damn you!* are deliberatedly affective rather than hortatory in their intent.


## 7.5   Affix Hopping and *Do* Support

The **affix hopping transformation** is required in every clause that contains a tense marker in the verb phrase. The d(eep) structures of verb phrases always place affixes in front of the verbs that they will attach to in s(urface) structures.

> *John **pres** be -**ing** go.*
> *John **is going**.*

> *John **past** shall have -**en** eat it.*
> *John **should** have **eaten** it.*

The affix hopping transformation moves each verb affix once in order to attach it as a suffix to the verb on its immediate "right."

   Let us now look at the following sentences to find out why the first three do not contain the auxiliary verb *do* but the last three do contain that verb:

> *Is Mary singing?*
> *The cat hasn't been eating it.*
> *You WILL take it.*

*Did John go to the movies?*
*The cat didn't eat it.*
*John DID take it.*

As we will discover in the pages that follow certain transformations require the splitting of the verb phrase. We will find that we often must split the initial tense constituent and any accompanying modal, *be*, or *have* constituents from the rest of the verb phrase. Such splitting will result in separating the verb phrases in the above sentences as follows before any transformations apply:

*Mary [pres be] [-ing sing]*
*the cat [pres have] [-en be -ing eat] it*
*you [pres will] [take] it*

*John [past] [go] to the movies*
*the cat [past] [eat] it*
*John [past] [take] it*

This separation into the above constituent structure will be required so that we can either move the first constituent, i.e., the one on the "left," or insert some other constituent between the two. For example, we may have to invert the subject and the leftmost constituent of the verb phrase in forming a question:

*[pres be] [Mary] -ing sing*
*[past] [John] go to the movies*

Or we may have to insert a constituent such as *[n't]* or stress *[']* in forming a negative sentence or an emphatic one:

*the cat [pres have] [n't] [-en be -ing eat] it*
*the cat [past] [n't] [eat] it*

*you [pres will] ['] take it*
*John [past] ['] [take] it*

Because each of these clauses contains a tense marker (either present or past) it must undergo affix hopping. We can easily perform this affix hopping in three of the above sentences:

*be pres Mary sing -ing*
*the cat have pres n't be -en eat -ing it*
*you will pres take it*

However, it is impossible to perform affix hopping in the other three cases because there is no verb over which the affix can be hopped. In these cases we must provide *do* by means of the ***do support transformation*** so that we can eventually hop these unsupported affixes:

> *past **do** John go to the movies*
> *the cat past **do** n't eat it*
> *John past **do** ' take it*

Affix hopping can now apply:

> ***do** past John go to the movies*
> *the cat **do** past n't eat it*
> *John **do** past ' take it*

The final results are as follows:

> *Did John go to the movies?*
> *The cat didn't eat it.*
> *John DID take it.*

## 7.6   Questions

**Question**-formation raises a number of interesting issues when we try to account for the various relationships we find among the different question types. Two kinds of question are fairly easy to describe structurally: the **echo question**, including the kind containing an interrogative pronoun, and the **tag question**:

> *You're going?*
> *You did **what**?*
> *He's going, **isn't he**?*

In the first case the question is signaled by a pitch change on the final word and/or the presence of a stressed *wh-* pronoun, e.g., *what, where, when*, etc., within the utterance; the second case requires that a tag be formed in a very precise way.

Both types of echo question can have statement-like structure:

> *You're going?*
> *You're going.*

*You did what?*
*You did something.*

It is not at all clear how the d(eep) structures of the first two differ but differ they must. Perhaps there is some kind of "echo-question" constituent in the d(eep) structure of the first sentence that is absent in the d(eep) structure of the second sentence. That is just one possibility but we will not pursue the matter any further. The echo question with the *wh-* pronoun has a similar d(eep) structure to the statement with *something*. In this case it is simply the presence of this pronoun which makes a sentence in which it occurs a question.

Tag formation is also fairly straightforward since just about any statement can be tagged and all we must do is specify this as a possibility for any statement. Once a statement is tagged, the precise form of the tag is clearly mandated (as we saw in chapter 6).

When we turn to **yes-no questions** and **wh- questions**, we can note the following important similarities. In **non-embedded clauses** both usually require **subject-verb inversion**:

**Are you** *going?*
*Who(m)* **do you** *want as a partner?*

However, in **embedded clauses** there is no such inversion:

*He asked whether* **you are** *going.*
*He asked who(m)* **you want** *as a partner.*

An embedded *yes-no* question requires *whether* (or sometimes *if*) to introduce it and this same *whether* is also used with embedded **alternative questions**:

*Are you going?*
*He asked* **whether** *you are going.*

*Are you going* **or not?**
*He asked* **whether or not** *you are going.*

A possible unifying solution is that all questions have d(eep) structures that contain a *question* constituent of some kind, possibly as an initial constituent in the d(eep) structure in what is sometimes referred to as the **Comp**, i.e., complementizer, position (so that the basic clause structure is really Comp + S rather than just S alone). Every sentence therefore has the following d(eep) structure at its highest level of organization:

A question therefore has the following initial organization:

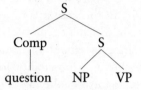

Some d(eep) structures also have a *wh-* word as one of their constituents. We will use four sentences as examples of what happens:

> *Are you going?*
> *Who(m) do you want as a partner?*
> *He asked whether you are going.*
> *He asked who(m) you want as a partner.*

We can represent the relevant parts of the d(eep) structures of these questions as follows:

> **question** *you pres be -ing go*
> **question** *you pres want **who** as a partner*
> *he past ask [**question** you pres be -ing go]*
> *he past ask [**question** you pres want **who** as a partner]*

The **question transformation** moves constituents and is required in each of the above structures. Any movement of a constituent requires that there be a position in the d(eep) structure to which it can be moved, e.g., an empty subject position as in the passive transformation or, as here, an available Comp position in the d(eep) structure. We can say that it is triggered by the presence of the *question* constituent and is sensitive as to whether or not the clause in which it applies is or is not embedded. The question transformation requires the inversion of the subject and tense plus any following modal, auxiliary, or *be* in a non-embedded clause but not in an embedded clause where no such structural change occurs. The results of applying the question transformation to each of the above d(eep) structures are as follows:

> ***pres be*** *you -ing go*
> ***pres*** *you want **who** as a partner*

*he past ask [question **you pres** be -ing go]*
*he past ask [question **you pres** want who as a partner]*

The question transformation therefore brings about inversion in the first two instances but not in the second two. This inversion replaces *question* with the inverted verb phrase in the first two cases;

**pres** *be you -ing go*
**pres** *you want who as a partner*

The resulting structures now must undergo the **wh- movement transformation**, i.e., any constituent that is a *wh-* word must be moved either to replace the question if it is still there or to be adjoined to a verb phrase that has already been moved to the Comp position. If there is no *wh-* word to move, as in the third case (an embedded *yes-no* question), *whether* (or sometimes *if*) is substituted for *question*:

*pres be you -ing go*
**who** *pres you want as a partner*
*he past ask [**whether** you pres be -ing go]*
*he past ask [**who** you pres want as a partner]*

The second sentence requires the introduction of the verb *do* (the *do* support transformation) to carry the tense marker isolated as a consequence of inversion, giving us:

*who pres **do** you want as a partner*

After the affixes are moved (the affix hopping transformation) and the clause boundary markers removed, we find ourselves with the following four s(urface) structures:

*Are you going?*
*Who(m) do you want as a partner?*
*He asked whether you are going.*
*He asked who(m) you want as a partner.*

(From these examples of embedded questions we can also see that many **noun clauses** are quite clearly embedded questions.)

This solution relates the various question types, accounts in a principled way for the relationships we observe between embedded and non-embedded questions, and shows how *whether* functions in English in embedded questions. (We can actually call it a **complementizer** in this use.)

Finally, we should note that in some varieties of English the inversion rule for questions also applies in embedded clauses, i.e., in those varieties of the language that allow sentences such as:

*He asked **could** he do it.*
*He asked me when **could** he sing.*

## 7.7   Relatives

A **relative clause** is an embedded clause. Any noun phrase may have as its constituents another noun phrase and an embedded clause with its own internal Comp constituent. This embedded clause contains as one of its constituents a noun phrase that is identical to the noun phrase with which the embedded clause is in construction. Here are some examples. (The triangle △ indicates that we are not concerned with the precise structural details of what appears below that triangle.)

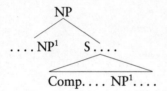

The two occurrences of $NP^1$ indicate that the NPs are identical.

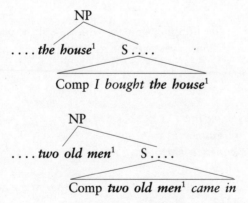

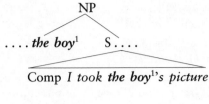

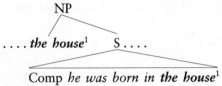

Such structures would produce the following noun phrases containing embedded relative clauses:

> *the house*[1] [Comp *I bought the house*[1]]
> *the house **which/that/** ( ) I bought*
>
> *two old men*[1] [Comp *two old men*[1] *came in*]
> *two old men **who/that** came in*
>
> *the boy*[1] [Comp *I took the boy*[1]*'s picture*]
> *the boy **whose** picture I took*
>
> *the house*[1] [Comp *he was born in the house*[1]]
> *the house **in which/where** he was born//**which/that/** ( ) he was born in*

The **relative transformation** substitutes a relative pronoun for the NP in the embedded clause and then moves that relative pronoun to the Comp position in the embedded clause. It is the position filled by *question* in the d(eep) structure of a question and eventually by *whether* in an embedded *yes-no* question. In relative clauses it is filled by the **complementizer** *that* so that possibly a fuller statement of the actual d(eep) structure underlying a relative clause is as follows:

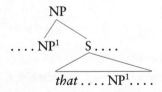

In certain circumstances *that* may be replaced by a relative pronoun or may be deleted. We can then recast the above structure as follows to produce the following d(eep) structures for relative clauses:

> the house[1] [*that I bought the house*[1]]
> two old men[1] [*that two old men*[1] *came in*]
> the boy[1] [*that I took the boy*[1]*'s picture*]
> the house[1] [*that he was born in the house*[1]]

In the first example the relative transformation allows three possibilities: the substitution of a relative pronoun – in this case *which* for *that*, the use of *that*, or the deletion of *that*:

> the house **which** I bought
> the house **that** I bought
> the house I bought

In the second example only the first two possibilities are allowed when the pronominalized noun phrase is the subject of the verb of the embedded clause:

> two old **men who** came in
> two old **men that** came in

In the third example some other constituent is moved – in this case *picture* – along with the pronominalized noun phrase and *that* must be deleted:

> the boy **whose picture** I took

In the last example there are alternative possibilities. We can substitute *which* for *that*, use *that*, or delete *that*:

> the house **which** he was born in
> the house **that** he was born in
> the house he was born in

If another constituent is moved along with the pronominalized constituent, *that* must be deleted:

> the house **in which** he was born

If, however, the whole prepositional phrase – in this case *in the house* – in which the relevant noun phrase occurs is pronominalized, we require a special relative pronoun – in this case *where* – to match the "place" orientation of the prepositional phrase. Such relatives replace *that*:

> the house **where** he was born

We can also note the similarity of relative clauses (including what are some-times called **free relative clauses**) to **embedded questions** and clauses which we have called **adverb clauses**:

> I *visited the place **where he was born**.* (relative clause)
> *She asked him **where he was born**.* (embedded question)
> *He died **where he was born**.* (adverb clause)

> *The boy **who left it** is outside.* (relative clause)
> *He wanted to know **who left it**.* (embedded question)

Relative clauses also have a certain freedom of movement. Whereas they appear to originate in d(eep) structures immediately following the noun phrases they modify, they may sometimes be moved out of the total noun phrases in which they are located. They move to a later position, i.e., undergo **right movement,** in the sentence in which they occur. Only restrictive relative clauses can be moved in this way.

> *The books **that John had labored so long to acquire** were damaged.*
> *The books were damaged **that John had labored so long to acquire**.*

> *A man **who knew something about it** approached us.*
> *A man approached us **who knew something about it**.*

Such right movement can apply in noun phrases to move constituents other than relative clauses. In the first of the following examples a restrictive noun clause is moved and in the second a prepositional phrase:

> *The story **that I'm not serious about the job** has been spread.*
> *The story has been spread **that I'm not serious about the job**.*

> *A book **about her bizarre adventures** was published just last month.*
> *A book was published just last month **about her bizarre adventures**.*

Relative clauses may also be the origin of certain modifying verb phrases of the following kind:

> *the branch **broken in the storm***
> *the boys **playing in the garden***

The origins might be as follows:

> *the branch **which was broken in the storm***
> *the boys **who are/were playing in the garden***

We can account for these verb phrases by deleting the relative pronoun, tense, and *be*. Similar verb phrases may be found in places in sentences other than directly after the noun phrases they modify restrictively:

> *The men left quietly, **broken in spirit**.*
> ***Broken in spirit**, the men left quietly.*

While the above phrases, which we have elsewhere called **phrasal adjuncts**, may possibly be accounted for through the process described above, plus some additional statement to account for the possibility of movement of the phrases, it is quite clear that not all phrases of this kind can be accounted for in this way:

> *Being of sound mind, the man declined the offer.*
> *Having consulted our lawyer, we accept your proposal.*
> *After completing the assigned task, she resigned.*

In each case there is a clear subject-verb relationship between the subject of the finite verb and the verb ending in *-ing* but one that the above statement does not capture:

> *\*The man was being of sound mind.*
> *\*We are having consulted our lawyer.*
> *\*After she was completing the assigned task.*

# 7.8   Exercises

1   Provide a d(eep) structure for each of the following sentences and explain the transformations required to derive the s(urface) structure. The first and sixth are done for you.

  (a)   He is going.
        (*he pres be -ing go*
           affix hopping
        *he be pres go -ing*)
  (b)   He has been going.
  (c)   She likes the car.
  (d)   She will buy a new car.
  (e)   She has a good job.
  (f)   Does she have a good job?
        (*question she pres have a good job*
           question
        *pres she have a good job*
           do support

*pres do she have a good job*
 affix hopping
*do pres she have a good job*)
(g)  Has she a good job?
(h)  The decision has been made.
(i)  She was approached by a stranger in the park.
(j)  He was recaptured last week.
(k)  Stand up!
(l)  Was it stolen?
(m)  Bill was sent away.
(n)  Was Sally elected treasurer at the meeting?
(o)  John has been dismissed.
(p)  Are Bill and Tom coming tonight?

2  Provide a d(eep) structure for each of the following sentences and explain the transformations required to derive the s(urface) structure. The first and the fifth are done for you.

(a)  The girl took the cake.
 (*the girl past take the cake*
  affix hopping
 *the girl take past the cake*)
(b)  The cake was taken by the girl.
(c)  The girl took the cake and the books.
(d)  The cake and the books were taken by the girl.
(e)  The cake was taken.
 ( [ ] *past be -en take the cake by* [ ]
  passive
 *the cake past be -en take by* [ ]
  affix hopping
 *the cake be past take -en by* [ ]
 *the cake be past take -en*)
(f)  Sally and George took the cake.
(g)  The cake was taken by Sally and George.
(h)  The grapes are being eaten by John.
(i)  Was she told about it?
(j)  Mary sent a letter to Bill.
(k)  A letter was sent to Bill.
(l)  The boy with the red hair took it.
(m)  It was taken by the boy with the red hair.

3  Provide a d(eep) structure for each of the following sentences and explain the transformations required to derive the s(urface) structure. The first and the fifth are done for you.

(a)  The man who came to dinner left early.
 (*the man*[1] [*that the man*[1] *past come to dinner*] *past leave early*
  relative
 *the man* [*who past come to dinner*] *past leave early*
  affix hopping
 *the man* [*who come past to dinner*] *leave past early*)

(b)    The car he bought is a lemon.
(c)    The employee who was dismissed sued the firm.
(d)    The dog that bit me is usually friendly.
(e)    The place to which they are going is cold now.
       (*the place¹ [that they pres be -ing go to the place¹] pres be cold now*
          relative
       *the place [to which they pres be -ing go] pres be cold now*
          affix hopping
       *the place [to which they be pres go -ing] be pres cold now*)
(f)    The place where they are going is cold now.
(g)    The boy at the back who spoke up is correct.
(h)    Smith, who is a friend of mine, is correct.
(i)    The boy at the back who spoke up and who is a friend of mine is correct.
(j)    The boy at the back who spoke up, who is a friend of mine, is correct.
(k)    She is the teacher whose classes I attended last year.
(l)    The dress, the material of which had been specially woven, caused a
       sensation.
(m)    Were the soldiers who were wounded evacuated quickly?

4   Provide a d(eep) structure for each of the following sentences and explain the
    transformations mentioned in this chapter that are required in order to derive the
    s(urface) structure. The first and sixth are done for you.

(a)    What does he want?
       (*question he pres want what*
          question
       *pres he want what*
          wh- movement
       *what pres he want*
          do support
       *what pres do he want*
          affix hopping
       *what do pres he want*)
(b)    Where are they going?
(c)    Who said that?
(d)    He is going where?
(e)    Where is he going?
(f)    What does he want to do?
       (*question he pres want to do what*
          question
       *pres he want to do what*
          wh- movement
       *what pres he want to do*
          do support
       *what pres do he want to do*
          affix hopping
       *what do pres he want to do*)
(g)    He wants to do what?
(h)    Whose shoes are these?
(i)    Along which road did they advance?

(j)     She wants to know if they are going.

(k)    She wants to know where they are going.

(l)     He gave it to the man who took what?

(m)   He left when John said what?

(n)    What did he say when John drank the wine?

(o)    He said I knew who(m)?

(p)    Who(m) did he say I knew?

(q)    What was happening at the time?

(r)     What can you do about it?

(s)     He asked what I did for a living.

(t)     What do you do for a living?

(u)    Was John given all the help he needed?

(v)    Where were they recaptured?

(w)   He asked if his laundry was ready.

# 8
# Rules and Principles

We will now turn our attention to a variety of other issues that we must consider if we are to attempt to uncover some of the subtle relationships that exist among different sentence types. We will consider these relationships mainly within the transformational framework outlined in the previous chapter. However, certain other general rules and principles will also appear to be useful.

## 8.1  Negatives

Negation requires the presence of a negative constituent in a clause. In the d(eep) structure this constituent is part of the Comp. Consequently *He isn't going* would have the following d(eep) structure:

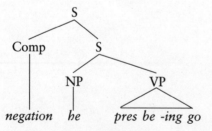

The **negative transformation** introduces *n't* (or *not*) after the first *be, have,* or modal verb in the verb phrase, or in the absence of one of these after the tense marker. We have the following situations therefore after the application of the negative transformation in a variety of d(eep) structures, including the one given above:

> *the boy pres be **n't** -ing go*
> *the girl past have **n't** -en leave*

*the car pres be n't red*
*he pres have n't a dime*
    or
*he pres n't have a dime*
*it past n't rain yesterday*

The last two structures require the *do* support transformation because the tense marker is not followed immediately by a verb:

*he pres do n't have a dime*
*it past do n't rain yesterday*

After affix hopping throughout we derive the following sentences from the above:

*The boy isn't going.*
*The girl hadn't left.*
*The car isn't red.*
*He hasn't a dime.*
    or
*He doesn't have a dime.*
*It didn't rain yesterday.*

We should note that the negative transformation sometimes requires additional changes in the words of the negative sentence that results, e.g., changes like *some* to *any*, *something* to *anything*, and *somewhere* to *anywhere*, as in the following examples:

| | |
|---|---|
| *I have some apples.* | *I don't have any apples.* |
| *He said something sensible.* | *He didn't say anything sensible.* |
| *I've seen him somewhere.* | *I haven't seen him anywhere.* |

Negated imperatives require an additional *don't* as in *Don't do it!* Apparently the function of *do* in such imperatives is merely to carry the negative constituent. Imperatives with initial *Let's* are also negated with *don't* as in *Don't let's tell him!* or with *not* as in *Let's not do it then!* Forms like *Bless you!* and *Damn you!* cannot be negated (*Don't bless you! *Don't damn you!*). They are not genuine imperatives.

## 8.2 Dative Movement

Typical **ditransitive verbs (Vdt)** require d(eep) structures with three complement constituents: an empty indirect object constituent (the [X] below), a

direct object constituent (the [Y] below), and a prepositional phrase constituent (the Prep [Z] below):

**Vdt  [X]  [Y]  Prep[Z]**

Here are examples of ditransitive verbs with the [X] constituent empty and
the [Y] and [Z] constituents filled:

| **Vdt** | **[X]** | **[Y]** | **Prep[Z]** |
|---------|---------|---------|-------------|
| *I gave* | [ ] | *[a dollar]* | *to* [*Mary*] |
| *I promised* | [ ] | *[a treat]* | *to* [*him*] |
| *I sold* | [ ] | *[a lemon]* | *to* [*my friend*] |
| *I baked* | [ ] | *[a cake]* | *for* [*Mary*] |

We will consider this structure to be the basic one in that it places the direct
object immediately after the verb (when the [X] constituent is empty) and it
also contains the preposition that actually occurs with [Z]. A **dative movement transformation** allows the NP that fills [Z] to be moved to fill [X] and
deletes the preposition in doing so:

| **Vdt** | **[X]** | **[Y]** | **Prep[Z]** |
|---------|---------|---------|-------------|
| *I gave* | [*Mary*] | *[a dollar]* | |
| *I promised* | [*him*] | *[a treat]* | |
| *I sold* | [*my friend*] | *[a lemon]* | |
| *I baked* | [*Mary*] | *[a cake]* | |

In most varieties of English the dative movement transformation may not
occur if the [Y] position is filled by a pronoun:

*I gave **it** to Mary.*          ? *I gave Mary **it**.*
*I promised **it** to him.*       ? *I promised him **it**.*

The passive transformation may apply to ditransitive verbs either before or
after dative movement applies. If it applies to the initial structures given
above for the four sentences, the results are as follows when there is no dative
movement:

*A dollar **was given** (by me) to Mary (by me).*
*A treat **was promised** (by me) to him (by me).*
*A lemon **was sold** (by me) to my friend (by me).*
*A cake **was baked** (by me) for Mary (by me).*

Note that the *by* phrase has more than one possible location and it may also
not occur at all in s(urface) structure if there is no subject specified in the

d(eep) structure. If there is dative movement then we have the following results after the further application of the passive transformation:

*Mary **was given** a dollar (by me).*
*He **was promised** a treat (by me).*
*My friend **was sold** a lemon (by me).*

(The passive transformation cannot apply in the last sentence: *\*Mary was baked a cake by me* is ungrammatical.)

In the above cases any *by* phrase must occur in final position. Because dative movement does not usually occur when the [Y] position is filled by a pronoun, the following passives are dubious:

*?Mary was given **it** (by me).*
*?He was promised **it** (by me).*
*?My friend was sold **it** (by me).*

We can compare such sentences with the following passives in which there has been no dative movement:

***It** was given (by me) to Mary (by me).*
***It** was promised (by me) to him (by me).*
***It** was sold (by me) to my friend (by me).*

There seems to be a strong preference for the use of the dative movement transformation when the direct object of a verb is "heavy" and the indirect object is "light." English sentences appear to have a preference for heavy weight at the end, hence the previously noted right movement of constituents out of noun phrases. Dative movement seems distinctly preferable in cases like the following:

*I gave the book that he had been trying to find **to him**.*
*I gave **him** the book that he had been trying to find.*
*I told the fairy tale about Goldilocks and the three bears **to the children**.*
*I told **the children** the fairy tale about Goldilocks and the three bears.*

## 8.3 Reflexives

Reflexive pronouns pose an interesting problem. How do we account for the pronouns in the following sentences (not all of which are reflexives)?

*John hurt **himself**.*
*John hurt **him**.*

*The workers made **themselves** some tea.*
*The workers made **them** some tea.*

*Please help **yourself**!*
**Please help **you**!*
**Please help **himself**!*

One solution is to propose that when there is a second occurrence of a noun phrase in the d(eep) structure of a sentence, under certain conditions of identity and dominance one or other of the noun phrases must be **reflexivized** by means of the **reflexive transformation**:

*John[1] hurt John[1]*
*John hurt **himself**.*

*the workmen[1] made the workmen[1] some tea*
**The workmen** made **themselves** some tea.

*Please you[1] help you[1]*
*Please help **yourself**!*

In this last case, an imperative, we have previously indicated that it is possible to postulate the presence of a *you* in the d(eep) structure. In this view **Please hurt himself!* is ungrammatical because there is no *he* in the d(eep) structure of the sentence and **Please help you!* is ungrammatical because of a failure to reflexivize when reflexivization is necessary.

Sometimes there is no reflexivization where we might expect it and on other occasions a choice is available between a reflexive and a non-reflexive pronoun. For example, whereas *He had his wife beside him* is possible **He had his wife beside **himself*** is not because reflexives do not occur in **locative** adverbials. However, the following variants are possible:

*She closed the door behind **her**/**herself***. (in which *she*, *her*, and *herself* all refer to the same person)
*I wrapped the towel around **me**/**myself***.
*As for **me**/**myself**, I don't care.*
*For someone like **you**/**yourself**, it must be a shock.*

In this last example it is the presence of *yourself* that is difficult to explain because the sentence contains no other instance of a *you* pronoun to bring about reflexivization.

An alternative explanation of reflexivization is that in such cases as the above there is really no difference between d(eep) and s(urface) structure. Instead the grammar contains a set of principles to account for the interpretation of pronouns. In *John hurt himself*, *himself* must refer back to *John*, but in *John hurt him*, *him* cannot refer back to *John*, and so on. In this view *\*Please help himself!* would be uninterpretable so far as *himself* is concerned and would, like *\*Please help you!*, be ungrammatical.

## 8.4   *There* Insertion

Under certain conditions it is possible – even necessary – to insert an unstressed expletive or non-referential *there* at the beginning of a clause through what appears to be a transformational process. Here are some examples of such a **there insertion transformation**:

> *There's a man outside to see you.*
> *There are/There's two reasons for that.*
> *There's not much to say.*
> *There's been an accident.*
> *There have been many different accounts of what occurred.*

Cases such as these seem to require the presence of the verb *be*, possibly in conjunction with a modal and/or auxiliary verb, and a noun phrase lacking a certain "definiteness." For example, the following sentences are usually not possible with unstressed *there*:

> *\*There's **Peter** outside to see you.*
> *\*There's **the man** outside to see you.*

There are, however, instances like:

> *There's **the opportunity** at last!*
> *There's **John**, for example.*

We appear to have d(eep) structures such as the following underlying the first set of sentences given above, not all of which could result in actual sentences in English:

> *a man is outside to see you*
> *two reasons for that are*
> *not much to say is*

*an accident has been*
*many different accounts of what occurred have been*

The *there* insertion transformation inserts *there* initially in the Comp position and inverts the subject and tense (plus *be* or *have*) of the verb phrase. In some varieties of English there may be no change in subject-verb agreement as a result of this inversion; consequently, we have *There **are two reasons** for that*. In other varieties the inserted *there* becomes the new subject and imposes singular agreement on the verb; consequently, we have ***There**'s two reasons for that*. We should also note that tag formation can be applied to structures that have undergone *there* insertion. In such cases *there* is treated as a pronoun subject: ***There**'s a man outside, isn't **there**?*

We will have more to say about *there* insertion in a later section on **raising** because of examples such as the following:

*There **must** be an answer to it.*
*There **appears** to be a sound reason for it.*
*There **happens** to be a right answer.*
*There **seems** to be a mistake.*

In such examples *there* insertion is found with verbs other than *be* or *have* directly following *there*.

## 8.5 Complements

There are three distinct kinds of **complement** structure:

*I noticed **John's excessive arguing**.*
*I noticed (**that**) **he had done it**.*
*I want **to go**.*

One possible origin for the first kind of complement, **possessive *-ing* complementation,** is a d(eep) structure like:

*I noticed [John argued excessively]*

The embedded subject *John* appears as a genitive *John's* and the embedded verb *argue* as an *-ing* participle *arguing*. Other changes such as that of *excessively* to *excessive* and its repositioning also occur. The passive transformation can also apply to sentences containing such complements, which must therefore be object noun phrases in the original structure:

*John's excessive arguing was noticed (by me).*

In the second kind, *that* **complementation**, a possible origin is:

*I noticed [that he had done it]*

The embedded noun clause is a finite clause, i.e., one that contains a tensed verb. In this case the complementizer *that* – it is in the Comp position – may be deleted. Again the resulting complement may be moved when the verb it follows undergoes passivization but the complementizer *that* is retained:

*That he had done it was noticed (by me).*

The third kind of complement in *I want to go* is called *for . . . to* **complementation**. It also occurs in the following sentences:

*I want to go.*
*I want him to go.*
*I expect to go.*
*I expect him to go.*
*He expects him to go.*
*The girls expect to go.*

The embedded clause in this case is tenseless so its verb is shown in the non-finite form, i.e., the form preceded by *to*. The clause is embedded as the complement of the verb of the main clause. We can see that this is so if we look closely at *I want him to go*. What is wanted is not "him" but "him to go." The tenseless clause must also have a subject. The following are possible d(eep) structures for the above sentences with the identical noun phrases co-indexed and each embedded clause shown as having *for* as a constituent in its Comp:

$I^1$ *want* [*for* $I^1$ *to go*]
*I want* [*for he to go*]
$I^1$ *expect* [*for* $I^1$ *to go*]
*I expect* [*for he to go*]
*he*$^1$ *expects* [*for he*$^2$ *to go*]
*the girls*$^1$ *expect* [*for the girls*$^1$ *to go*]

In this transformational approach when the subjects of the two clauses, i.e., the matrix and the embedded clauses, are identically indexed, the subject of the embedded clause is deleted by the **equi deletion transformation**. When the subjects of the two clauses are not identically indexed, the subject of the embedded clause becomes the object of the verb in the matrix clause and, if it is a pronoun, appears in its object case form. In most varieties of English *for* is also deleted before the new object or before *to* if there is no new object.

> I *want* **to** *go.*
> I *want* **him to** *go.*
> I *expect* **to** *go.*
> I *expect* **him to** *go.*
> He *expects* **him to** *go.*
> The girls *expect* **to** *go.*

In equi deletion there is a problem with postulating what happens when the subjects contain **quantifiers** like *all*, *everyone*, and *no one*. For example, it cannot be the case that sentences such as the following:

> **All people** *expect to grow old.*
> **Everyone** *hopes to win.*
> **No one** *wants to be the one chosen.*

have d(eep) structures like:

> *\*all people*$^1$ *expect* [*for* **all people**$^1$ *to grow old*]
> *\*everyone*$^1$ *hopes* [*for* **everyone**$^1$ *to win*]
> *\*no one*$^1$ *expects* [*for* **no one**$^1$ *to be the one chosen*]

This is still another instance of the difficulty of accounting structurally for English quantifying expressions.

We can also extend *for . . . to* complementation and equi deletion to account for other structures, e.g., those involving adjective complements and ditransitive verbs:

> **John**$^1$ *is eager* [*for* **John**$^1$ *to please*]
> John *is eager to please.*

> I *asked* **him**$^1$ [*for* **he**$^1$ *to go*]
> I *asked him to go.*

It is also possible to try to account for the above grammatical phenomena in another way. Rather than use a transformational account, we could propose that what happens in such sentences is that the grammar contains a set of principles to assign interpretations to pronouns and to mark them for case, i.e., as subjects and objects. It would interpret *him* in *I want him to go* as the subject of *go* and affirm that its case is correct because of its position in relation to *want*. It would also specify that *\*I want me to go* is uninterpretable, and that *He expects him to go* must be interpreted to refer to two different people.

## 8.6   Raising

In a transformational approach the creation of new objects in sentences like *I want **him** to go* and *I expect **him** to go* is called **raising**. In each case a constituent has been taken from an embedded clause and raised to become a constituent of the matrix clause. That this is so can be seen not only from the object case marking on *him* but also from the possibility of forming a passive for the sentence *I **expect** him to go*, i.e., *He **was expected** to go (by me)*. The passive transformation requires the presence of a direct object in the clause to which it applies. Therefore, *him* must be in the same clause as *expect* when the passive transformation applies. However, the pronoun originated in another "lower," i.e., embedded, clause from which it was "raised." In *I expect **him** to go* we have the subject of an embedded clause raised to become the object in a matrix clause. This process is called **subject to object raising**.

Here are some further possible examples of raising:

> *My **cousin** seems happy.*
> *My **cousin** appears to be happy.*
> *There happens to be a right answer.*
> *The **band** failed to appear.*
> *It began to rain.*
> *John happened to see me.*
> *John has to go.*
> *It kept on snowing.*
> *There must be an answer to it.*

In this view the relevant d(eep) structures of these sentences appear to be structures of the following kind in each of which the matrix clause has an empty subject slot that is eventually filled by the subject of the embedded clause:

> [ ] *seems* [*for **my cousin** to be happy*]
> [ ] *appears* [*for **my cousin** to be happy*]
> [ ] *happens* [*for **there** to be a right answer*]
> [ ] *failed* [*for **the band** to appear*]
> [ ] *began* [*for **it** to rain*]

[ ] *happened* [*for* **John** *to see me*]
[ ] *has* [*for* **John** *to go*]
[ ] *kept on* [*for* **it** *snowing*]
[ ] *must* [*for* **there** *to be an answer to it*]

Note that in each case the verb in the embedded clause is a non-finite verb, therefore marked by *to* if not already marked by *-ing*. (*To be* is also omissible as we can see since *My cousin seems happy* appears to be derived from *My cousin seems to be happy*.) In these sentences an embedded subject is raised to become a matrix subject; hence we have **subject to subject raising**.

Raising would also seem be involved in sentences such as the following:

*John is certain to please.*
*John is easy to please.*

We can postulate the following d(eep) structures for these sentences:

[ ] *is certain* [*for* **John** *to please* [ ]]
[ ] *is easy* [*for* [ ] *to please* **John**]

In the first case the embedded subject *John* becomes the matrix (or raised) subject and in the second case the embedded object becomes the matrix (or raised) subject, a process sometimes referred to as **object to subject raising** or **tough movement** (because it is difficult to explain and works with *tough*, as in *John is tough to please*). We can contrast the d(eep) structures of these sentences not only with each other but also with the d(eep) structure of the superficially similar *John is eager to please*, which was discussed in the previous section. In this case there is no raising, just an instance of equi deletion:

*John*[1] *is eager* [*for* **John**[1] *to please*]

Raising would also be involved in each of the following sentences:

*I don't think he's going.*
*I don't suppose he knows that.*

These sentences would have the following d(eep) structures:

*I think* [*that he isn't going*]
*I suppose* [*that he doesn't know that*]

Such d(eep) structures could also be used to produce the following sentences, which mean the same as the sentences given above:

*I think he isn't going.*
*I suppose he doesn't know that.*

However, in the first pair of sentences we find the negative *n't* raised from the embedded clause to the matrix clause. These are examples of **negative raising**. It should also be pointed out that such sentences can have question tags formed on their embedded clauses:

*I don't think he's going, is he?*
*I don't suppose he knows that, does he?*

The question tags are positive in each case. This fact suggests that the tags are formed while the embedded clauses still contain *n't*, i.e., before negative raising occurs:

*I think [that he isn't going] [is he]*
*I suppose [that he doesn't know that] [does he]*

Sentences like *Sally doesn't seem to care* and *He doesn't appear to under-stand* will therefore show both subject to subject raising and negative raising:

[ ] *seems [for Sally n't to care]*
[ ] *appears [for he n't to understand]*

These various sentences also illustrate the importance of *do* support in the formation of many negative clauses.

It would also be quite possible to extend the concept of raising to cover still other sentences:

*John must go.*
[ ] *must [for John to go]*

*John left.*
[ ] *past [for John to leave]*

*John has left.*
[ ] *pres [[ ] have -en [for John to leave]]*

In this last case raising would apply twice. First it would give us:

[ ] *pres [John have -en leave]*

A second round of raising gives us:

*John* pres have -en leave

Affix hopping then applies:

*John* have *pres* leave *-en*
*John has left.*

An alternative to a raising account in sentences like *Fred happened to kick it, John seemed angry, Sally began to sing,* etc. would involve an explanation of how predicates like *happen, seem, begin,* etc. require certain roles structures. For example, *Fred* in the first sentence cannot be construed to have any kind of agent role in relation to *happen* but only in relation to *kick,* the basic relationship in *John seemed angry* is not between *John* and *seemed* but between *John* and *angry,* and *Sally* is in an experiencer role in relation to *sing* and in no role relationship at all to *began.* However, what "happened" was that "Fred kicked it," what "seemed" was that "John was angry," and what "began" was "Sally's singing," so the role relationships must be interpreted accordingly.

## 8.7  Extrapositioning

An embedded clause may sometimes be moved and the non-referential pronoun *it* inserted in the position which the clause occupied:

[*that he should go*] *was decided*
*It was decided* (*that*) *he should go.*

Without such **extrapositioning**, sentences such as the one above are at the very least awkward:

*That he should go was decided.*

Sometimes extrapositioning is obligatory:

*He made it clear that she was to go.*
*\*He made* (*that*) *she was to go clear.*

*We took it for granted* (*that*) *they were going*
*\*We took that they were going for granted.*

*They thought it a great mistake that we had told them.*
*\*They thought that we had told them a great mistake.*

We also have sentences such as the following:

> *It seems (that) John likes Mary.*
> *It happens (that) I love her.*

The d(eep) structures of these sentences appear to be the following:

> [ ] *seems* [*that John likes Mary*]
> [ ] *happens* [*that I love her*]

Unlike the examples above in the discussion of raising, the verb in the embedded clause in each case is tensed. The result is that *it* must be inserted to
fill the subject position in the matrix clause and the embedded clause must
be left where it is. We can now account for the structural differences between
the following sentences:

> *John seems to like Mary.*
> *It seems John likes Mary.*

The d(eep) structure of the first sentence contains an untensed verb in the
embedded clause whereas the d(eep) structure of the second sentence contains
a tensed verb in the embedded clause:

> [ ] *seems* [*for John to like Mary*]
> [ ] *seems* [*that John likes Mary*]

The first d(eep) structure requires raising *John* to be the subject of *seems* and
the second requires the insertion of *it* to provide a subject for *seems*.


# 8.8   Clefting

There are two kinds of clefting transformation used for focusing, **clefting**
itself and **pseudo-clefting**. Clefting allows one to focus on a particular part
of a structure by employing *it is* or *it was* as a sentence introducer and recasting part of the original sentence as a relative clause. We can cleft a
sentence like *Fred drove his car last night in the city* in a variety of ways:

> *It was **Fred** who drove his car last night in the city.*
> *It was **his car** that Fred drove last night in the city.*
> *It was **last night** that Fred drove his car in the city.*
> *It was **in the city** that Fred drove his car last night.*

Pseudo-clefting focuses by means of an initial *wh-* word followed at some point by the verb *be* (or by *do* if the focused constituent is a verb phrase). The embedded clause in this case is a type of noun clause. Once again using the above sentence, we can pseudo-cleft it as follows:

> *What Fred drove last night in the city was **his car**.*
> *What Fred did last night in the city was **drive his car**.*
> *When Fred drove his car in the city was **last night**.*
> *Where Fred drove his car last night was **in the city**.*

## 8.9   Pronominalization, Substitution, and Ellipsis

Many of the following kinds of structural change in English may be accounted for either transformationally or through use of a set of interpretative principles: many third-person pronominal forms, various substitutions, and ellipses.

Some examples of **pronominalization** that need to be accounted for include:

> **Joan** *took **her** coat and left.*     [**Joan**$^1$ *took **Joan**$^1$'s coat and left*]
> **He** *hurt **himself**.*              [**he**$^1$ *hurt **he**$^1$*]
> *Sit **yourself** down!*            [**you**$^1$ *sit **you**$^1$ down*]
> **Mary** *is proud of **herself**.*        [**Mary**$^1$ *is proud of **Mary**$^1$*]

We can compare two of these sentences with the two that follow:

> **He** *hurt **him**.*               [**he**$^1$ *hurt **he**$^2$*]
> **Mary** *is proud of **her**.*        [**Mary** *is proud of **she***]

(We are assuming that the changes of *he* to *him* and *she* to *her*, i.e., marking for object case, occur automatically by rule at some later point in the derivation.) In the last two cases the *him* and *her* must refer to different persons than the subject pronouns of the sentences. We can also note that the very first sentence above (**Joan** *took **her** coat and left*) could also be ambiguous: she may have taken a coat belonging to some other female ([**Joan**$^1$ *took **she**$^2$ coat and left*]). Within an interpretative framework pronominalization is not explained transformationally but by a set of principles so that *He hurt him* is grammatical only if there are two different people involved. In this same account *Joan took her coat and left* would allow for alternative interpretations.

Pronominals do not necessarily "follow their antecedents" as we can see from the following examples:

*Knowing what **they** did, **Joan and Mary** refused the offer.*
*When **he** graduates, **John** is going to Paris.*
*The girl **he** likes says **Fred** is great.*
*The fact that **she** is talented doesn't mean **Mary** will be a success.*

In the following sentences **substitutes** are given in boldface and the structures substituted for are given in parentheses immediately following the substitutes:

*I like Updike's novels but she likes **those** (the novels) of Bellow.*
*She said she would be good and **that** (good) she was.*
*Mary sings and Sally **does** (sings) too.*
*They said the pears would be ripe and **so** (ripe) they were.*
*Mary sings beautifully and **so does** (sings beautifully) Sally.*
*Are you going? I hope **so** (I am going).*
*I told Jack to leave the room and he **did so** (left the room).*
*John goes to Toronto on Wednesdays and Sally **does so** (goes to Toronto) on Fridays.*
*Did she leave? I believe **not** (she did not leave).*
*I rushed to the store but he wasn't **there** (at the store).*
*He said he left it here, but I don't think he **did** (left it here).*
*She spoke to the boy at the back and to the **one** (boy) at the front.*
*She spoke to the girl wearing jeans in the hall and also to the **one** (girl wearing jeans) in the playground.*
*Mary's old house is prettier than Sally's new **one** (house).*

Finally, **ellipses** of various kinds occur in the following sentences. The non-ellipted structure is given in boldface and the ellipted constituent is given in parentheses.

*I **like** jazz, Fred (likes) the classics, and Sam (likes) light opera.*
*John won't **come** but Fred might (come).*
*I **gave** Sally a rose and (I gave) Fred a peach.*
*He **paid for it** but there was no need to (pay for it).*
*I'**ll speak to the group** this week and Mary ('ll speak to the group) next week.*
*He **does it** more often than she (does it).*
*He **can** go with us or (he can) stay at home.*
*Mary's **house** is prettier than Susan's (house).*
*These **books** are more expensive than those (books).*
*He might **tell Sarah** and I certainly hope he will (tell Sarah).*
*She says she's **sorry** if you are (sorry).*
*Kim **plays in an orchestra** regularly but Lee (plays in an orchestra) only intermittently.*

*Because I will* (take part in the competition), *John will* **take part in the**
  **competition.**
*I write* (books), *he edits* (books), *and she publishes* **books.**
*She's* **taller that John is** (tall).

Ellipsis is principled in operation and must be accounted for in some way. A
simple illustration of the need for such an account can be seen in the following sets of sentences in which there is contraction in both verbs in the second
sentence and in the first verb of the third sentence; however, the last sentence
with a contracted second verb is not grammatical:

*I* **am** *not going but* **they are** *going.*
*I'm not going but* **they're** *going.*
*I'm not going but* **they are.**
*I'm not going but* **they're.**

*I* **will** *do it and he* **will** *do it too.*
*I'll do it and he'll do it too.*
*I'll do it and he* **will** *too.*
*\*I'll do it and he'll too.*

Evidently verb contraction is not allowed once a following verb phrase constituent is ellipted.

  What we appear to need is a set of rules or principles that allows us to do
two things: one is to recover the d(eep) structure of a sentence at every step
in its generation and the other is to be able to specify the order in which
various transformations and rules apply. In one view of what such a set
might contain any ellipted or moved constituent leaves behind a trace [t] of
itself. Consequently, the sentences *John won't come but Fred might, John is*
*eager to please, John is easy to please, I'm not going but they are, I'll do it*
*and he will too,* and *What did he want?* each have a trace in the place
indicated below, with the source of each trace indicated in parentheses:

*John won't come but Fred might* [t]. (come)
*John is eager* [t] *to please.* (John)
*John is easy to please* [t]. (John)
*I'm not going but they are* [t]. (going)
*I'll do it and he will* [t] *too.* (do it)
*What did he want* [t]? (what)

We will use the final sentence above *What did he want?* to show a complete
derivation:

d(eep) structure          *question he past want what*
                            question
                          *past he want what*
                            *wh-* movement
                          *what past he want* [t]
                            *do* support
                          *what past do he want* [t]
                            affix hopping
s(urface) structure       *what do past he want* [t]
                          *what did he want?*


# 8.10   Exercises


1   Provide a d(eep) structure for each of the following sentences and show the transformations required to derive the s(urface) structure. The first three are done for you.

(a)   I want to know whether he's going.
      (*I¹ pres want [for I¹ to know [question he pres be -ing go]]*
         question
      *I¹ pres want [for I¹ to know [whether he pres be -ing go]]*
         equi deletion
      *I pres want [[t] to know [whether he pres be -ing go]]*
         affix hopping
      *I want pres [[t] to know [whether he be pres go -ing]]*)
(b)   What does he want to do?
      (*question he¹ pres want [for he¹ to do what]*
         equi deletion
      *question he pres want [[t] to do what]*
         question
      *pres he want [[t] to do what]*
         *wh-* movement
      *what pres he want [[t] to do [t]]*
         *do* support
      *what pres do he want [[t] to do [t]]*
         affix hopping
      *what do pres he want [[t] to do [t]]*)
(c)   He didn't go.
      (*negation he past go*
         negative
      *he past n't go*
         *do* support
      *he past do n't go*
         affix hopping
      *he do past n't go*)
(d)   Couldn't they tell him the answer?

(e)    Please yourself!
(f)    She hurt herself when she fell.
(g)    She talks to her every day.
(h)    She talks to herself all day.
(i)    He wouldn't give me the book I wanted.
(j)    Don't hurt yourself!
(k)    The shed in which it was stored burned down.
(l)    There's a man at the door.
(m)    There must be a pen around here somewhere.
(n)    He likes to party.
(o)    I consider you a friend.
(p)    I believed Mary to be innocent.
(q)    I want to go.
(r)    I want him to go.
(s)    He wants him to go.
(t)    I am happy to oblige.
(u)    There isn't any time for it.
(v)    They are anxious to help them.
(w)    They are anxious to help themselves.

2   Provide a d(eep) structure for each of the following sentences and show the transformations required to derive the s(urface) structure. The first three are done for you.

(a)    He seems content.
       ([ ] *pres seem* [*for he to be content*]
          raising
       *he pres seem* [[t] *content*]
          affix hopping
       *he seem pres* [[t] *content*])
(b)    It began to rain.
       ([ ] *past begin* [*for it to rain*]
          raising
       *it past begin* [[t] *to rain*]
          affix hopping
       *it begin past* [[t] *to rain*])
(c)    I happened to notice her.
       ([ ] *past happen* [*for I to notice her*]
          raising
       *I past happen* [[t] *to notice her*]
          affix hopping
       *I happen past* [[t] *to notice her*])
(d)    He is certain to please them.
(e)    He is difficult to please.
(f)    He is eager to please.
(g)    There appears to be no reason for it.
(h)    I don't think he'll do it.
(i)    It was agreed that John would do it.
(j)    It seems he's ready for it.
(k)    He doesn't seem to be ready for it.

(l)    John seems to like Mary.
(m)   It seems John likes Mary.
(n)    I believe it inevitable that it will fail.
(o)    They considered it foolish to press on.
(p)    He considered it wise to quit.
(q)    John imagined him kissing Sally.
(r)    John imagined himself kissing Sally.
(s)    John imagined him kissing himself.
(t)    John imagined himself kissing himself.
(u)    John is too crazy to live with.
(v)    Fred needs someone to work for.
(w)   Fred needs someone to work for him.
(x)    It's clear it's impossible for pigs to fly.
(y)    Which prize did John think Fred believed I'd won?
(z)    What hotel did you hear it's rumored I'm alleged to have been seen going
       into?

3   Show as best you can how the following sentences are quite different in their
    grammatical structures.

    (a)    The tribunal required the firm to rehire the complainant.
    (b)    The tribunal required the complainant to be rehired.
    (c)    The tribunal required the complainant to reapply for the position.

4   Show as best you can how the sentences in each of the following pairs are
    quite different in their grammatical structures.

    (a)    Did he say who did it?
           Who did he say did it?
    (b)    He wants a song to sing.
           He wants to sing a song.
    (c)    Who has seen your friend?
           Who has your friend seen?

5   How would you use data such as the following sentences provide to argue that
    the matrix clause in each sentence has no other NP than *I* and that both the
    subject and object of *shave* are recoverable, i.e., that in each case you quite
    clearly know who got shaved and, except in the last two, who did the shaving?

    (a)    I wanted to shave myself.
    (b)    I wanted him to shave himself.
    (c)    I wanted him to shave me.
    (d)    I wanted to shave him.
    (e)    I wanted him to be shaved.
    (f)    I wanted to be shaved.

# 9
# Sounds and Systems

A language is a system of sounds as well as a system of meanings. We will therefore now turn our attention to English pronunciation. In this chapter we will be concerned with such matters as exactly what we mean by "sounds" and "systems of sounds." Our immediate concern will be with finding answers to questions such as the following: What are the sounds of English? How might we best describe them? How many sounds does a word like *train* have? Why is *slkop* not a possible English word? How do we usually spell the sounds we have? And so on. In later chapters our concern will be with how we combine sounds to form larger structural units such as words, phrases, clauses, and sentences.

## 9.1   Contrastive Sounds

Each language has its own system of contrastive sounds, and utterances in the language are formed by combining sounds out of that system. No two systems are alike, for what counts phonetically as a "sound" in one language may or may not count as a "sound" in another language.

We say that sounds are **contrastive** because they are used not only to form utterances but to distinguish utterances from one another. For example, two utterances may differ because one contains a sound the other does not have, or one has one sound in a particular place and the other has a different sound in that same place:

He saw the ape.
He saw the tape.

He bought a cat.
He bought a mat.

In the first pair of utterances *ape* contrasts with *tape* and in the second pair *cat* contrasts with *mat*. *Tape* contains a sound that *ape* does not have, but *cat* and *mat* each have the same number of sounds, with the difference in this case being that *cat* and *mat* begin with different sounds: We will call pairs of the *cat-mat* kind **minimal pairs**. Minimal pairs of utterances differ in that one member of the pair has one sound in a particular place and the other has another, therefore contrastive, sound in the same place. By "sound" we also mean a distinctive unit in the pronunciation of a language which can occur in various places in that language. We will call such units **phonemes**. Many other English words contain instances of the sounds spelled here by *c* and *m*: *cap, can, cane*; *map, mane*. *Cap* and *map*, *can* and *man*, and *cane* and *mane* are also further minimal pairs because of this initial contrast.

If we use English words pronounced in isolation – what are often referred to as the **citation forms** of words – we can attempt to see how many different initial consonant sounds there are for such words in the variety of English we are using as our source of data. We will also confine our attention to words of one syllable. (We will attempt definitions of both **consonant** and **syllable** later.) We will also use words that both begin and end with single consonant sounds and employ a set of symbols to record those consonants, or **consonant phonemes**. In this case these are the consonant phonemes of English because the language we are concerned with is English, and phonemes are always the phonemes of some language. We will also enclose these phonemic symbols within diagonal strokes, e.g., /p/ or /b/.

From the above source we can establish the following list of initial consonant phonemes in English if we look for minimal pairs, triples, etc.:

/p/    *pin, bin, tin, din*
/b/    *bin, pin, tin, din*
/t/    *tin, din, pin, bin*
/d/    *din, tin, pin, bin*
/č/    *chin, gin, tin, din* (č is called "c wedge" or "c hachek")
/ǰ/    *gin, shin, tin, din* (ǰ is called "j wedge" or "j hachek")
/k/    *kin, Ginn, tin, din*
/g/    *Ginn, kin, tin, din*
/f/    *fin, tin, din; fan, van*
/v/    *van, fan, can, tan*
/θ/    *thin, tin, din, fin* (θ is called "theta")
/ð/    *then, den; this, kiss* (ð is called "eth")
/s/    *sin, tin, din; sip, zip*
/z/    *zip, sip, ship, chip*
/š/    *ship, chip, tip, dip* (š is called "s wedge" or "s hachek")
/m/    *men, then, den*
/n/    *nip, ship, pip, rip*

/r/    *rip, ship, chip, pip*
/l/    *lip, rip, nip, dip; let, yet*
/y/    *yet, let; yell, dell*
/h/    *hip, lip; hot, rot*
/r/    *rot, lot; rip, lip*

We can now apply the same procedure to final consonants in English mono-syllabic words. We will also use the same symbol as before for a particular contrastive sound when the sound seems to be phonetically very similar or identical. For example, we will say that the last sound in *pen, Dan, soon,* and *run* is the same /n/ as the first sound in *nip, no, now,* and *neat.* At some point we will have to specify what we mean by "phonetically very similar" and "same sound," but again we will delay doing so for a while. Applying the same procedure, we arrive at the following list of consonant phonemes in final position:

/p/    *nip, nib; nap, nab*
/b/    *nib, nip; rob, rot*
/t/    *rot, rob, rod*
/d/    *rod, rot; rid, rich, ridge*
/č/    *rich, ridge, rid*
/ǰ/    *ridge, rich, Rick, rig*
/k/    *rick, rich; deck, deaf*
/g/    *rig, Rick, rip*
/f/    *deaf, deck; safe, save*
/v/    *save, safe; rave, raise*
/θ/    *pith, pin; Beth, Ben*
/ð/    *soothe, soon; bathe, bake*
/s/    *race, raise; mass, mash*
/z/    *raise, race; jazz, jam*
/š/    *mash, mass; fish, fizz*
/m/    *rim, ring, rid*
/n/    *run, rum, rung*
/ŋ/    *rung, rum, run* (ŋ is called "eng")
/l/    *dell, deck; sail, safe*

This last list is not identical to the first list. The list of final consonants includes /ŋ/, not found in the first list, but does not include the /y/, /w/, /h/, and /r/ from that list.

If we look at further minimal pairs in English and do not restrict our attention to the monosyllabic words used above, we may discover still an-other possible consonant phoneme /ž/:

/ž/ *seizure, Caesar; measure, mesher* (ž is called "z wedge" or "z hachek")

However, we will not be able to find a great many illustrative minimal pairs with /ž/ as one of the members in contrast to most of the other consonants for which many minimal pairs exist. Ideally, we would like to find a minimal pair for every pair of consonants. Better still would be several minimal pairs showing the contrast in several positions, e.g., initially, finally, and within words, as /p/ and /b/ contrast in *pin* and *bin*, *nap* and *nab*, and *staple* and *stable*. Consonants like /p/ and /b/ do indeed show great contrastive ability in all positions, but consonants like /ŋ/ and /ž/ have much more limited contrastive possibilities.

Pairs of phonemes for which we can find many minimal pairs, e.g., /p/ and /b/ (e.g., *pin* and *bin*) or /p/ and /t/ (e.g., *pin* and *tin*) carry a big **functional load** in the language, i.e., they are used frequently to distinguish among words. In contrast a pair like /θ/ and /ð/ has a small functional load with *thigh* and *thy* and *ether* and *either* being the only easily discoverable pairs for this contrast.

We did not show /r/, /y/, /w/, and /h/ in word-final position. In this variety of English only /r/ appears in this position, in contrasts like the following:

/r/   *bit, bid, beer; beat, bead, beer*

We will have more to say about /r/ in this position later and about the relationship it has to the vowels that precede it. The other three consonants do not occur finally in this variety of English, just as /ŋ/ does not occur initially and /ž/ occurs only medially.

Here then are the English consonant phonemes with each described according to its essential phonological characteristics. We will have more to say about these characteristics in the next section. The parenthesized terms are sometimes omitted from the descriptions.

| | |
|---|---|
| /p/ | voiceless bilabial stop |
| /b/ | voiced bilabial stop |
| /t/ | voiceless (apico)alveolar stop |
| /d/ | voiced (apico)alveolar stop |
| /č/ | voiceless alveopalatal affricate |
| /ǰ/ | voiced alveopalatal affricate |
| /k/ | voiceless (dorso)velar stop |
| /g/ | voiced (dorso)velar stop |
| /f/ | voiceless labiodental fricative |
| /v/ | voiced labiodental fricative |
| /θ/ | voiceless dental fricative |

/ð/   voiced dental fricative
/s/   voiceless alveolar fricative
/z/   voiced alveolar fricative
/š/   voiceless palatal fricative
/ž/   voiced palatal fricative
/m/   bilabial nasal
/n/   alveolar nasal
/ŋ/   (dorso)velar nasal
/y/   front glide
/w/   back glide
/h/   glottal
/r/   retroflex
/l/   lateral

We can now apply the same procedure to English **vowels**. Once again we will employ monosyllabic English words and confine our attention to a particular variety of English:

/i/   *beat, bit, bet, bat*
/ɪ/   *bit, beat, bet, bat*
/e/   *bait, bet, bit, bat*
/ɛ/   *bet, bait, bat, but* (ɛ is called "epsilon" or "open e")
/æ/   *bat, bet, bait, but* (æ is called "ash" or "digraph")
/u/   *boot, bait, bet, but*
/ʊ/   *full, fool; wood, weed*
/o/   *boat, bet, boot, but*
/ɔ/   *bought, boat, boot, but* (ɔ is called "open o")
/ə/   *but, boot, boat; nut, nought* (ə is called "schwa")
/a/   *not, nought, nut; lot, lit, let*
/aɪ/  *bite, bit, bait, bet*
/aʊ/  *bout, bite, bit, beet*
/ɔɪ/  *boil, bile, Bill; soil, sail, sell*

In this variety of English we can find all the above vowel contrasts and no others. We can also describe the vowels by their essential phonological characteristics about which we will have more to say in the next section.

/i/   high front tense vowel
/ɪ/   high front lax vowel
/e/   mid front tense vowel
/ɛ/   mid front lax vowel
/æ/   low front vowel
/u/   high back tense vowel

/ʊ/   high back lax vowel
/o/   mid back vowel
/ɔ/   low back vowel
/ə/   mid central lax vowel
/a/   low central vowel
/aɪ/  low central front-rising diphthong
/aʊ/  low central back-rising diphthong
/ɔɪ/  low back front-rising diphthong

English consonant and vowel phonemes are spelled in a variety of ways. Many of the spellings are infrequent and a few are unique. What follows is a fairly comprehensive listing of the different spellings (**graphemes**) one may encounter. We should note that this list is for the variety of English that we are concentrating on here for the purposes of exposition; speakers of other varieties of English may not agree with some of the assignments. We should also note that on occasion more than one interpretation is given for some particular combination of letters: for example, in *sign* it is not at all clear whether /aɪ/ is represented in spelling *i* or *ig* and /n/ by *gn* or *n*.

## Consonants

/p/   *pen, span, sample, nip, slipper, hiccough*
/b/   *ban, rib, nimble, rabble, cupboard*
/t/   *ten, stop, bat, writer, latter, baked, debt, Thomas, Ptolemy, victuals*
/d/   *den, leaden, said, loved, ladder, riddle, bdellium, dhoti*
/č/   *chip, pitch, rich, righteous, nature, Christian, fixture*
/ǰ/   *judge, gin, region, midget, suggest, sergeant, pigeon large, Norwich, change, soldier, adjacent*
/k/   *cap, kin, quiet, crack, locker, seek, frantic, fox, scheme, chorus, mechanic, khaki, critique, quote, havoc, conquer, succumb, chloride, queue, Sikh*
/g/   *goal, dig, gaggle, guest, plague, ghost, exact, Pittsburgh, blackguard*
/f/   *fan, rifle, if, sniff, rough, photograph*
/v/   *vain, even, of, serve, give*
/θ/   *thin, path, athlete*
/ð/   *then, bathe, brother*
/s/   *so, pass, pussy, city, tense, psychology, science, whistle, democracy, receive, answer, listen, quartz, assert, accent, sword, descent, bus, fuss, dance, fix, parcel*
/z/   *zip, jazz, fuzzy, begs, visor, roses, xerox, peas, scissors, exact, please, raspberry*

/š/    shop, sure, fashion, ration, glacial, dish, mission, machine,
       mention, mansion, conscious, crucial, ocean, luxury, chalet
/ž/    measure, decision, azure, beige, regime
/m/    man, ham, important, mummy, sitcom, come, crumb, autumn
/n/    nap, gnaw, knee, pneumonia, mnemonic, skinny, sin, sign, cognac
/ŋ/    singer, finger, sank, sang, anxious
/y/    you, few, fuel, spaniel, feud, beauty, music, fiord
/w/    win, whine, queen, language, choir, switch, anguish, one
/h/    happy, who, ahead
/r/    rap, girl, hurry, Mary, her, rhyme, wring
/l/    lull, little, salt, Lloyd


## Vowels


/i/    meet, meat, be, mete, deceive, reprieve, key, quay, valley, museum,
       people, Caesar, ravine, pity, stadium
/ɪ/    fit, imp, been, myth, pretty, sieve, women, build, busy, England
/e/    gate, bay, great, rain, vein, eight, gauge, reign, they, straight,
       (double) bass, ballet, cafe, sundae, archaic, Ralph
/ɛ/    pet, penance, says, said, quest, let, bread, friend, any, heifer,
       bury, jeopardy
/æ/    pat, laugh, plaid, half, comrade, meringue
/u/    do, moot, blue, duty, rude, super, through, too, two, move, chew,
       fruit, shoe, uncouth, deuce, duet, newt, view, Sioux, Hugh
/ʊ/    bull, put, could, wolf, foot, woman
/o/    vote, moat, so, sow, sew, hoe, dough, beau, owe, bolt, control,
       poet, brooch, mauve, yeoman, yolk
/ɔ/    caught, bought, fall, stalk, flaw, awe, automatic, water, Santa
       Claus
/ə/    the stressed vowels in sun, putt, son, does, dove, tough, flood,
       was, come; the unstressed vowels in comma, alone, telegraph,
       harmony, difficult, hybrid, harmonious, rented, houses, agreeable,
       woman, women, apple, support
/a/    hot, bottle, father, balm, cough, knowledge, sausage, yacht
/aɪ/   bite, type, fight, sign, indict, by, dye, tiger, aisle, choir, hybrid,
       island, die, height, buy, aye, eiderdown, eye, riot, bind, guile, pi
/aʊ/   now, bough, doubt, loud, down
/ɔɪ/   boy, boil, buoy, Reuters


## Vowels followed by r


/ir/   hear, here, pier, beer, weird
/er/   bear, bare, fair, heir, Eire, where, scarce, Mary, fairy

/ɛr/    merry, ferry, perish
/ær/    marry
/ur/    poor, tour, demure, sure
/or/    bore, pour, boar, door, oar, aura, fort
/ər/    the stressed vowels in cur, myrtle, purr, burn, scourge, thirst, earth, work, masseur; the unstressed vowels in worker, figure, sailor, liar
/ar/    park, heart
/aɪr/   fire, pyre
/aʊr/   hour, power

(English spelling is often criticized because it is not "phonetic." Some of that criticism is justified, but not all. Spellings like bough, cough, tough, through, though, and thorough are exceptions rather than the rule. George Bernard Shaw's suggestion that fish could just as easily be spelled ghoti was absurd. There are easily discoverable general spelling patterns in English; moreover, the pronunciations of written words are usually much more easily predicted than the spellings of spoken words.)

## 9.2   Distinctive Characteristics

In the preceding section we used minimal pairs, triples, etc. to discover the contrastive consonants and vowels, i.e., the phonemes, for one variety of English. We also assigned each phoneme a brief phonological description. We will turn our attention now to those descriptions and in doing so, make reference to the diagram of the **vocal tract** (figure 1).

**Consonants** and **vowels** are produced by interfering in some way with the egressive airstream as it proceeds from the chest and out of the mouth and/ or nose. The distinction between consonants and vowels resides in the type of interference: with consonants the interference leads to a marked increase in the turbulence associated with that flow of air; on the other hand, vowels do not produce like turbulence. As we will see in chapter 13, vowels also form the peaks of syllables, whereas consonants are peripheral entities in syllables.

Consonants may be **voiced** or **voiceless**. Voicing is an effect produced in the glottis by the vocal cords (also called vocal folds). If the vocal cords vibrate during the production of a sound, that sound is a voiced sound; if they do not vibrate, that sound is a voiceless sound. In the following two rows of words, those in the first row begin with voiced sounds and those in the second row begin with corresponding voiceless sounds:

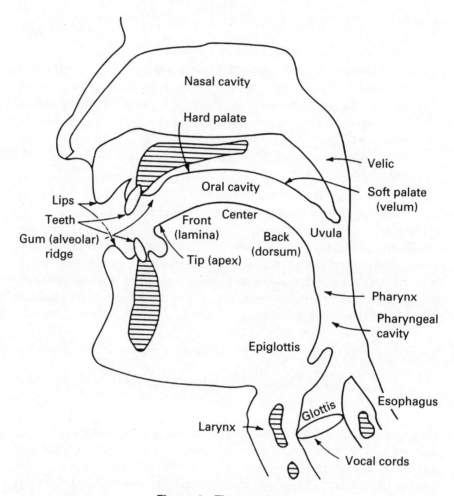

**Figure 1**  The vocal tract

*bat din gap vat thy zip jeep*
*pat tin cap fat thigh sip cheap*

The /š/ of *ship* is voiceless; there is no contrast initially in English in words with its voiced counterpart /ž/. The /h/ of *hot* is also voiceless. All English consonants are voiced except those just described as voiceless. This means that, except for /h/, those consonants for which no voiced-voiceless characterization was given in the list in the previous section of this chapter must be regarded as voiced; /m/ and /n/, for example, are voiced and have no voiceless counterparts.

Consonants are characterized by turbulence in the airflow during their production. There are various kinds of turbulence and reference to these varieties is used in further characterizing consonants. The airflow may be completely stopped at a place in the mouth and concurrently prevented from finding an exit through the nose. Consonants produced in this way are called **stops** (or **plosives**). The place of stoppage is also sometimes indicated by naming the particular part of the lower jaw which is moved to cause the stoppage and the point on the upper jaw at which that stoppage occurs. Sometimes only the second bit of information is given. To say of a stop that it is a bilabial stop is to indicate that the lower lip stopped the airstream at the upper lip. In a dorsovelar stop, /k/ or /g/, the back of the tongue, the dorsum, has stopped airstream at the back of the hard palate. In this last case sometimes only the hard palate, the velum, is mentioned because only the back of the tongue could make such a closure.

**Nasals** are very similar to stops. However, in this case while there is a complete stoppage of the air in the mouth, the airstream is allowed to escape through the nose via the velic opening. The point of articulation on the upper jaw (and sometimes the articulator on the lower jaw) are also used in the description of nasals: /ŋ/ is therefore a dorsovelar nasal. All English nasals are voiced. We can compare the nasals in the first of the following two rows with the corresponding voiced stops in the second row:

*man nip rim sang*
*bad dip rib sag*

**Fricatives** are produced with an incomplete closure in the mouth and complete closure of the nasal passage. The airstream is forced through the incomplete closure with noticeable turbulence. Fricatives may be voiced or voiceless. Fricatives are also described in terms of their place of articulation. Consequently, /š/ is a voiceless palatal fricative.

**Affricates** are sounds which begin with a complete stoppage of air like stops but the stopped air is released with the kind of turbulence associated with fricatives. There is a single pair of English affricates, one voiceless /č/ and the other voiced /ǰ/.

The **retroflex** /r/ and the **lateral** /l/ are both voiced. The tip of the tongue is curled back in the production of the retroflex and the airstream is forced over it. The airstream is forced around the sides of the tongue in the production of the lateral.

The **glides** /y/ and /w/ are both voiced. In the production of /y/ (the front or palatal glide) the front of the tongue is bunched high in the front of the mouth and the lips are spread; in the production of /w/ (the back or labiovelar glide) the tongue is bunched high in the back of the mouth and the lips are rounded. These glides do not have the very noticeable turbulence of the other consonants and are like vowels in many respects. Consequently, they are sometimes called **semi-consonants**. They do, however, fill positions in words that are usually filled by consonants.

|      | Front | Center | Back |
|------|-------|--------|------|
| High | i     |        | u    |
|      | ɪ     |        | ʊ    |
| Mid  | e     | ə      | o    |
|      | ɛ     |        |      |
| Low  | æ     | a      | ɔ    |

**Figure 2**   English vowels

The **glottal** /h/ is voiceless. It is not characterized by any other features than voicelessness and friction in the vocal cords (or glottis).

All English vowels are voiced. There are simple vowels (also called **monophthongs**) and **diphthongs**. A simple vowel consists of one sound and there is little or no movement of the tongue associated with its production. A diphthong is a vowel during the production of which there is considerable tongue movement to the extent that it is necessary to specify both the starting and ending positions of the vowel. In the variety of English we are describing there are eleven simple vowels and three diphthongs.

Vowels are described by how **high** or **low** (or intermediate **mid**) the tongue is positioned in the mouth, by how **front** or **back** (or intermediate **central**) it is positioned, and by the **tenseness** or **laxness** of the tongue and the muscles that control it. As with consonants we do not describe features which are predictable or which are not distinctive. For example, all English front vowels are produced with spread lips and are **unrounded**. All English back vowels are produced with rounded lips and can be described as **rounded**. However, the unrounded-rounded quality is predictable from the frontness-backness quality so need not be specified here.

The high vowels are /i/, /ɪ/, /u/, and /ʊ/. The first pair are high front vowels produced with the tongue both high and front in the mouth; the second pair are high back vowels with the tongue both high and back in the mouth. However, /i/ and /u/ are tense, whereas /ɪ/ and /ʊ/ are lax. The mid vowels are /e/, /ɛ/, /o/, and /ə/. The tongue is not so high as with the high vowels nor is it at its lowest possible position in the mouth. There is a tense-lax distinction between the front vowels /e/ and /ɛ/, but /o/ is the only mid back vowel. The low vowels are /æ/, /a/, and /ɔ/. The first is front, the second central, and the third back. There is no contrastive tense-lax distinction in the low vowels. The mid-central vowel /ə/ is produced in the center of the mouth; it is neither high or low nor front or back. It is also lax. Figure 2 shows the relative positions of the vowels in the mouth.

The diphthongs are of two types: the /aɪ/ and /aʊ/ type and the solitary /ɔɪ/. In the first two the pronunciation begins with the tongue in the low

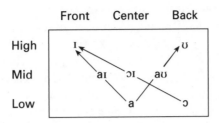

**Figure 3** English diphthongs

central area: in the case of /aɪ/ the tongue thrusts upward and forward in the mouth (and the lips remain spread); in the case of /aʊ/ the tongue pulls upward and backward in the mouth (and the lips round). In contrast, /ɔɪ/ begins with the tongue in the low back position and during the production of the diphthong there is both raising and fronting of the tongue. The lips also unround. Figure 3 shows the diphthongs.

The above description of English consonants and vowels makes use of articulatory features, that is, it refers to the physical movements associated with the production of the phonemes. Because we are discussing phonemes, that is, contrastive sound units, we have also restricted the descriptions to the essential defining features of each phoneme. We have not included statements about predictable features, e.g., that nasals are voiced or that back vowels are rounded.

It is also possible to use other systems of classification in describing the phonemic system of English. One frequently used system uses **distinctive features** to describe the differences we noted above. For example, sounds can be described as being **continuants** or noncontinuants. Continuants are sounds that allow the airstream to proceed through the mouth unblocked, e.g., sounds such as fricatives, vowels, and /l, r, w, y/. Sounds may also be **consonantal** or not; consequently, consonantal /l/ and /r/ are distinguishable from nonconsonantal /w/ and /y/. A **voiced-voiceless** distinction also distinguishes sounds such as /b, d, g/ from /p, t, k/. An **anterior-nonanterior** distinction separates the anterior consonants /m, n, p, t, b, d, f, θ, s, v, ð, z, l/, i.e., those consonants produced with the involvement of the tip of the tongue or lips from nonanterior consonants. A **coronal-noncoronal** distinction separates coronal consonants made in the alveolar and palatal area, i.e., /n, t, d, θ, s, š, ð, z, ž, č ǰ, l, r/ from those produced elsewhere. In this system each phoneme is described in terms of the minimum set of distinctive features required to differentiate it from all the others.

## 9.3 Systems

There is more than one possible way of describing English phonemes. We chose to describe the phonemic system of English – or to be more accurate, one variety of English – using the principle of distinctive contrast in utterances that are minimally different from one another. We then proceeded to describe the articulatory characteristics of the sounds, or phonemes, we discovered, and we also excluded redundant, or predictable, characteristics. In grouping "sounds" together, we also decided that certain sounds were the "same" as other sounds. Consequently, there are numerous assumptions built into what we did. Let us now look at a few of these.

We ascribed phonemic status to /č/ and /ǰ/; however, /č/ may be a combination of /t/ and /š/, and /ǰ/ may be a combination of /d/ and /ž/. The decision to call /č/ and /ǰ/ separate phonemes and not sequences of phonemes really rests on criteria we have not discussed. There criteria are distributional in nature. English words do not begin with sequences of stop followed by fricative, not even when the stop and the fricative are **homorganic**, i.e., made in the same position. We find no instances of *tsin, *pfine, and *dzoo. Some such sequences do occur at the ends of words but usually only over a meaning boundary, e.g., between a noun and a plural ending or between a verb and a third person singular ending as in *cats*, *walks*, and *bends*. However, /č/ and /ǰ/ occur quite freely at the beginnings and endings of words and, in doing so, behave like other consonant phonemes. Therefore, we conclude that each is a single phoneme and not a sequence of phonemes.

The /ž/ phoneme, however, is only tenuously established in the system we described above. It has a very limited distribution, occurring in many varieties of English only between vowels in words like *measure* and *precision*. If it occurs in words liks *garage*, *beige*, and *Jeanne*, it sounds somewhat "foreign." The phoneme /ž/ is a late addition to the English language and not a very productive one, i.e., we hardly ever use it to form minimal pairs of words with other consonants. The phonemes /ŋ/, /y/, /w/, and /h/ are not without their problems too. The first occurred contrastively only in final position and the last three occurred contrastively only in initial position. Like /ž/, /ŋ/ is a relatively late addition to the English phonemic system, if indeed it is fully established there at all. In some accounts of English phonemes /ŋ/ does not appear as a phoneme. Words like *sing* and *drink* are said to contain /n/ rather than /ŋ/, i.e., to be phonemically /sɪng/ and /drɪnk/ respectively. This /n/ is then realized by a velar nasal before the /g/ and /k/ in such words, and then the /g/ is predictably deleted in words like *sing*. We will return to this problem in chapter 12.

If we look more closely at /y/ and /w/, we will see that in their articulation these phonemes resemble the final parts of the diphthongs /aɪ/ and /ɔɪ/ in the first case and of the diphthong /aʊ/ in the second case. Such a resemblance has prompted claims that /aɪ/ and /ɔɪ/ are really /ay/ and /ɔy/ and that /aʊ/ is really /aw/. This solution "corrects" a distributional anomaly in the consonantal system in that it allows /y/ and /w/ to appear after vowels as well as before them. However, such a solution does not seem to be particularly well motivated. Speakers of English do not intuitively think that the final sounds in words like *my* /maɪ/, *boy* /bɔɪ/, and *now* /naʊ/ are consonants, no matter how we represent those sounds in the written form of the language. They also almost certainly will agree that each word has but a single consonant sound followed by a single vowel sound. Moreover, it may be hard to convince them that the following are somehow minimal pairs in English:

| | | |
|---|---|---|
| *dog, die* | /dag/, day/ | (not /daɪ/) |
| *hot, how* | /hat/, haw/ | (not /haʊ/) |
| *talk, toy* | /tɔk/, tɔy/ | (not /tɔɪ/) |

In a further extension of this kind of reasoning the whole vowel system is reinterpreted to remove the tense-lax contrast by reinterpreting tense vowels as sequences of lax vowel plus either /y/ or /w/, depending on whether the vowel is front or back. The actual number of vowels is also reduced. The result is the following equivalents for the vowels given in the first section of this chapter. An illustrative word is also given in each case.

| | | |
|---|---|---|
| /i/ | /iy/ | *beat* |
| /ɪ/ | /i/ | *bit* |
| /e/ | /ey/ | *bait* |
| /ɛ/ | /e/ | *bet* |
| /æ/ | /æ/ | *bat* |
| /u/ | /uw/ | *food* |
| /ʊ/ | /u/ | *full* |
| /o/ | /ow/ | *boat* |
| /ɔ/ | /ɔ/ | *bought* |
| /ə/ | /ə/ | *but* |
| /a/ | /a/ | *hot* |
| /aɪ/ | /ay/ | *bite* |
| /aʊ/ | /aw/ | *bout* |
| /ɔɪ/ | /ɔy/ | *boil* |

## 9.4 Phonemic Sequences

Numerous restrictions apply in the sequencing – or **clustering** – of phonemes within English utterances. As we will see in the final chapter, in a certain kind of speech – **allegro speech**, i.e., fast speech – some of these restrictions may be relaxed, but it is useful to think that the restrictions exist and are relaxed rather than that slow and fast speech make use of two independent systems. We will not state all of the restrictions here, only a few of the more interesting ones.

No more than three consonants can occur in a cluster at the beginning of an utterance. If three do occur, the first must be /s/ and the next consonant must be a voiceless stop, therefore one of /p/, /t/, or /k/. The third consonant must be one of /r/, /l/, /y/, or /w/ although not all combinations with /l/ or /w/ are possible. (In the following examples the # sign refers to the boundary of an utterance, either the beginning or the end.)

$$
/^{\#}\text{s} \quad \begin{matrix} & \text{r} \\ \text{p} & \text{l} \\ \text{t} & \\ \text{k} & \text{y} \\ & \text{w} \end{matrix} \quad -/
$$

Some example words are:

| *sprint* | *sclerosis* | *spume* | *squelch* | *stretch* |
|---|---|---|---|---|
| /sprɪnt/ | /sklərósəs/ | /spyum/ | /skwɛlč/ | /strɛč/ |

Not all possibilities occur, however. For example, there are no English words beginning with */#spw-/, */#stw-/, or */#stl-/, and /#skl-/, as in *sclerosis*, is rare. Considerably more variety is possible in two-consonant initial clusters. However, many beginnings are excluded, among them the following: */#lr-/, */#dz-/, */#tz-/, */#rs-/ */#rt-/, */#pn-/, */#dl-/, and so no. Many other initial clusters are infrequent: /#šr-/ as in *shred*, /#sf-/ as in *svelte* and *sphinx*, /#θw-/, as in *thwart*. Words pronounced with some of them may sound "foreign": /#ŋk-/ as in *Nkomo*, /#pw-/ as in *pueblo*, /#ts-/ as in *tsetse fly* and *Tsar*, /#šn-/ as in *Schnapps*, and even /#šw-/ as in *schwa*. In this connection we can note that when we take words from other languages into English, while we often preserve certain aspects of the foreign spelling, we usually change their sounds and their clusters to conform to the structure of English. We can see how this is so in the initial consonants of the following words in which the foreign cluster is maintained in English spelling but not in English pronunciation.

| *Dvorak* /#v-/ or /#dəv-/ | *pneumonia* /#n-/ | *bdellium* /#d-/ |
|---|---|---|
| *pterodactyl* /#t-/ | *psychology* /#s-/ | *mnemonic* /#n-/ |

In addition, */#ŋ-/ and */#ž-/ are not found initially in English words (unless *Jeanne* is pronounced in the French manner).

Utterance endings are less restricted in their clustering possibilities, but once again not every possibility can occur. For example, final clusters like the following are not possible in English: */-tz#/, and */-rzt#/. The restriction here is one of voicing: the consonants in such clusters must be either all voiced or all voiceless so that *boots* must be /buts/ not */butz/ and *parsed* must be /parzd/ or /parst/ but not */parzt/ or */parsd/. Sequences of consonants within utterances consist of possible final sequences followed by possible initial sequences.

Five of the English vowels can occur only before another phoneme in an utterance. Such vowels are called **checked vowels**; vowels with no such restriction on their occurrence are called **free vowels**. This indicated checked vowels occur as follows in the variety of English we are describing:

/ɪ/     *rim, sin, fill, lingual, discover, women, been, breeches*

/ɛ/     *deaf, inspect, expose, relent, tell, egg, mess, sweat, economic, leisure, many, ten*

/æ/     *factual, map, sad, accent, man, half, dance, bath, glass, aunt, laugh, plaid, staff, apricot, relapse*

/a/     *hop, knot, log, cot, closet, tonsil, off, bomb*

/ʊ/     *good, book, bull, could, soot, wolf*

In stressed syllables /ə/ is also a checked vowel:

/ə/     *cup, buzz, son, sun, duck, blood, tough, blush, stubble, shovel, dungeon, Monday*

(In other varieties of English some of the above words may contain a different phoneme from the one indicated.)

In the variety of English described here the maximum sequence of vowels is two. The first of these vowels must be a tense vowel or diphthong. (In the following examples the stressed syllable is indicated by an acute accent.)

| | |
|---|---|
| *idea* | /aɪdíə/ |
| *chaos* | /kéas/ |
| *duel* | /dúəl/ |
| *slower* | /slóər/ |
| *royal* | /rɔ́ɪəl/ |
| *allowance* | /əláʊəns/ |

## 9.5   Neutralization

At least two of the issues we have mentioned in preceding sections bring up the issue of **neutralization**. A phonemic contrast may be lost in certain environments; when this happens the contrast is said to be neutralized. We saw the first example of neutralization when we tried to find minimal pairs

for /r/ in word-final position. In that discussion we said that *beer* contrasts
with both *beat* /bit/ and *bit* /bɪt/. However, *beat* and *bit* are themselves a
minimal pair. Is *beer* then to be /bir/ or /bɪr/? Other pairs before /r/ give us
the same problem:

| *bait, bet*   | *bare* | /ber/ or /bɛr/? |
| *pool, pull*  | *poor* | /pur/ or /pʊr/? |
| *boat, bought* | *bore* | /bor/ or /bɔr/? |

What we observe here is the loss of the usual tense-lax distinction in a specific
environment, in this case before /r/. The distinction is neutralized. There are
really no good grounds for deciding the issue of which vowel actually occurs
in the neutralized environment. We will be consistent and use the tense vowel
symbol in such neutralized environments, i.e., we will represent *beer* as
/bir/, *bare* as /ber/, *poor* as /pur/, and *bore* as /bor/. (If, in addition, *boor* and
*bore* are not distinguished, then we have a further neutralization to /bor/.)
We must remember what we are doing though: in using the phonemic sequence /bir/, we must be aware that because of the /r/ that follows the /i/ the
vowel is no longer tense rather than lax although the symbol we have chosen
to use is one for a tense vowel. The tense-lax distinction is no longer relevant
here. Some linguists have proposed that an entirely new symbol be used in
such an environment in which a distinction is not maintained, i.e., it is
neutralized. That symbol would represent the **archiphoneme** that is said to
occur in such an environment. That solution – with [bIr] for *beer* – is possible
but we prefer not to use such an entity.

Tense and lax vowels are also neutralized both before another vowel and
in word final position, i.e., there is really no distinction between /i/ and /ɪ/
in words like *idea* and *pretty*. We will use the free vowel /i/ rather than the
checked vowel /ɪ/ in such circumstances, i.e., /aɪdíə/ and /príti/ rather than
/aɪdíə/ and /prítɪ/.

Neutralization is also responsible for why we can have English words
beginning with /#sp-/, /#st-/, and /#sk-/ but not with */#sb-/, */#sd-/, and
*/#sg-/. The voiced-voiceless distinction is neutralized in stops that follow an
initial /#s-/ in English. Once again we might be tempted to show this fact by
using an archiphoneme in describing the stops that do occur, e.g., to show
*spin* as /sPɪn/ or /sBɪn/, but we choose not to do so. (We will return in the
next chapter to a further mention of neutralization in connection with pairs
of words like *writing* and *riding*.)

## 9.6  Transcriptions

Now that we have dealt with the basic issues involved in describing the
contrastive sounds of English we can see what the phonemic structure of

certain English words is like. In the following phonemic transcriptions of English words stressed syllables (in polysyllabic words only) are shown under an acute accent. Many unstressed vowels are best transcribed with the phoneme /ə/ (called "schwa") that we used in words like *nut* and *cut*. For example, that phonemic symbol will be used to transcribe many unstressed vowels in English words

| about | coma | ended | passes | total |
|-------|------|-------|--------|-------|
| /əbáut/ | /kómə/ | /éndəd/ | /pǽsəz/ | /tótəl/ |

The same symbol is used because these are examples of the same phoneme, the stressed and the unstressed variety. Both occur in a word like *Russia* /rɔ́šə/. Unstressed /ə/ occurs with great frequency in English. It is also possible to pronounce some of these unstressed syllables with /ɪ/ rather than /ə/. (Although it has been suggested that a minimal pair *Rosa's* and *roses* exists, it is doubtful that unstressed /ɪ/ contrasts with unstressed /ə/.)

In each of the following words there are also as many vowel phonemes (either simple vowels or diphthongs) as there are syllables. We will not try to define syllable until chapter 13 but will assume for present purposes that information as to the number of syllables in English words is readily accessible to native speakers of the language.

| | | | |
|---|---|---|---|
| *man* | /mæn/ | *drink* | /drɪŋk/ |
| *repeal* | /rəpíl/ | *foul* | /faul/ |
| *pens* | /pɛnz/ | *happens* | /hǽpənz/ |
| *atlas* | /ǽtləs/ | *passion* | /pǽšən/ |
| *both* | /boθ/ | *Ritz* | /rɪts/ |
| *example* | /əgzǽmpəl/ | *bottle* | /bátəl/ |
| *anxious* | /ǽŋkšəs/ | *helpless* | /hélpləs/ |
| *cook* | /kuk/ | *chrome* | /krom/ |
| *please* | /pliz/ | *pleasure* | /pléžər/ |
| *steeple* | /stípəl/ | *feature* | /fíčər/ |
| *boring* | /bórɪŋ/ | *poor* | /pur/ |
| *married* | /mǽrid/ | *baby* | /bébi/ |
| *beers* | /birz/ | *puck* | /pək/ |
| *buttered* | /bátərd/ | *breaded* | /brédəd/ |
| *baked* | /bekt/ | *axed* | /ækst/ |
| *accepted* | /əkséptəd/ | *sunk* | /səŋk/ |
| *glimpsed* | /glɪmpst/ | *screams* | /skrimz/ |
| *able* | /ébəl/ | *mischievous* | /mísčəvəs/ |
| *bears* | /berz/ | *scrabble* | /skrǽbəl/ |
| *exist* | /ɛgzíst/ | *poison* | /pɔ́ɪzən/ |
| *ideas* | /aɪdíəz/ | *oases* | /oésiz/ |

## 9.7  Exercises

1  Write out each of the following words in the phonemic notation employed in the text. If the word has two or more syllables mark the syllable that has primary stress. The first three are done for you.

waves (/wevz/), worked (/wərkt/), insomnia (/ɪnsámnyə/ or /ɪnsámniə/), joked, delayed, passionate, pulling, rapacious, pleasant, limitless, atomic, bargaining, illness, apprenticeship, greedy, dullish, peace, Joyce's, tomatoes, toxic, presence, woolen, allowance, opened, occupied, Freddie, pea stalks, aroused, teacher, peace talks, woman, commotion, teethed, steeples, snatched, seizure, instinctive, bundle, lessen, feature, women, settle, lesson, fricatives, wolves, tenth, chosen, rippled, ached, canoe, selectional, sceptre, constrained, emphasized, singer, innocent, realism, Josephine, finger, president, trinket, gurgles, precedent, uproar, duckling, fixture, bullet, sympathy, reality, factional, verbless, rapidly, backwards, astronomical, treasonous, fingered, belonged

2  Write out your pronunciation of each of the following words in the phonemic notation employed in the text. What other pronunciations are you familiar with? How would you write these phonemically? The first three are done for you.

bade (/bæd/ and /bed/), status (/stǽtəs/ and /stétəs/), leisure (/léžər/ and /lížər/), matrix, data, apparatus, patriotic, azure, apical, amen, diphthong, asphalt, comrade, Wednesday, garage, economics, deity, ate, solder, missile, trait, dilemma, derisive, shone, controversy, schedule, mischievous, comely, been, Ralph, Anthony, hegemony, athlete, film, often, herb, historical, hotel, thorough, alms, palm, clothes, nephew, handsome, kiln, comptroller, lieutenant, advertisement, every, factory, family, century, diphtheria, polka, comely, distribute, controversy, demonstrable, clandestine, applicable

3  Write out each of the following words in the phonemic notation employed in the text. What other pronunciations are you familiar with? How would you write these phonemically? The first three are done for you.

fiduciary (/fɪdúsyəri/ or /fɪdúšəri/ or /fɪdúšri/), dukedom (/dúkdəm/ or /dyúkdəm/ or /júkdəm/), cordial (/kórdyəl/ or /kórdiəl/ or /kórǰəl/), Indian, issue, picture, racial, ensure, appreciate, controversial, graduate, adversary, secretary, medicine, realism, laboratory, century, factory, slavery, forgery, burglary, easily, lamentable, news, tune, due, nuclear, which, when, paws, pores, pours, pause, clerk, Derby

4  Write out the following words containing vowel sequences in the phonemic notation employed in the text. The first three are done for you.

prosaic (/prozéək/), client (/kláɪənt/), Suez (/suéz/ or /súəz/) dial, neon, Maria, fluid, ruin, bias, suicide, poem, poetry, Noah, cruel, weird

5  Name the distinctive characteristic (or feature) that operates to distinguish the following pairs of words. The first one is done for you.

peel/pill (the tenseness – or laxness – of the vowel), dens/dense, wren/Len, pin/bin, peel/pool, batter/backer, sin/sing, me/may

6  Supply half a dozen minimal pairs for each of the following contrasts. A few examples of the first pair are provided.

/t - d (*ten, den; pat, pad; cuttle, cuddle*), t - p, f - v, l - r, š - z, t - s, t - n, y - w, s - š, m - n, m - ŋ, f - θ, k - f, l - s, p - ŋ, f - m/

7  Some speakers of English have no contrast between the vowels of *cot* and *caught*. Others have a vowel in *bath* and *father* that is different from the vowel(s) in either *cot* or *caught*. *Cat* has a different vowel again. Use the following list of words to determine just what vowel contrasts you have.

cot, caught, dog, cross, long, laugh, half, cat, calm, father, path, dance, law, cause, farm, rather

8. Which vowels have been neutralized in those varieties of English in which *merry* and *Mary* are pronounced alike? What has happened when *marry* is also not distinguished from either of them? How would you propose to handle such neutralizations in the phonemic notation?

9  Which of the following words are incorrectly spelled?

develop, accommodation, (to pay a) compliment, vocal cords, recede, diphthong, its (ingredients), pronunciation, (the) principal (reason), asphalt, separate, (the ship's) complement, (a) discrete (number), receive, proceed, stationery (and ink), (a scientific) principle, occurred, it's (raining), (Please be) discreet, guttural, millennium, minuscule, privilege, government, (a) stationary (vehicle), all right, idiosyncrasy, (the book is) hers.

# 10
# Phonetic Realization

In the previous chapter we were concerned with how the sound system of English allows users of the language to distinguish one utterance from another. Sounds were described as somewhat abstract reference points – called **phonemes** – that speakers aim at in order to keep utterances distinctive from one another. We offered an account of what appear to be the essential characteristics of each reference point and used articulatory facts rather than distinctive features to do so. In this chapter we will describe the articulations of phonemes in considerably more detail and, in doing so, point out some of the important variations that occur in the actual pronunciations of the different phonemes.

## 10.1 Allophonic Variation

The phoneme /p/ occurs twice in the word *pop*, at the beginning and at the end /pap/. It is also the second sound in the word *spot* /spat/. If we examine carefully how the /p/ is pronounced on each occasion, we will find that there are noticeable differences. We record the actual pronunciations that occur in **phonetic notation** and use square brackets [ ] to do so. A phonetic notation of an utterance records all the details of pronunciation we are able to distinguish in that utterance. In transcribing an utterance phonetically, we note down everything we hear in that utterance whether or not it might have any kind of structural importance in the language. We will use a modified version of the **International Phonetic Alphabet (IPA)** in the transcriptions that follow. The IPA is perhaps the best known system of phonetic notation in existence.

Returning to the examples above, we would record that the initial sound in *pop* is followed by a small puff of air – it is **aspirated** – but the final sound in *pop* is not. Indeed that final sound may be **unreleased**, i.e., the lips may not even open. On the other hand, the second sound in *spot* is not aspirated and is most certainly released into the vowel. The final sound in *spot* may also be unreleased. A phonetic notation would record these words as follows if the final sounds are unreleased. (Symbols such as [ʰ] and [˺] are called **dia-critics**.)

*pop*  [pʰap˺]
*spot*  [spat˺]

What we see here are variant pronunciations of the phoneme /p/: [pʰ], [p], and [p˺]. The variant pronunciations of a phoneme are called the **allophones** of that phoneme. Most phonemes have more than one allophone. Moreover, it is possible to predict where each allophone of a particular phoneme occurs because the allophones of a phoneme are usually in **complementary distribution** with one another. In the case of /p/, for example, an initial /p/ in a word is always realized by the aspirated allophone [pʰ], a /p/ after an initial /s/ is an unaspirated [p], and a final /p/ is often realized by the unreleased allophone [p˺]. Note that in the latter case we said *often* not *always*. In certain positions more than one possibility may exist for the realization of a phoneme. In a word like *top* the final voiceless stop /p/ may actually be realized by the unreleased allophone [p˺] or by the aspirated allophone [pʰ]. When there is this kind of choice between allophones, we say that the allophones are in **free variation**.

We can show the above information about /p/ in the form of a pronunciation rule:

$$/p/ \rightarrow \begin{cases} [p^h] \ /^{\#}- \\ [p^˺] \text{ or } [p^h] \ /-^{\#} \\ [p] \text{ elsewhere} \end{cases}$$

This rule says that /p/ is pronounced [pʰ] initially in utterances (after #), is pronounced as either [p˺] or [pʰ] finally in utterances (before #), and is pronounced [p] elsewhere. An alternative formulation of this rule is as follows:

$$/p/ \rightarrow [p]$$

$$[p] \rightarrow \begin{cases} [+\text{aspirate}] \ / \begin{cases} \#_- \\ (-^{\#}) \end{cases} \\ [-\text{release}] \ / \ (-^{\#}) \end{cases}$$

This rule says that /p/ is essentially a voiceless bilabial stop [p]. If it occurs initially (after #), it must be [+aspirate], therefore [pʰ], and if it occurs finally it may be aspirated, the parentheses (  ) in the rule indicating the possibility of such a choice. If it occurs finally, it may also be [−release], therefore [p˺] if it is not already aspirated. Elsewhere /p/ occurs as [p].

The two rules given in the second set above apply serially, that is, the product of the first rule [p] becomes the input of the second rule, the rule for aspiration and release. However, the second rule, where curly bracketing is used, applies disjunctively, i.e., only one of the horizontal lines applies within such a bracketing. If such rules were not read disjunctively, a final /p/ could be both apirated and unreleased; however, an aspirated unreleased stop is impossible.

We will use the kind of description given in the second set of rules above in the discussion that follows. It allows us to use the characteristics which we assigned to the English phonemes in the previous chapter as the starting point for each phoneme. For example, in the discussion of /p/ in that set the [p] in the first rule (/p/ → [p]) represents just those characteristics which we used to define the distinctiveness of /p/ in the last chapter: voicelessness, bilabial position, and stop quality.

A system of rules also allows us to make generalizations. The phoneme /p/ is not alone in having the above characteristics: all voiceless stops are aspirated initially in English utterances, may or may not be aspirated or unreleased finally, and are unaspirated elsewhere. We can write a rule of the following kind to express this generalization:

$$\begin{bmatrix} +\text{stop} \\ -\text{voice} \end{bmatrix} \rightarrow \begin{Bmatrix} [+\text{aspirate}] / \begin{Bmatrix} \#_- \\ (-^\#) \end{Bmatrix} \\ [-\text{release}] / (-^\#) \end{Bmatrix}$$

This rule states that any voiceless stop must be aspirated initially and may be aspirated or unreleased finally. Note that the curly bracketings indicate that this rule as a whole and an internal part once again apply disjunctively. We can actually further refine this rule for voiceless stops if we consider more data. A comparison of the pronunciations of words like *taste* and *tomatoes* and *tack* and *attack* shows that there can also be considerable aspiration of voicelesss stops at the beginning of stressed syllables, e.g., in *taste*, *tack*, and *attack*. However, only light aspiration occurs in *tomatoes* when the initial syllable is unstressed. In general, phonetic features of the kind we are discussing are best understood to be **gradient** features, i.e., showing characteristics of a more-or-less kind, rather than **categorical** features, i.e., are either present or not. That is, aspiration is not just a feature that is or is not present; rather it is one, which when present, is present in varying amounts in different circumstances.

We will now turn our attention to some of the more important allophones of English, first of all looking at consonant phonemes and then at vowel phonemes. As we have noted above, voiceless stops are aspirated initially and may be aspirated or unreleased finally. Voiced stops, however, are never aspirated but may be unreleased finally: *pod* /pad/ may be [pʰad] or [pʰad˺].

The /t/ phoneme has some additional interesting allophones in certain varieties of English. In some dialects a solitary /t/ between a stressed syllable

and an unstressed syllable becomes voiced and is articulated as a quick tap
of the tongue on the alveolar ridge – technically a **flap**. This flapped allophone
sounds very much like a /d/. Phonetically, *batter* is [bærɾ], the [ɾ] here indicating the combination of voicing and flapping that occurs. We can state
the necessary rule for /t/ in this position in this variety of English as follows:

$$[t] \rightarrow \begin{bmatrix} +\text{voice} \\ +\text{flap} \end{bmatrix} / \ [+\text{stress}] - [-\text{stress}]$$

This rule says that [t], the basic phonetic realization of /t/, adds the phonetic
features of voicing and flapping between a stressed vowel and an unstressed
vowel. The rule does not mention vowels directly, but it does not need to do
so because only vowels can be stressed. That information is therefore redundant, i.e., entirely predictable. In other varieties of English /t/ in the same
environment is pronounced as a glottal stop [ʔ], i.e., the closure is made in
the vocal cords and not on the alveolar ridge. So we have a pronunciation
for *batter* which is phonetically [bæʔɾ]. We need the following rule for such
varieties:

$$[t] \rightarrow [+\text{glottal}] \ / \ [+\text{stress}] - [-\text{stress}]$$

This rule simply substitutes a glottal place of articulation for the alveolar
place of articulation and realizes /t/ as [ʔ] rather than [t] between a stressed
vowel and an unstressed vowel.

   One general feature of the alveolars /t/, /d/, and /n/ and of the velars
/k/, /g/, and /ŋ/ is that their precise positions of articulation vary. For example, before a front vowel each has a more forward point of articulation and
before a back vowel a more retracted point of articulation. If we consider the
/t/ of *Tom* to represent the norm of this phoneme, with its alveolar articulation, then the /t/ of *team* is articulated a little more forward on the alveolar
ridge and the tip of the tongue may actually come into contact with the upper
teeth. However, in the pronunciation of *tomb* the tip of the tongue is well to
the back of the alveolar ridge. We might want to show the differences phonetically as follows: [tʰ] in *Tom*, [t̪ʰ] in *team*, and [t̠ʰ] in *tomb*. Likewise, the
/k/s at the beginnings of *keep*, *calm*, and *cool* differ in position, the closure
in *keep* being made much further forward (in the back of the mouth in this
case) than the closure at the beginning of *cool*, in which it is really very far
back: [k̟ʰ] in *keep*, [kʰ] in *calm*, and [k̠ʰ] in *cool*. We can observe similar
forward and back differences in the following pairs:

| | | | |
|---|---|---|---|
| *deam* | [d̪] | *doom* | [d̠] |
| *niece* | [n̪] | *noose* | [n̠] |
| *geese* | [g̟] | *goose* | [g̠] |

The nasals themselves have still other interesting allophones. Normally nasals are voiced but voiceless allophones can occur after an initial /s/, as in *snap* [sn̥æp] and *Smith* [sm̥ɪθ], or even after an initial /š/ in those varieties of English with words like *Schnapps* and *shmuck* pronounced as [šn̥æps] and [šm̥ʌk]. Here the subscripted diacritic indicates voicelessness. The rule is as follows:

[+nasal] → [–voice] / [#s–]

The bilabial nasal /m/ is sometimes pronounced not with the two lips as [m] but with the lower lip and the top teeth, i.e., as a labiodental [ɱ]. This is likely to be the pronunciation heard in such words as *comfort, Stamford, Humphrey, symphony, infant,* and *Banff.* Here a rule is needed to specify the change in the point of articulation of /m/ before the labiodental fricative /f/. What has happened is that the nasal has assimilated to the following sound in its place of articulation. **Assimilation** is a process in which one sound changes in some way to become more like another sound in its environment. The voicing of /t/ between vowels that we mentioned earlier is an instance of assimilation – vowels are voiced – and the devoicing of nasals after the voiceless initial [s] is still another example. Assimilation frequently explains allophonic variation but not all allophonic variation can be accounted for in this way. Assimilation does not, for example, account for the initial aspiration of voiceless stops.

If we return to the word *Stamford* above, we can point out that there is another word very like it, *Stanford.* In slow and deliberate speech the two words are likely to be distinguished as ['stæmfərd] and ['stænfərd] respectively. However, in quick and casual pronunciations of these names no distinction may be made and both nasals may be realized as labiodentals, hence ['stæɱfərd] for both words. In that case either both nasals /m/ and /n/ have the same allophone [ɱ], a labiodental allophone before a labiodental fricative, or only one of the nasals has such an allophone and the spelling of one of these words for such quick casual pronunciations is not very reliable. We will leave this issue unresolved, for although there are certain interesting theoretical problems in assigning the same allophone to two different phonemes or, alternatively, claiming that two phonemes in the same position have but a single phonetic realization, such problems are beyond the scope of our treatment here. We will accept the fact that *Stamford* and *Stanford* are kept apart in very careful speech styles and that one of the consequences of speaking quickly and casually is that certain distinctions made in very careful speech can disappear.

/m/, /n/, and /ŋ/ are sounds that are capable of being sustained: you can say [mmmm] and so on, but not *[dddd]. If you try to pronounce /d/ or repeat instances of it, you must say [də] or [dədədə]. When nasals appear finally in unstressed syllables, as at the ends of *redden* or *Grab 'im!* or as realizations of *and* in *top'n' bottom*, *nip'n' tuck*, and *touch'n' go*, they may be used to pronounce whole syllables as **syllabic nasals**: [m̩], [n̩], and [ŋ̩]. In the above examples we are likely to have the following phonetic realizations of the total syllable in which each occurs:

| | |
|---|---|
| *redden* | [n̩] |
| *Grab 'im!* | [m̩] |
| *top'n' bottom* | [m̩] |
| *nip'n' tuck* | [n̩] |
| *touch'n' go* | [ŋ̩] |

We should note once again that the spelling is not a particularly good indicator of which syllabic nasal appears in the last three cases. Which nasal appears is determined by the position of the following consonant: we have a labial [m] before a labial [b], an alveolar [n] before an alveolar [t], and a velar [ŋ] before a velar [g]. This is another case of assimilation. Once again we have a problem. Are the [m], [n], and [ŋ] that we find here all allophones of /n/ when they are realizations of the reduced word *and*? Or are they realizations of /m/, /n/, and /ŋ/ respectively? We prefer the first solution: a rule that allows /n/ to have variants which assimilate in position to following consonants. If this solution results in a phonetic segment like [m] belonging on some occasions to /m/ and on others to /n/ that is not an unreasonable solution. Speakers of English do regard all the *n*s in the above expressions to be the "same" *n*. Our preferred solution also acknowledges this similarity.

At one time some linguists would not accept the possibility that a phonetic segment like [m] might be assignable to two, or even more, phonemes. They wanted a principle which would not only take into account how phonemes are realized in sounds – which is what we are doing – but which would also explain how sounds are processed into phonemes. (The technical term for this principle is **biuniqueness**.) In trying to explain the latter, however, they also excluded grammatical and semantic information, e.g., any knowledge that the [m], [n], [ŋ] in the above are instances of *and*. Such concerns now seem quite unjustified and such goals completely unrealizable. That is why we prefer the solution given here, a solution which also acknowledges that while listeners are processing the sounds that make up each of the above expressions, they are also concurrently processing the syntax and the meaning.

The retroflex and the lateral also have voiceless allophones, [r̥] and [l̥], after voiceless consonants in the same syllable:

| | | |
|---|---|---|
| *crane* | [kʰr̥en] | (compare *grain* [gren]) |
| *pleat* | [pʰl̥it] | (compare *bleat* [blit]) |

Other words with similar voiceless allophones for /r/ and /l/ are *three* [θr̥i], *shred* [šr̥ɛd], *flack* [fl̥æk], and *slap* [sl̥æp]. The rule in this case states that the retroflex and the lateral become [–voice] after a voiceless segment in the same syllable. In a word like *train* we can also observe sometimes an **affricated** quality in the initial [tʰɽ], the aspirated consonant and the devoiced retroflex, so that *train* sometimes sounds like [čṛen] (and *drain* sometimes sounds like [ǰren]). This affrication can be very noticeable in some varieties of English.

English /l/ is often a "dark *l*" in its phonetic realization [ɫ], i.e., it is pronounced with the tongue bunched back in the mouth. This dark *l* is found in most varieties of English after a vowel, e.g., *fill* [fɪɫ] and *fool* [fuɫ]. However, a "clear *l*" is also possible in English, particularly before high front vowels, as in *leek* and *lick*, ([lik] and [lɪk]). In contrast, words like *look*, *luck*, and *lack* usually have a dark *l*: [ɫʊk], [ɫʌk], and [ɫæk].

Both the /r/ and the /l/ can appear as syllabics just like the nasals. The final /r/ and /l/ in *ripper* and *ripple* are realized as syllabics:

> *ripper*    [rɪpṛ]
> *ripple*    [rɪpl̩]

Even the stressed /ər/ combination has this syllabic quality to it. In this case the vowel may have more prominence phonetically that the consonant and we have [ɚ], or the consonant may have greater phonetic prominence than the vowel and we have [ṛ]. Consequently, a word like *bird* may have two slightly different pronunciations:

> *bird*   [bɚd]   or   [bṛd]

However, each pronunciation is phonemically /bərd/. The phonetic realizations indicate only that some speakers give emphasis to the vowel and others give it to the consonant but all have both the vowel and the consonant. We will have more to say later about those varieties of English which do not pronounce /r/ at all in this environment.

There are some rules that apply throughout the vowel system and are particularly noticeable in their effects when they apply to stressed syllables. All vowels have slightly longer variants before following voiced sounds than before the corresponding following voiceless sounds. The vowel in *bid* [bɪ·d] is therefore longer than the vowel in *bit* [bɪt]. The exceptions are vowels before nasals or /l/ with either followed by a consonant, e.g., *pint* in contrast to *pine*, *pink* in contrast to *pin*, and *belt* in contrast to *bell*, and vowels before voiced consonants when the following syllable is unstressed, e.g., *mannish* in contrast to *man*, *muddy* in contrast to *mud*, and *crudely* in contrast to *crude*. Stressed vowels have still longer variants before silence of any kind, e.g., at the ends of words or utterances, e.g., *allow* in contrast to *allowed* and *sigh* in contrast to *sighed*. Tense vowels and diphthongs also show a tendency for the tongue to move to a higher position and such movement most easily occurs under either of the two previously mentioned conditions. What this means is that the vowel /i/, for example, has a slightly longer variant in *bead* than in *beat* (and there may be some tongue movement as well). It will have an even longer variant in *bee* and the tongue movement will be even greater. Phonetically we have:

    *beat*  [bit]    *bead*  [bi·d]    *bee*  [biː]

A very informal statement of the general rule for all vowels (ignoring the exceptions given above) would be:

$$[+\text{vowel}] \rightarrow \begin{cases} [+\text{long}] & / - [+\text{voice}] \\ [+\text{longer}] & / - [^{\#}] \end{cases}$$

Another rule would specify the further raising of the tongue position ([+higher]) for tense vowels and diphthongs. This last rule would account for the fact that the vowels in words like *day* and *sew* can show considerable movement as well as length: [deɪ̯] and [soʊ̯] respectively.

    Vowels also tend to be nasalized [ ˜ ] before nasals:

    [+vowel] → [+nasal] / –[+nasal]

We find examples like the following:

    *rip*  [rɪp]    *rim*  [rɪ̃·m]
    *bit*  [bɪt]    *bin*  [bɪ̃·n]
    *bag*  [bæ·g]    *bang*  [bæ̃·ŋ]

In *rim* and *bin* and in the last pair of examples, *bag* and *bang*, we have also indicated the vowel length that is apparent when the vowel is followed by a voiced consonant. In *rip*, therefore, we have as it were the prototypical allophone of /ɪ/ – it is short and completely oral. In *rim* we have another allophone – it is nasalized (and a little longer). As we noted in the previous chapter, a vowel like /ɪ/ is also a **checked vowel**, i.e., it is always found before a consonant; consequently, it has no still longer variant or a variant involving tongue raising. On the other hand, the unchecked (or **free vowel**) /i/ has more allophones because of its greater freedom of occurrence, e.g., [i] in *beat*, [i·] in *bead*, [ĩ·] in *beam*, and [iː] in *bee*.

## 10.2 Transcriptions

At the end of the previous chapter we provided a list of words transcribed in phonemic notation. We will now present the words on that list written in phonetic notation. A stressed syllable in a polysyllabic word is preceded by [']. Note too that /ə/ has two distinct allophones: [ʌ] (called "caret" or "wedge") in stressed syllables and [ə] in unstressed syllables.

| | | | |
|---|---|---|---|
| *man* | [mæ·n] | *drink* | [drɪŋk⌐] |
| *repeal* | [rə'pʰi·ł] | *foul* | [faʊ·ł] |
| *pens* | [pʰɛ̃nz] | *happens* | ['hæpn̥z] |
| *atlas* | ['ætłəs] | *passion* | ['pʰæšn̥] |
| *both* | [boθ] | *Ritz* | [rɪts] |
| *example* | [əg'zæmpl̥] | *bottle* | ['baɾl̥] |
| *anxious* | ['æŋkšəs] | *helpless* | ['hɛłpłəs] |
| *cook* | [kʰʊk⌐] | *chrome* | [kʰrõ·m] |
| *please* | [pʰl̥i·z] | *pleasure* | ['pʰlɛžr̥] |
| *steeple* | ['st̥ipl̥] | *feature* | ['fičr̥] |
| *boring* | ['bɔrɪ̃ŋ] | *poor* | [pʰu·r] |
| *married* | ['mærid] | *baby* | ['bebi] |
| *beers* | [bi·rz] | *puck* | [pʰʌk⌐] |
| *buttered* | ['bʌɾr̥d] | *breaded* | ['brɛdəd] |
| *baked* | [bekt⌐] | *asked* | [æskt⌐] |
| *accepted* | [ək'sɛptəd] | *sunk* | [sʌ̃ŋk⌐] |
| *glimpsed* | [glĩmpst⌐] | *screams* | [skr̥ĩmz] |
| *able* | ['ebl̥] | *mischievous* | ['mɪsčəvəs] |
| *bears* | [bɛ·rz] | *scrabble* | ['skr̥æbl̥] |
| *exist* | [ɛg'zɪst⌐] | *poison* | ['pʰɔɪzn̥] |
| *ideas* | [aɪ'di·əz] | *oases* | [o'esiz] |

## 10.3   Regional and Social Variations

English is, of course, pronounced differently in various parts of the English speaking world. Leaving aside such matters as differences in the actual rate of speaking – in some places people speak more slowly and in others they speak more quickly than we may be used to – and ignoring for the present matters of stress, pitch, and intonation, we can note some of the following kinds of difference. In different varieties of English speakers may make use of different phonemes in certain words. For example, we can find different pronunciations that may or may not be regarded as acceptable for each of the following words:

*clerk* ([ər] or [ar]), *tomato* ([a] or [e]), *bath* ([a] or [æ]),
*either* ([i] or [aɪ]), *news* ([n] or [ny]), *tune* ([t] or [ty] or [č]),
*when* ([w] or [hw]), *soot* ([u] or [ʊ] or [ʌ]),

*happy* ([h] or nothing), *herb* ([h] or nothing),
*calm* ([l] or nothing), *singing* ([n] or [ŋ]), *lever* ([i], or [ɛ]),
*missile* ([l] or [aɪl]), *leisure* ([ɛ] or [i]), *schedule* ([š] or [sk])

Sometimes these differences can be fairly clearly associated with a particular region, e.g., *bath*, *clerk*, *missile*, *lever*, *when*, etc.; or the association may be mainly due either to social class or to the formality of language use, e.g., *singing* and *happy*; or there may be a combination of these two sets of factors; or the choice may be largely a matter of individual preference, e.g., *either*.

More subtle are differences in allophonic selection. It is fairly easy to describe the two common pronunciations of *either* in phonemic terms: /íðər/ and /áɪðər/. But how does one describe the different pronunciations of *bird* and *here*, for example a southern British English pronunciation and a typical Chicago pronunciation, or the various pronunciations of *house* and *writer* that one is likely to encounter in the English-speaking world? What we can attempt to do in each case is try to account for the variants by stating the particular rules that give us the allophones of the variety we wish to describe. In the examples just given, what rules do we need to account for the absence of certain qualities normally associated with /r/ in *bird* and *here* and for the particular qualities we sometimes observe in the stressed syllables of *house* and *writer* and in the medial consonant of this last word?

Let us look at words like *bird* and *here* first. We can observe that some speakers of English do not pronounce an /r/ either finally in a word or before a consonant in the same syllable in the manner we have previously indicated for /r/ pronunciation. Indeed, if /r/ occurs in a final unstressed syllable in a word, it may be dropped entirely so that words like *under*, *sailor*, *liar*, and *picture* are pronounced with a final schwa as ['ʌndə], ['selə], ['laɪə], and ['pʰɪkčə] respectively. They are also all quite clearly words with two syllables. In stressed syllables the /r/ is undoubtedly still present in some way because *bird* is usually distinguished from *bud*. What happens is that the quality of the vowel changes; the so-called **non-rhotic** or **r-less dialects** usually do make distinctions in pairs of words such as the following:

| | | | |
|---|---|---|---|
| *bird* | *bud* | *dire* | *die* |
| *beard* | *bead* | *hire* | *high* |
| *moored* | *mood* | *byre* | *buy* |
| *tired* | *tied* | *lyre* | *lie* |

When the /r/ is in word final position, sometimes **homophony** may result: *pour* and *paw* and *lore* and *law* may be pronounced alike. Or they may be distinguished by the first word having a schwa-like realization of the /r/:

*pour* [pʰɔə̯]   *paw* [pʰɔː]
*lore* [ɬɔə̯]   *law* [ɬɔː]

The [ə̯] indicates that this schwa is non-syllabic: *pour* and *lore* are clearly words of one syllable. Words like *hire* and *high* in the above list may then be distinguished as [haɪə̯l] and [haɪː] respectively.

In certain varieties of English an /r/ at the end of a word is realized as schwa (or is unrealized) at the end of an utterance or if the next word begins with a consonant. If the next word begins with a vowel, the /r/ is fully pronounced:

*fair* [feə̯]   *fair price*   [feə̯'pʰrаɪs]   *fair amount* [ferə'maʊnt]

This *r* is sometimes referred to as a **linking *r***. In some non-rhotic varieties of English there is a rule which in certain circumstances introduces a phonetic [r] between pairs of words the first of which ends in a vowel (when pronounced in isolation) and the second of which begins with a vowel (and sometimes before the addition of the *-ing* suffix to verbs). The rule that introduces this **intrusive *r*** is a completely phonetic rule, i.e., the [r] does not derive directly from the underlying phonemic structure of the words. It can therefore result in pronunciations like *the idear of it* and *redrawring boundaries* as well as *fair amount*.

As we indicated previously, phonemic vowel contrasts before /r/ are sometimes **neutralized**, e.g., the /i/–/ɪ/ contrast in words like *beer*. But still further neutralization is possible. In some varieties of English the vowels in *Mary*, *merry*, and *marry* are distinguished, the words having the /e/, /ɛ/, and /æ/ phonemes respectively, with [e], [ɛ], and [æ] as the phonetic realizations. In other varieties the first two words are pronounced the same: the /e/–/ɛ/ contrast is lost and both words are pronounced with [ɛ]. In still other varieties all three phonemic vowel contrasts are realized as [ɛ] in this position before /r/; there is complete neutralization and the words become homophones.

Returning to the words *house* and *writer*, we observe a number of interesting pronunciation variants. The phonemic diphthongs /aʊ/ and /aɪ/ may not be realized phonetically by diphthongs at all. Certain varieties of English prefer long monophthongs in both words instead of diphthongs. Such realizations occur in certain varieties of southern United States speech so that we get pronunciations like [haːs] rather than [haʊs].

In still other varieties of English it is the first part of the diphthong that shows the variation we are interested in. In this case the first part of the diphthong is centered so that we have [əʊ] rather than the expected [aʊ]. Consequently, *house* is pronounced as [həʊs] not [haʊs]. There are even varieties of English in which this last rule applies only when the consonant that follows the diphthong is a voiceless consonant. The rule may also apply to the /aɪ/ diphthong as well. It results in pairs of words like *house* /haʊs/ and *houses* /háʊzəz/ having different phonetic realizations of the /aʊ/ phoneme. In *houses* the consonant that follows the diphthong is voiced – it is /z/ – so the centering rule for the first part of the diphthong does not apply. We therefore have the following phonetic realizations of *house* and *houses* in this variety:

   *house* [həʊs]   *houses* ['haʊ·zəz]

If we look at the pronunciations of the words *write*, *writer*, and *rider* in various dialects of English we will find considerable variation. Our basic rules give us the following phonemic representations and phonetic realizations of these words:

   *write*    /raɪt/     [raɪt]
   *writer*   /ráɪtər/    ['raɪtɽ]
   *rider*    /ráɪdər/    ['raɪ·dɽ]

In the *r*-less varieties of English we would expect the last two words to end in schwa rather than the syllabic [ɽ] and we do find pronunciations like ['raɪtə] and ['raɪ·də] in those varieties. In still other varieties, probably *r*-less, we will find a glottal stop in *writer* but not in *rider* when /t/ has this glottal realization in this position, hence *writer* is ['raɪʔə] and *rider* is ['raɪ·də]. We would also expect and do find varieties which show a strong tendency to monophthongize the diphthong or to change the diphthong into a very long low vowel, e.g., *rider* pronounced as ['raːdə]. But we also find pronunciations such as the following:

   *write*    [rəɪt]
   *writer*   ['rəɪɾɽ]
   *rider*    ['raɪ·dɽ]

How do we account for the last two pronunciations, which are really very much alike everywhere except in the quality and length of their stressed vowels? We can account for the [ɾ], which, as we said earlier, is phonetically almost indistinguishable from [d], if we remember that in certain varieties of English a /t/ between a stressed syllable and an unstressed syllable becomes a voiced flap. What is of particular interest here though are the centralization of the first part of the diphthongs in *write* and *writer* and the vowel lengthening in *rider*. Such centralization occurs only before voiceless consonants and such lengthening occurs only before voiced consonants. However, in the phonetic realization of *writer* we have centralization before a voiced segment [ɾ] but no lengthening of the diphthong.

   The difficulty can be resolved if we take the position that speakers of

English have a set of phonological contrasts, i.e., phonemes, available to them out of which they construct distinguishable utterances. When they realize these contrasts, they do so by using a set of phonetic realization rules which produce the actual utterances they use. These rules differ from variety of English to variety of English. The rules must also be ordered so that some apply before others. Let us assume then that in the variety of English just described there are three relevant pronunciation rules. The first rule (R1) says that the /aɪ/ – and we could add /aʊ/ – has its first segment centered before certain voiceless consonants. The second rule (R2) says that all vowels and diphthongs are lengthened before voiced consonants (in specified environments). The third rule (R3) says that the /t/ is pronounced [ɾ], i.e., as a voiced flap, between a stressed vowel and an unstressed vowel.

If we apply these three rules when necessary to *write*, *writer*, and *rider*, we will see that although the first two rules are not ordered in relation to each other since they deal with quite different matters, both must precede the third rule if we are to account for the above forms. (The syllabic [ɹ̩] is here introduced along with the last rule that applies to the word but is, of course, the product of some other rule.)

| *write*  | /raɪt/  | (R1) [rəɪt]   | (R2)  |                | (R3)           |
|----------|---------|---------------|-------|----------------|----------------|
| *writer* | /ráɪtər/| (R1) ['rəɪter]| (R2)  |                | (R3) ['rəɪɾɹ̩] |
| *rider*  | /ráɪdər/| (R1)          | (R2)  | ['raɪ·dɹ̩]      | (R3)           |

An example such as this one clearly shows the need to postulate both a basic phonological form for each word in the language, i.e., a phonemic representation, and a set of ordered realization rules that will turn phonemic representations into pronounceable words.

# 10.4   Exercises

1   Write out the following words in both the phonemic notation we have been using and a phonetic notation. The first three are done for you.

tricked (/trɪkt/ and [tʰɹ̥ɪktˀ]), those (/ðoz/ and [ðo·z]), scenes, (/sinz/ and [sīnz]), leaves, gulf, yelp, mistletoe, emphatic, Betty, slow, fasten, sleep, team, kissed, creamy, flea, most, sparkle, thrilled, hissed, cast, splashed, ripple, penned, juice, crackled, coals, woken, inked, thatches, snap, pretty

2   Write out the following words in both the phonemic notation we have been using and a phonetic notation.

entrance, permit, rebel, video, audio, rodeo, particle, particular, jewelry, escape, illness, dryness, reasonable, perhaps, frantic, treason, sudden, thank, camphor, singer, finger, while, island, hurdle, bird, beard, bard, admire, hire, higher, fire, fly, flyer, reorder, reassign, resign, real, reality, realism, paws, pores, pours, pause, poor, pound, shutter, shudder, matter

3   Describe the phonetic difference or differences that exist in the boldfaced parts of each pair of words. Which differences are allophonic in nature? Which are phonemic? The first two are done for you.

tin, letter (t and tt are the same phoneme /t/ but different allophones: [tʰ] and [ɾ]); bat, bad (the as are the same phoneme /æ/ but different allophones: [æ] and [æ·]); bad, man; sin, sing; Tim, team; peel, pool; lose, lost; Canada, Canadian; space, spacious; face, phase; gripped, grabbed; path, paths; lose, loose; bed, Ben; play, plate; plain, plaint

4   Provide examples of each of the following rules in operation in English words:

(a)   $\begin{bmatrix} +stop \\ -voice \end{bmatrix}$   →   [+aspirate]

(b)   [+stop]        →   [−release]
(c)   [+vowel]       →   [+nasalization]
(d)   [+nasal]       →   [−voice]
(e)   [+retroflex]   →   [−voice]
(f)   [+vowel]       →   [+long]

5   Provide a full phonetic description of the sound represented by the boldfaced letter or letters in the following words. The first three are done for you.

trip (short high front unround lax vowel), pen (voiceless aspirated bilabial stop), full (dark voiced lateral), sigh, butter, load, kitten, cool, two, toys, lease, sad, main, crack, car, chat, snake

# 11

# Word Formation

In this chapter we will be concerned with how words are formed in English. So far we have used terms like **sound, syllable,** and **sentence** without attempting a rigorous definition of any one of them. **Word** is a similar term. Most discussions of language make constant reference to sounds, syllables, words, and sentences without insisting on rigorous definitions of any one of them. What simple definitions we do find are also often plainly inadequate. Sounds are not just those things we capture on paper through using the letters of the alphabet. If sentences are those "complete" utterances we choose to record in writing with capital letters at their beginnings and periods, question marks, and exclamation marks at their ends, how do we know when to use these punctuation marks? What are the actual signals of "completeness"? The same kinds of problems occur with the usual definitions of syllable and word.

In a real sense writing a grammar of English is an attempt to give an exact meaning to each of these four terms. Insofar as the grammar is complete the terms are defined. Unfortunately, we have no complete grammar of English so to that extent we are left with incomplete definitions. What we are attempting here is to show some of the essential features of the structure of English and, consequently, some of the factors that must be considered in talking in an insightful way about sounds, syllables, words, and sentences in English. In previous chapters we discussed issues associated with sentences and sounds. We will now turn our attention to words, and, still later, in chapter 13, we will have something to say about syllables.

## 11.1  Words and Lexemes

Linguists who try to define **word** must confront several issues. The most important of these is that if they try to define words using only one set of criteria, e.g., phonological (i.e., pronounceability in isolation), morphological (i.e., potential for taking affixes), semantic (i.e., as units of meaning), or syntactic (i.e., freedom of movement in clauses), they cannot cover all the data that must be accounted for. However, if they try to use criteria from all four domains, they get contradictory results. Is *un-* a word in *What does un-in unlikely mean?* Is *t* a word in *That t should be capitalized?* Is *Queen of England's* a word in *the Queen of England's children?* Is *kick the bucket* a word when it means the same as *die?* Is *n't* a word in *Don't do it now!* when it is quite clearly related to *not?* All five are words by some definition and yet they are not words, certainly not like *word* itself is a word.

One might be tempted to say that "words are what you find recorded in dictionaries" and leave the matter at that. But how does one know what to record in dictionaries, and why do dictionaries themselves produce different records? In fact, dictionaries do not record words; they record **lexemes**. And for our purposes the lexeme is perhaps a more useful classification than the word.

If dictionaries did record words, we would expect to find entries for *cat* and *cats*, for *bake, bakes, baked*, and *baking*, and for *long, longer*, and *longest*. What we find, however, is that only one word from each of these sets is recorded. The other members of the set are regarded as instances of the "same word." We will substitute the term **lexeme** for **word** in this last sense. A dictionary records lexemes. It assumes that the users of the dictionary understand that words can take various forms in various places in which they are used while remaining somehow the "same." These sames are the different realizations of a single lexeme.

We can also observe what a dictionary does with *bank*. *Bank* is one word but it has two clearly different meanings in the following sentences:

> The left **bank** of the river is steep at that point.
> He put all his remaining money in the **bank**.

*Bank* is therefore two different lexemes and any adequate dictionary of English will contain separate entries for *bank*[1] with the meaning it has in the first sentence above and *bank*[2] with the meaning it has in the second sentence. *Bank*[1] and *bank*[2] are **homonyms**, i.e., different lexemes that happen to be pronounced alike. English contains numerous homonyms, e.g., *like, sole, utter, fast, last, bear*, etc.

Some lexemes may be **polysemous**, i.e., contain a variety of related meanings. Lexemes like *play, book*, and *break* display closely related senses in the following examples:

> The children **played** in the yard.
> He **played** a minor role in our production.

*She borrowed a **book** from the library.*
*Did the same person write both the **book** and lyrics?*

*Who **broke** that plate?*
*He **broke** his silence after two decades.*

However, polysemy shades off into homonymy so that there is no easy test to determine whether *man* and *fair* in the following sentences are each instances of the same lexeme (therefore polysemous) or of different lexemes (therefore homonymous):

*He is a good **man**.*
***Man** is mortal.*

*She has a **fair** skin.*
*It was a **fair** decision.*

Therefore, even the concept of "lexeme" is not without its own problems! For example, we can note that *Webster's Third New International Dictionary* (1961) records three different lexemes *set* with 56 polysemous variants of one of these lexemes, 11 of the second, and 46 of the third. Other dictionaries, e.g., the 1989 edition of the *Oxford English Dictionary* give still other accounts of the word we spell *set*.

What we will do in the rest of the chapter is discuss lexemes rather than words. We will say, for example, that the lexeme *cat* can be realized in various word forms, e.g., *cat, cat's, cats,* and *cats'*, and we will attempt to describe these various word forms. In the discussion we will also meet other kinds of lexemes: anything cited in a naming context is a lexeme, e.g., *un-* in *Is un-a word?*; compounds like *icebox*; and even idioms like *kick the bucket, pull someone's leg, play fast and loose, round the bend,* etc.

Words themselves are also sometimes described as the smallest meaningful units of a language which can be moved freely. This is a useful definition if we remember that lexemes manifest themselves through words so that words are the local realizations of lexemes. Such a definition, however, tells us nothing about how words are constructed and it is this matter that we turn to now.

## 11.2  Morphology

In order to discuss word formation in English we need to establish certain basic concepts. The principal one is that words consist of one or more units of meaning with grammatical significance. In the pair *cat* and *cats* we can say that the first word contains one grammatically significant unit of meaning, "cat." In the second case there are two such units, "cat" and "plural." Moreover, in each case we can associate phonemes directly with those meanings, /kæt/ with "cat" and the final /s/ with "plural." We will call these units of meaning **morphemes**. *Cat* is comprised of a single morpheme and *cats* of two morphemes. In contrast to *cats*, in a word like *dogs* we also have two morphemes /dag/ "dog" and /z/ "plural." In this case the "plural" is realized by /z/ and not by /s/. It is quite clear, however, that it is the same "plural" that occurred before in *cats*. It is the same morpheme but a different phonemic realization of that morpheme. The different phonemic realizations of a morpheme are called the **allomorphs** of that morpheme; the allomorphs of a morpheme also occur in **complementary distribution** with each other, i.e., each allomorph has its own predictable environment.

When we can explain in phonological terms why one particular allomorph of a morpheme occurs rather than another, we have what is called **regular**, i.e., **phonological, conditioning** of the allomorph. For example, the /s/ allomorph of the "plural" morpheme regularly occurs after nouns ending in /t/ and the /z/ allomorph regularly occurs after nouns ending in /g/:

/s/   *hats, parts, rates, pets, goats*
/z/   *legs, bags, logs, kegs, jugs*

If we must cite the actual morpheme to which the allomorph attaches and specify the special form of that allomorph and therefore the special form of the resulting combination, then we have **irregular**, i.e., **morphological, conditioning** of the allomorph. For example, the **plurals** of English words such as *man* (**men**), *goose* (**geese**) and *child* (**children**) are irregular. *Men* is "man" plus "plural" just as *cats* is "cat" plus "plural," but we have to know this special fact about the word, i.e., that with *man* the pluralization process involves a vowel change in the noun and not affixation. Likewise, we have to learn the specific ways in which the plurals of *goose* and *child* are formed in English.

Returning to *cats*, we can further distinguish between /kæt/ and /s/. The morpheme /kæt/ is a **base**, i.e., it is a fundamental unit of meaning stripped of any kind of inflectional or derivational marking. **Inflectional** marking is the kind that occurs among the various words that compose a lexeme, e.g., *cat*, *cat's*, *cats*, and *cats'*. **Derivational** marking, on the other hand, creates one lexeme from another, e.g., **unkind** from *kind*, *goodness* from *good*, and *redoable* form *redo*, and *redo* in turn from *do*. So *kind* and *do* are also bases. A **stem** is any morpheme or combination of morphemes to which an inflectional suffix may be attached. *Cat* is a stem in *cats* and so is *kind* in *kinder* and *redo* in *redoes*. A **base** is any morpheme or combination of morphemes to which one can attach either an inflectional or derivational affix. All stems are therefore bases, but not all bases are stems. *Do* is a stem (and therefore also a base) when we attach the "third person singular" to it to form *does*, but it is to a base (not a stem) that we attach the derivational prefix "again," the *re-* of *redo*.

Morphemes may also be **free morphemes** or **bound morphemes**. "Cat" is quite free in that it can occur as a word by itself, as *cat*, but obviously "plural" is bound, for it never occurs by itself, as *\*s*. In English the commonest types of bound morphemes are inflectional suffixes and derivational prefixes and suffixes. From now on we will show all bound morphemes with a hyphen, e.g., the "plural" as /-z/ or *-s*. In certain words we may also find bound bases: *-couth* in **uncouth** and both *astro-* and *-naut* in **astronaut**.

Finally, we should note that when we talk about the meaning we associate with a particular morpheme we usually show that meaning in quotation marks so as to distinguish the meaning content from the actually occurring form. Such a distinction is a useful one, but one not without its difficulties. While it is possible to characterize a word like *cat* in this way, to speak of the content, or **lexical meaning**, "cat" and differentiate that from the actually occurring form /kæt/, it seems to make less sense to do so with the **grammatical meanings** associated with grammatical morphemes like *the, of, but, there* (as in **There's** *a man outside to see you*), and so on. Consequently, from now on we will refer to morphemes in the way that is most convenient at the time. We will probably prefer to refer to *cat* rather than "cat," but may refer to "plural" either as "plural," or as /-z/, or as *-s*, depending on whether we want to emphasize the "meaning," the basic phonological shape, or the most frequent realization in spelling of this morpheme.


# 11.3   Inflection


As a process, **inflection** usually involves only a small set of changes in words, e.g., English nouns are marked inflectionally only for "plural" and "genitive." The set, however, is likely to be extremely productive, i.e., it will apply to a large number of words and a particular set of inflections may establish a part-of-speech category. The meanings of inflections, i.e., "plural," etc. are also likely to form a very restricted set. They will be consistent, i.e., they are **transparent**: for example, "plural" is always unambiguously "more than one." The inflected English word classes are the nouns, pronouns, verbs, and adjectives, and English inflections are always suffixes. We will deal briefly with each of these classes in turn.

English **nouns** are inflected for "plural," for "genitive," and for a combination of both "plural" and "genitive":

regular     *cat, cats, cat's, cats'*
irregular   *man, men, man's, men's*

The regular "plural" and "genitive" morphemes are **homophonous**, i.e. they sound the same. The regular phonological realization of the morphemes is /-z/ so there is a /-z/ meaning "plural" and a /-z/ meaning "genitive." When a noun with regular inflection is both "plural" and "genitive" the two /-z/ morphemes are realized as /-z/ not */-zz/. Each morpheme has three regular allomorphs: a schwa is inserted before the /-z/ after nouns ending in any one of /s, z, š, ž, č, ǰ/ to produce the /-əz/ allomorph; the /-z/ devoices after voiceless consonants to produce the /-s/ allomorph; and elsewhere /-z/ occurs. The consequences for the "plurals" (/-z/), "genitives" (/-z/), and "plural genitives" (also /-z/) of *dish*, *cat*, and *pig* are:

*dishes, dish's, dishes'*    /dɪš/ + /-z/ → /díšəz/
*cats, cat's, cats'*         /kæt/ + /-z/ → /kæts/
*pigs, pig's, pigs'*         /pɪg/ + /-z/ → /pɪgz/

That is, the "plural," "genitive," and "plural genitive" of a regular noun are homophones.

Whereas the English "genitive" is always regular and is suffixed to either the base form or the "plural" form of the noun, the English "plural" is frequently irregular. We can therefore note the following regularities in the "genitive" as it is suffixed to either the base form or the "plural" form of the noun:

*man's, men's; foot's, feet's; goose's, geese's;*
*criterion's, criteria's; datum's, data's; sheep's, sheeps'*

However, the irregularities of the "plurals" of the above are quite noticeable:

*man, men; foot, feet; goose, geese;*
*criterion, criteria; datum, data; sheep, sheep*

There are various kinds of irregularity in such words. In *man, foot,* and *goose* there is vowel replacement, sometimes called a **replacement allomorph** to indicate that the noun is a "plural" noun, so *man* changes to *men, foot* to *feet,* and *goose* to *geese.* In *criterion* and *datum* there is deletion at the end of each word so that *criterion* becomes *criteria* and *datum* becomes *data* in the "plural." In *sheep* there is no change at all between the singular and the "plural" so we have a **zero allomorph** of the "plural" morpheme. If we add *wives* and *children* to our list, we will observe that there is a stem change in *wife* (to *wive-*) before the regular plural is affixed. Some other words that

behave like *wife* are *knife, wolf,* and *truth*. In *children* there is vowel replacement in the first syllable and an entirely new allomorph of the "plural," the
*-ren* ending. *Brethren,* the rare plural form of *brother* has some resemblance
to *child,* as does *ox,* with its "plural" *oxen*.

The morphology of the English personal **pronouns** is extremely irregular.
There are subject and object forms and two genitive forms, one characteristic
of attributive use, the **first possessive,** e.g., *my* in *It's **my** book,* and one characteristic of predicative or absolute use, the **second possessive,** e.g., *mine* in
*It's **mine**.* The whole set of personal pronouns is produced here in phonemic
notation in contrast to the spelling representation given in the first chapter:

Singular

| Person | Subject | Object | 1 Poss. | 2 Poss. |
|--------|---------|--------|---------|---------|
| 1 | /aɪ/ | /mi/ | /maɪ/ | /maɪn/ |
| 2 | /yu/ | /yu/ | /yor/ | /yorz/ |
| 3m. | /hi/ | /hɪm/ | /hɪz/ | /hɪz/ |
| 3f. | /ši/ | /hər/ | /hər/ | /hərz/ |
| 3n. | /ɪt/ | /ɪt/ | /ɪts/ | /ɪts/ |

Plural

| Person | Subject | Object | 1 Poss. | 2 Poss. |
|--------|---------|--------|---------|---------|
| 1 | /wi/ | /əs/ | /aʊr/ | /aʊrz/ |
| 2 | /yu/ | /yu/ | /yor/ | /yorz/ |
| 3 | /ðe/ | /ðɛm/ | /ðer/ | /ðerz/ |

While it is possible to attempt to break down pronouns like *him* and *them*
into component morphological parts with /hi/ and /hɪ-/ being considered
allomorphs of "he" and /ðe/ and /ðɛ-/ being considered as allomorphs of "they"
and the /-m/ in both cases being considered as an allomorph of "objective
case," such an exercise seems to be of dubious value. How can we pick out
all the other morphemes that we might want to claim are present in the above
set of pronouns, e.g., "first person," or "third person singular," or "feminine"?
What we have here is an extremely irregular set of personal pronouns. The
set does realize various combinations of meanings but any attempt to specify
in every case which bit of sound goes with which bit of meaning seems
uncalled for – except perhaps as an exercise in linguistic ingenuity!

There are two other inflectional patterns among English pronouns. *This*
and *that* have the plural forms *these* and *those.* The latter forms are definitely
bimorphemic: "this" plus "plural" and "that" plus "plural." However, once

again there seems to be little to gain by trying to tie particular sounds to particular meanings. The relative pronoun *who* has an objective case form *whom* (in some varieties of English) and a genitive case form *whose*.

From the point of view of inflection, English **verbs** are the most morphologically complicated word class. There are four basic inflections for a regular verb like *beg*: *begs*, the /-z/ of "present" (or "third person singular"); *begged*, the /-d/ of "past"; *begged*, the /-d/ of "past participle"; and *begging*, the /-ɪŋ/ of "present participle." In regular verbs the "past" and "past participle" morphemes are homophonous. However, only the "present participle" morpheme is regular throughout the verb system, but even here there are some anomalies, for verbs like *must* and *ought* have no present participle forms, e.g., *\*musting* and *\*oughting*.

The "present" morpheme in verbs is also homophonous with the "plural" and "genitive" morphemes in nouns. It is basically /-z/ and has the same phonological conditioning of its allomorphic variants: *catches* /kǽčəz/, *bakes* /beks/, and *begs* /bɛgz/. The regular "past" and "past participle" morphemes are both realized as /-d/. Once again there are three allomorphs. After alveolar stops, i.e., /t/ and /d/, a schwa is inserted to produce the /-əd/ allomorph. After the remaining voiceless consonants the /-d/ devoices to /-t/. Elsewhere the /-d/ occurs. So we have *waited* /wétɛd/, *asked*, /æskt/, and *begged* /bɛgd/.

(Sometimes, as, for example, in earlier chapters, the "past participle" morpheme is referred to as the *-en* ending rather than the *-ed* ending. This renaming is simply a matter of descriptive convenience: it conveniently distinguishes between two very frequently occurring and often homophonous inflections that distribute quite differently.)

The "past" and "past participle" morphemes are irregular in a variety of ways. In verbs like *bet*, *put*, *hit*, and *cut* there are **zero allomorphs** for both the "past" and "past participle," i.e., no overt marking. There is final consonant replacement in verbs like *lend*, *bend*, and *spend* so that we find final /t/ instead of /d/, e.g., *I bent* and *I have bent*. In verbs like *burn*, *learn*, and *spill* we have this same replacement in some varieties of English, e.g., *He burnt it*, whereas other varieties are quite regular, e.g., *He burned it*. In verbs like *feed*, *drink*, *swim*, and *hold* we have vowel **replacement** and sometimes the replacement may be different for the "past" and the "past participle" so that we have *I drank* but *I have drunk*. In verbs like *creep* and *weep* we find a combination of vowel replacement and the regular ending: *I crept* and *I have wept*. Verbs like *bring*, *catch*, *think*, *sell*, and *tell* change their vowels (and sometimes their consonants too) and add either /-t/ or /-d/: *brought*, *caught*, *thought*, etc. *Break*, *speak*, *wear*, *bite*, etc. have vowel replacement in both the "past" and "past participle" and the past participle is further marked by a final /-n/ or /-ən/: *I broke*, *I have broken*. The verb *go is* **suppletive** in its "past" form (*went*) and the "past participle" *gone* is also irregular. Finally, *be*, *have*, and *do* are quite irregular:

*be, have,* and *do*

| stem | present | past | past participle | present participle |
|------|---------|------|-----------------|--------------------|
| *have* | *has* | *had* | *had* | *having* |
| *do* | *does* | *did* | *done* | *doing* |
| *be* | *am* | *was* | *been* | *being* |
| | *are* | *were* | | |
| | *is* | | | |

In *be* there is morphological marking for "first person singular" in the "present" form of the verb. Such marking is found nowhere else in English; in all other verbs the "present" is marked only when the subject is "third person singular." In the "past" there is also a distinction between "first person singular" and "third person singular" on the one hand and all the other persons, again a unique distinction in the language. In addition the verb *be* is doubly **suppletive**, making use of three entirely different phonological bases in *am*, *was*, and *be*. Once again one could attempt to relate the semantic content of the various forms we find to the various phonemes that occur but, as with the personal pronouns, such an effort seems scarcely justifiable. (Notice too the frequently occurring but often condemned occurrence of *ain't* /ent/ as a negative variant.)

The **modal verbs** are deficient in their inflectional morphology: they are therefore sometimes referred to as **defective** verbs. *Will*, *shall*, *may*, and *can* have irregular "past" forms (*would*, *should*, *might*, and *could*) and no other variants. *Must* and *ought* have only those forms. There are verb forms like *cans*, *willed*, and **canning** but these are entirely different lexemes:

> He *cans* tomatoes on Tuesdays.
> She **willed** it to her nephew.
> We *were* **canning** the fruit at the time.

Some of the modals also have interesting variants before the negative **clitic** *n't* /-ənt/, e.g., *shan't*, *won't*, and *mustn't*.

The final inflected word class in English is the class of **adjectives** or at least the part of that class that can be inflected for "comparative" and "superlative." The regular endings are *-er* and *-est* in spelling:

> *fast   faster   fastest*

Some irregular forms do occur. For example, there are some **suppletive** forms:

> **good   better   best**
> **bad    worse   worst**

*Better* is "good" plus "comparative" and *worst* is "bad" plus "superlative." There are also irregularities like:

   *less   lesser   least*

In addition to the adjectives cited above a few others such as *long* and *strong* show a small change in their stems when either inflection occurs, e.g., /laŋ/, /láŋgər/, and /láŋgəst/. One proposal for dealing with such adjectives is to say that they have the underlying phonemic forms /laŋg/ and /straŋg/ respectively. These form are realized only before the above affixes. When there is no affix, the final stem consonant is deleted. A still more radical interpretation provides underlying forms like /lang/ and /strang/ for the two words. In this case the /n/ assimilates to the following /g/ and becomes [ŋ] and then the above deletion rule applies if no inflection is added. The phonological entity that we have referred to throughout as the /ŋ/ phoneme has numerous deficiencies in its distribution in English; this last solution is part of an attempt to eliminate it completely by deriving all phonetic realizations of [ŋ] from underlying /n/s by rules of various kinds. (We will take up this point again in chapter 12.)

   What we have just provided is a very brief description of English inflectional morphology. We have also confined our attention to the inflectional, morphology of standard varieties of the language. Non-standard varieties often preserve inflectional forms that have been eliminated from standard varieties or extend a morphological rule to cover forms not usually covered by that rule in standard varieties. In the following examples it is fairly easy to note the rules that have been used to produce the forms that occur:

   *I want three of **yous** to go.*
   *He hurt **hisself**.*
   *She **drunk** her milk slowly.*
   *Who **taked** it out?*
   *They **brung** it back a week ago.*

From what we have said above, we should now be aware that there is considerable irregularity in English nouns, pronouns, and verbs in standard varieties of English. Non-standard varieties are no less regular or irregular; their regularities and irregularities are just different regularities and irregularities. What happens is that when these do indeed differ from those of the standard varieties they are usually condemned. That is, however, a social condemnation not a linguistic one.

# 11.4   Derivation

As a process, **derivation** often involves many different kinds of changes in words. The derivational process is often inconsistent and it may also result in a word changing its part-of-speech category. Derivational affixes are sometimes **opaque**, i.e., they may appear to be somewhat variable in their meanings as they attach to different bases, e.g., *-ation* in *derivation* and *affixation*.

English has an extensive derivational morphology. Unlike inflectional affixes, which are always suffixes in English, derivational affixes may be either prefixes or suffixes. Moreover, an English word may contain more than one derivational affix whereas – if we exclude examples of irregular forms such as *men's* – it may contain no more than one inflectional affix. If there is one or more derivational suffixes and an inflectional suffix, the inflectional suffix must also follow any derivational marking: *kindnesses* is possible but *\*kindsness* is not. This last fact would seem to follow from the principle that derivational affixes create new lexemes and it is lexemes that we inflect.

One further observation is called for. We are concerned with the "productive" morphology of English, that is, with processes that are alive in the language. If we look at words like *receive, deceive,* and *conceive, refer, prefer,* and *defer,* and *obtain, retain,* and *detain,* we might be tempted to analyze each as bimorphemic. Each would contain a derivational prefix, *re-, de-, con-, pre-,* or *ob-,* and a bound base, *-ceive, -fer,* or *-tain*. We might even try to ascribe some meanings to *-ceive, -fer,* and *-tain* although it is not clear what exactly those meanings would be, just as it is not clear what meanings we could give to *re-, de-, con-, pre-,* and *ob-*. Some kind of morphological analysis is possible here but we will not attempt it. We will ignore it because we no longer, if we ever did, form new words using such morphemes. The process, if it existed, is now "frozen." A more likely explanation is that words such as these were borrowed into English in sufficient quantity that they have retained some of their morphological characteristics from the language of origin. However, we will resist this **etymological** justification for regarding these words as bimorphemic and treat them as single morphemes in each case. (We must note, however, that it is not at all clear exactly where we would draw the line between etymology and morphology; below, for example, we consider words like *aside* and *alive* to be bimorphemic, an analysis which depends on the *a-* prefix being still productive in the language.)

If we compare the above words with words like *redo,* **unkind,** and **pre-teen,** we can see that in the case of the last three words there is no question that each is bimorphemic and that the process of word formation in each case is a productive one. Any native speaker of English can use the processes to create new words: *restructure,* **unholy,** and **pre-industrial.** We can also observe a difference between the "dead" *re-* of **recreation** and the "live *re-* of *re-creation*. We must not carry this notion too far though: as we will see, there are serious restrictions on the use of derivational affixes in English.

When we add a derivational affix to a base, we sometimes change the word class of the original word: if we add *-ness* to *good* we change an adjective into a noun and if we add *-ful* to *help* we change a verb into an adjective. Sometimes the derivational affix does not change the word class at all: both *kind* and **unkind** are adjectives and **stepfather** is a noun just like *father*.

In the following examples of derivation we make no attempt to be exhaustive; we wish merely to illustrate the variety to be found in English derivational morphology. If we look at prefixes first, we can observe that the following prefixes are often class changing:

| | |
|---|---|
| *a-* | *aside, alive* (noun or verb to adjective) |
| *be-* | *becalm, bewitch* (adjective or noun to verb) |
| *en-* | *enslave, entrain* (noun to verb) |

Most prefixes do not usually change the word class of the words to which they are affixed. The following prefixes go on nouns:

| | |
|---|---|
| *anti-* | *anti-war, anti-tank* |
| *arch-* | *archduke, archbishop* |
| *co-* | *co-worker, co-producer* |
| *ex-* | *ex-president, ex-husband* |
| *fore-* | *forefathers, forebears* |
| *in-* | *in-house, in-group* |
| *inter-* | *interstate, inter-office* |
| *mid-* | *midstream, midair* |
| *mini-* | *mini-dress, mini-contest* |
| *non-* | *non-smoker, non-believer* |
| *post-* | *post-war, postproduction* |
| *step-* | *stepfather, stepson* |
| *sub-* | *subsurface, sub-lieutenant* |
| *super-* | *superman, superstructure* |

The following prefixes go on verbs:

| | |
|---|---|
| *circum-* | *circumnavigate, circumscribe* |
| *co-* | *co-occur, cohabit* |
| *counter-* | *counterattack, counteract* |
| *de-* | *deregulate, demystify* |
| *dis-* | *disobey, distrust* |
| *fore-* | *foretell, forestall* |
| *inter-* | *interchange, interact* |

| | |
|---|---|
| *mis-* | *misrepresent, misconstrue* |
| *out-* | *outspend, outlast* |
| *over-* | *over-regulate, oversupply* |
| *re-* | *resubmit, redecorate* |
| *sub-* | *sublet, subdivide* |
| *un-* | *unwrap, unload* |
| *under-* | *underestimate, under-report* |

The following prefixes go on adjectives:

| | |
|---|---|
| *a-* | *asymmetrical, amoral* |
| *dis-* | *disloyal, disrespectful* |
| *i-* | *illegal, irregular* |
| *im-* | *impossible, implausible* |
| *in-* | *intolerable, inhospitable* |
| *non-* | *non-transferable, nonexistent* |
| *over-* | *overanxious, overabundant* |
| *pre-* | *prehistoric, pre-industrial* |
| *trans-* | *transcontinental, trans-oceanic* |
| *ultra-* | *ultralight, ultrasonic* |
| *un-* | *unkind, unhappy* |

We should note that *i-*, *im-*, and *in-* in the above list are really allomorphic variants of the same prefix meaning "not." The basic form of the prefix is *in-* and, in speaking, we **assimilate** the consonant to the position of the following labial, e.g., *imbalance*, *impotent*, and *infamous*. Before words that begin with *r* or *l* the final consonant is actually lost; it is merely a spelling convention to double the *r* or *l* in words like *irregular* and *illegal*.

Adding a suffix to a word often produces a change of word class. Therefore, we will describe suffixes from the perspective of the resulting word class.

The following suffixes may be used to form nouns:

from nouns

| | |
|---|---|
| *-dom* | *kingdom, earldom* |
| *-ess* | *hostess, actress* |
| *-ette* | *statuette, diskette* |
| *-ful* | *handful, armful* |
| *-hood,* | *nationhood, parenthood* |
| *-ist* | *violinist, stylist* |
| *-let* | *piglet, booklet* |
| *-ship* | *friendship, kingship* |

| | |
|---|---|
| -ster | *gangster, mobster* |
| -y | *mummy, pussy* |

from verbs

| | |
|---|---|
| -age | *drainage, wastage* |
| -al | *referral, trial* |
| -ant | *informant, inhabitant* |
| -ation | *examination, proclamation* |
| -ee | *employee, payee* |
| -er | *employer, worker* |
| -ing | *founding, building* |
| -ion | *protection, delegation* |
| -ment | *enjoyment, deployment* |
| -th | *growth, health* |

from adjectives

| | |
|---|---|
| -dom | *freedom, wisdom* |
| -ism | *idealism, realism* |
| -ist | *fatalist, loyalist* |
| -ity | *sanity, rapidity* |
| -ness | *goodness, brightness* |
| -th | *width, length* |

The following suffixes may be used to form verbs:

from nouns

| | |
|---|---|
| -ify | *typify, beautify* |
| -ize | *decimalize, publicize* |

from adjectives

| | |
|---|---|
| -en | *brighten, widen* |

The following suffixes may be used to form adjectives:

from nouns

| | |
|---|---|
| -al | *national, fatal* |
| -en | *wooden, golden* |

| *-ish* | *girlish, foolish* |
| *-ful* | *painful, armful* |
| *-ian* | *Canadian, Parisian* |
| *-ic* | *organic, demonic* |
| *-less* | *headless, guiltless* |
| *-like* | *manlike, godlike* |
| *-ly* | *beastly, womanly* |
| *-ous* | *virtuous, courageous* |
| *-y* | *rainy, muddy* |

from verbs

| *-able* | *agreeable, affordable* |
| *-ful* | *helpful, harmful* |
| *-ive* | *assertive, active* |
| *-less* | *helpless, harmless* |

from adjectives

| *-ish* | *yellowish, smallish* |

The following suffixes may be used to form adverbs:

from adjectives

| *-ly* | *calmly, hopefully* |

from other sources

| *-ward(s)* | *westward, backwards* |
| *-ways* | *crossways, sideways* |
| *-wise* | *length-wise, time-wise* |

The above lists are by no means exhaustive: there are still other derivational affixes and some of the above are usable in ways that are not described here. A derivational affix may also produce different meanings depending on what it is affixed to. We will illustrate this point by referring to a prefix *dis-* and a suffix *-ation*. The prefix *dis-* appears in *dislike* and *disapprove* and also in *disembark, disappear, dispossess,* and *dismount.* In the first two examples it produces an **antonym** of the verb: *like-dislike* ("not like") and *approve-disapprove* ("not approve"). However, *embark* and *disembark,* and the other verbs in the second group are not antonyms. Rather *dis-* in this case "reverses" the action specified by the verb so that one can only disembark after having embarked, dismount after having mounted, and so on. The suffix *-ation* is even more complicated and we can observe some of the variety of the resulting meanings in a word like *classification* where it can mean any one of the "act of," the "result of," or the "system of" classifying, as in:

> The ("act of") **classification** *took years to complete.*
> He appealed the ("result of") **classification.**
> I prefer the Dewey ("system of") **classification.**

*Classification* may only be a single lexeme but a comprehensive dictionary would have to record at least the kinds of meanings given here as **polysemous** sub-variants of the meaning of that lexeme.

Some derivational prefixes appear to be attached to bases which are themselves bound. This seems to be particularly the case with certain "negative" prefixes, for many people have no positive freely occurring bases for the following negatives yet each appears to be bimorphemic: **uncouth** (*couth?*), **unkempt** (*combed?*), **illicit** (*licit?*), **inept** (*apt?*), **impeccable**, **implacable**, **inane**, **insipid**, **inscrutable**, **intrepid**, **incorrigible**, **disdainful**, **discordant**, **disgruntled**, **nondescript**, and **nonplussed**.

When two or more derivational suffixes occur in a word there is a definite order in which they occur. For example *-ation* occurs before *-al*, as in *derivational*. The same *-al* occurs before *-ize*, as in *industrialize*. However, *-ize* must occur before *-ation*, as in *synthesization*. We could even put an *-al* on the last word if we wished: *synthesizational*. The same kind of ordering can be seen with *-ic*, *-al*, *-ist*, and *-ic* again: *poetical*, *herbalist*, *communistic*, and *tribalistic*.

Some of the derivational possibilities the language offers are not used. The meaning of *\*ungood* is quite transparent but apparently we do not use a derivational process to create a "meaning" which already exists in the language. In this case we already have *bad* with its simple monomorphemic structure. Likewise, we do not have *\*stealer* because we already have *thief*. This explanation may account for why certain forms do not occur, why for example we have *curious* and *curiosity* but not *furious* and *\*furiosity* – we already have *furiousness*. Because we have *wisdom* and *ability* we do not need *\*wiseness* and *\*ableness* and because we have *disloyal* and *improper* we do not need *\*unloyal* and *\*unproper*.

Words may contain several derivational affixes. If they do, they will have a definite **constituent structure**. *Kindness* and *disembark*, each composed of two constituents – we consider *embark* to be a single morpheme – give us no problem:

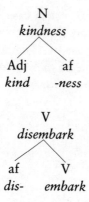

```
        N
     kindness
      /    \
   Adj      af
   kind    -ness


        V
    disembark
      /    \
    af      V
   dis-    embark
```

When we add further affixes, either inflectional or derivational, we still have a definite constituent structure. The following examples show the hierarchical constituency of several more words with once again the word class indicated as noun (N), verb (V), or adjective (Adj), and affixes as (af).

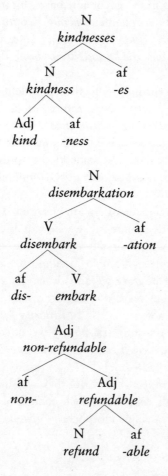

```
              N
          kindnesses
          /        \
        N           af
     kindness      -es
      /    \
   Adj      af
   kind    -ness


              N
        disembarkation
          /        \
        V           af
    disembark     -ation
      /    \
    af      V
   dis-    embark


            Adj
       non-refundable
        /          \
      af            Adj
     non-        refundable
                   /      \
                  N        af
               refund    -able
```

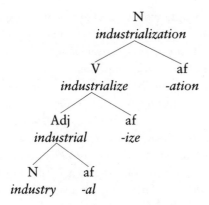

## 11.5   Compounding

In the previous section we were concerned with the formation of words containing a single **base.** A word with a single base and one or more derivational affixes is a **complex word.** In this section we will be concerned with words formed from two (or more) bases. Such words are called **compound words.**

Word compounding is a very productive process in English for forming new words. Compound words may often be recognized in speech from the stress pattern that many of them carry: full stress on their first constituent and a reduced stress on their second. We will use the acute and grave accent markers as follows (′ ‵) to show this stress pattern. For example, in the following list the first member of each pair is a compound and the second a phrase consisting of a modifier and a noun with a different stress pattern, secondary stress and main stress (ˆ ′):

<table>
<tr><td>′  ‵</td><td>ˆ  ′</td></tr>
<tr><td>blackbird</td><td>black bird</td></tr>
<tr><td>icebox</td><td>ice statue</td></tr>
<tr><td>darkroom</td><td>dark night</td></tr>
<tr><td>car park</td><td>car lights</td></tr>
</table>

The above stress pattern is typical of many compounds regardless of the word classes from which they are formed. However, some combinations that do not have this pattern are also very like compounds: they may sometimes be included in this category or treated separately as syntactic compounds, e.g., *trade union, bank holiday, carbon dioxide, speed limit, sign language, Fifth Avenue, smoked meat, bow tie, cold war, apple pie, foul play, glottal stop, cottage cheese, Lake Louise,* and so on. So far as spelling is concerned, compounds are sometimes written as single words (*daylight, watchdog, airborne*), sometimes as hyphenated words (*garden-fresh, in-group, easy-going*), and sometimes as two words (*life insurance, bath towel, mental hospital*). Spelling, therefore, is not a reliable indicator of compound status.

Compounds may be **endocentric** or **exocentric**. An endocentric compound is one that can substitute for one of its component parts. Endocentric compounds are also fairly transparent in meaning. For example, a *rattlesnake* is a kind of *snake*, a *girlfriend* is a kind of *friend*, and a *windmill* is a kind of *mill*. These are all endocentric compounds. However, a *redneck* is not a kind of *neck*, a *hotdog* is not a kind of *dog*, a *highbrow* is not a kind of *brow*, and a *loudmouth* is not a kind of *mouth*. These are all exocentric compounds. An exocentric compound has a meaning which cannot be said to derive from the sum of its parts. A *redneck* refers to a type of person, just as do *highbrow* and *loudmouth*, and a *hotdog* refers to a type of food. Exocentric compounds are often quite opaque in meaning.

We can attempt to give some kind of syntactic reading to most compounds and indeed various attempts have been made to classify endocentric compounds according to their presumed syntactic bases. For example, we might attempt to give readings of the following kinds to the compounds cited:

| | |
|---|---|
| *swimsuit* | a suit (to wear) for swimming |
| *hangman* | a man who hangs others |
| *goldfish* | a fish of gold color |
| *earthquake* | the earth quakes |
| *mind reader* | one who reads minds |
| *soap opera* | the opera sells soap |
| *sunburn* | the sun causes burns |
| *pickpocket* | one who picks (things out of) pockets |
| *girlfriend* | the friend is a girl |
| *bulldog* | the dog is like a bull |
| *drawbridge* | the bridge can be drawn up |

In such attempts disagreements soon arise concerning the syntactic bases that must be postulated for many of the compounds. There is also no reason to believe that compounds necessarily have a syntactic base. Word compounding is after all a lexical, i.e., word-formation, process not a syntactic process.

We will give some examples of different kinds of English compounds. Once again we will make no attempt to be exhaustive. We will also proceed word class by word class. Noun compounds are formed from various combinations:

| | |
|---|---|
| noun and noun | *boyfriend, death blow, acid rain, bagpipes, blood-test, newspaper* |
| verb and noun | *cut-throat, hovercraft, pickpocket, rattlesnake, watchdog, chewing gum* |

| noun and verb | *nosebleed, skyscraper, striptease, sunrise,* |
| | *bus-stop, house-keeping, boat-ride* |
| verb and verb | *hearsay, make-believe* |
| adjective and noun | *fast-food, blackboard, madman, greenhouse* |
| particle and noun | *in-group, off-Broadway, bystander, overcoat* |
| verb and particle | *put-down, fallout, teach-in, leftover, hold-up* |

Verb compounds are formed as follows:

| noun and verb | *carbon-date, color-code, sightsee, gatecrash* |
| adjective and verb | *fine-tune* |
| particle and verb | *outlast, overbook, undermine* |
| adjective and noun | *brown-bag, bad-mouth* |

Adjective compounds are formed as follows:

| noun and adjective | *leadfree, grass-green, duty-free,* |
| | *garden-fresh, class-conscious* |
| noun and verb | *man-eating, man-made, breathtaking,* |
| | *airborne, color-blind* |
| adjective and adjective | *bitter-sweet, red-hot, icy-cold* |
| adjective and verb | *good-looking, easy-going* |
| particle and noun | *in-depth, offside, underground* |
| particle and verb | *hard-hitting, well-read* |
| verb and particle | *see-through, tow-away* |
| particle and adjective | *wide awake, oversensitive* |

There are also compound adverbs like *overnight* and *flat-out*.

Still another kind of compound is the **neo-classical compound** in which the combining elements are Greek or Latin in origin: *astrophysics, hydroelectric, aquanaut, anglophile, homophobe, pseudo-science, sociobiology, francophone, technophobe,* etc. There is perhaps no clear distinction between such compounds and complex words.

# 11.6  Conversion and Other Processes

Still another way of forming new words in English is by **conversion** or **functional shift**. One way of looking at this process is to say that a word may be shifted from one word class into another word class without the addition of a derivational affix. Once shifted, the word may take on all the usual inflections of the new word class. In such a view we turn the noun *bottle* into a verb and the verb *fight* into a noun when we use them in the following ways:

> *Are you going to* **bottle** *the fruit?*
> *It was a fair* **fight**.

Here then are what appear to be some cases of conversion with the apparent direction of shift indicated. Some illustrative sentences follow.

| | |
|---|---|
| noun to verb | *bottle, mail, skin, coat, glue, mother, group, elbow* |
| verb to noun | *call, guess, need, walk, retreat, catch, swim, cover* |
| adjective to verb | *better, empty, dirty, calm, lower, dry* |
| adjective to noun | *poor, daily, crazy, comic, regular, heavy* |
| particle to noun | *up, down, how, why* |
| particle to verb | *down* |

> *He* **elbowed** *his way through the crowd.*
> *My* **needs** *are few.*
> *What was your best* **catch**?
> *She tried to* **empty** *the container.*
> *Stop playing the* **heavy**!
> *We've had a lot of* **ups** *and* **downs** *recently.*
> *He tried to* **down** *the medicine in one gulp.*

Another interpretation of such facts is to say that some words may belong concurrently to two or more word classes. In this view we assign no primacy to any particular word class. For many of the above words that might appear to be a reasonable solution. It might also receive some support from an additional set of words like the following:

| noun/adjective | verb | noun/adjective | verb |
|---|---|---|---|
| *súspect* | *suspéct* | *ímport* | *impórt* |
| *súrvey* | *survéy* | *ábstract* | *abstráct* |
| *pérmit* | *permít* | *fréquent* | *frequént* |
| *présent* | *presént* | *récord* | *recórd* |
| *ábsent* | *absént* | *súbject* | *subjéct* |

In this set of two-syllable words the nouns and adjectives on the one hand and the verbs on the other have different stress patterns. There also seems to be little reason to say that the noun or adjective has any kind of primacy over the verb or vice versa. A second set further complicates the issue because of another kind of change:

| noun   | verb    | noun   | verb    |
|--------|---------|--------|---------|
| *house*  | *house*   | *advice* | *advise*  |
| *abuse*  | *abuse*   | *proof*  | *prove*   |
| *mouth*  | *mouth*   | *device* | *devise*  |
| *breath* | *breathe* | *wreath* | *wreathe* |
| *refuse* | *refuse*  | *belief* | *believe* |

There is no stress difference in such pairs when there is more than one syllable in the word: however, the noun in each case ends in a voiceless fricative whereas the verb ends in a voiced fricative. Once again we could say that we convert a noun to a verb in each case and that voicing of the final fricative accompanies that conversion. Or we may prefer to list the nouns and verbs separately and merely note the close phonological relationship that exists in the final fricatives.

The shift proposal seems to be more valid for a word like *poor*. When *poor* is used after *the*, it can still take *very* in front of it, as in *The **very poor** will lose*. It still retains some of its adjective quality. It cannot be pluralized either: *\*the poors*. Perhaps this is not conversion at all but a form of **ellipsis**: *The very poor (**people**) will lose*. In contrast, we can still talk about *various ups and downs*, *the dailies*, and *downing a pint of beer*.

**Back-formation** is a process in which a word originally comprised of a single constituent is analyzed as having two constituents and one of them is then removed to form a new word. For example, *peddler* was reanalyzed as being composed of *peddle* and *-er* and a new word *peddle* entered the language through back-formation. Some other examples are *burgle* from *burglar*, *edit* from *editor*, *afflict* from *affliction*, *negate* from *negation*, *intuit* from *intuition*, *surreal* from *surrealist*, *housekeep* from *housekeeper*, *baby-sit* from *baby-sitter*, *televise* from *television*, *pea* from an older form *pease*, and *self-destruct* from *self-destruction*.

**Clipping** involves the omission of part of a word: ***memo**(randum)*, ***sit**(uation)* ***com**(edy)*, ***lab**(oratory)*, ***hippo**(potamus)*, ***ad**(vertisement)*, ***condo**(minium)*, ***deli**(catessen)*, ***taxi**(cab)*, *(taxi)**cab***, *(in)**flu**(enza)*, *(re)**fridge**(erator)*, *(air)**plane***, *(para)**chute***, and ***gym**(nasium)*.

**Blending** creates a new word out of two old words: *smog (**smoke** and **fog**)*, *brunch (**breakfast** and **lunch**)*, *motel (**motor** and **hotel**)*, *chunnel (**channel** and **tunnel**)*, *Spanglish (**Spanish** and **English**)*, and *pulsar (**pulse** and **quasar**)*.

**Acronyms** are words formed from the initials of other words: *NATO*, *UNICEF*, *AIDS*, *AWOL*, *WASP*, *BASIC*, *VAT*, *GNP*, and *UCLA*. Some like *WASP* and *AIDS* can be pronounced like ordinary words; others like *GNP* and *UCLA* must be spelled out. *Yuppie* and *dink* are recent acronyms now written like ordinary words.

**Reduplication** makes use of rhyme: ***flower-power**, **hobnob**, **razzle-dazzle**,* *fuddy-duddy, helter-skelter, walkie-talkie,* and *teeny-weeny.* Examples like *sing-song, flip-flop, tip-top, zig-zag, riff-raff, tittle-tattle, flim-flam,* and *mish-mash* also show vowel alternation.

**Invention** brings other words into the language: *Xerox, Teflon, Kodak, Kleenex, Dacron,* and *fax.*

An **idiom** is a combination of two or more words in which the combination takes on a unique meaning, that is, a meaning which in no way derives from the sum of the parts. Idioms are therefore just like all the other lexemes we have been considering and must be treated as new meaning entities in the language. English contains a vast number of idioms. All of the following are idioms in English:

> He **kicked the bucket.**
> I **met up with** him in Rome.
> **Shut up!**
> I'll **go along with** it.
> He **got away with** it.
> It was **raining cats and dogs.**
> His uncle **passed away.**
> I was only **pulling your leg.**
> They **took** him **to the cleaners.**

The idiomatic nature of such expressions is soon apparent if we try to make any changes in them:

> *\*The bucket was kicked by him.*
> *\*I met down with him in Rome.*
> *\*Shut down!*
> *\*I'll come along with it.*
> *\*He got with it away.*
> *\*It's raining kittens and puppies.*

None of the above is possible as it would be if the syntax of the original did not contain an idiom.

## 11.7   Exercises

1   Are the following italicized words examples of homonymy or polysemy?

a mountain/kitchen *range*, a *case* of beer/measles, the human/space *race*, a *free* meal/press, some *rare* beef/books, a *light* blow/color

2    Each of the following plurals is irregular. Explain the irregularity in phonemic terms. The first one is done for you.

women (/ɪ/ replaces /ʊ/ in the first syllable.), feet, children, deer, data, theses, wives

3    Each of the following verbs is irregular in either its past tense or its past participle or in both. Explain the irregularity in phonemic terms. The first one is done for you.

sleep (In both the past tense and past participle /ɛ/ replaces /i/ in addition to the regular process of adding the suffix /-t/.), put, go, break, get, read, drive, be, sell, seek, spend, keep, take, begin, sink, do, bite, lie, see, weave

4    How many morphemes are there in each of the following words? What meaning do you associate with each of these morphemes? What problems do you find? The first one is done for you.

lobster (One only. The -ster looks like the ending of *gangster, mobster,* etc., but whereas we have the words *gang* and *mob*, and -ster may mean something like "member" or "performer," we have no word *lob* connected to *lobster* and there is no concept of membership or performance here.), amoral, reinstitutionalized, unkempt, mobster, deceitful, belfry, deplaned, zoological, hippopotamus, Billy, laughter, lukewarm, cranberry, muskrat, November

5    Are the following possible English words? If not, why not?

wiseness, savageness, strongness, severeness, cycler, typer, raper, stealer, shop assister

6    Examine the final -er in each of the following words. In which words is it a morpheme? How many homophonous morphemes are there?

bigger, baker, diner, order, worker, dinner, player, brother, trailer, widower, friendlier, slipper, cylinder, painter, rubber, planter

7    How would you analyze the following words? Consider the following questions. How is the prefix *un-* usually used? How many morphemes are there in each word? For example, if there are two morphemes in *uncouth* is there a word *couth* to which we can attach *un-*? Compare *kind* and *un-* in *unkind*.

unkempt, inept, uncouth, nonplussed, impeccable, implacable, inane, incorrigible, intrepid, disdainful, disgruntled, discordant, insipid, nondescript, inscrutable

8    In which of the following words is -ic a derivational suffix? Is the solution always clear?

Arabic, arithmetic, arsenic, catholic, choleric, comic, cubic, fatalistic, frantic, heretic, metric, phonetic, politic, psychic, rhetoric, topic

9  What phonological changes occur in each base form when you add -*ic* in the first of the following sets and -*ous* in the second?

   (a)  alcohol, angel, catastrophe, diplomat, dynamo, economy, German, harmony, history, magnet, ocean, parasite, volcano
   (b)  advantage, courage, grace, harmony, industry, miracle, peril, study, vice

10  How would you analyze the following italicized constituents? Are these examples of still another type of compound?

   *parent–teacher* association, *Army–Navy* game, *faculty–student* committee, *federal–provincial* relationships, *teacher–student–child* interaction

11  Are the following words compounds? Or is the second morpheme in each case a derivational suffix?

   gentleman, topsail, careful, saucepan, brimstone, welcome, Plymouth, Monday, Highgate

12  Diagram the constituent structure of each of the following words or phrases. (They are deliberately given without spaces or hyphens.) What problems do you find? The first one is done for you below.

   repossession, freetrader, otherworldliness, nonjudgmental, antinuclear-armamentscampaign, exformercigarettesmoker, prolifer, dispassionately, deputychairmanship

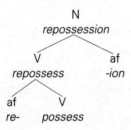

# 12
# Words and Sounds

In this chapter we will be concerned with two aspects of the pronunciation of words. One has to do with the different degrees of loudness given to the pronunciation of vowels in polysyllabic words and phrases. The other concerns certain regular relationships that hold between various consonants and vowels in morphemes, e.g., between the consonants in pairs of words like *space* and *spacious* and *face* and *facial* and the vowels in pairs of words like *sane* and *sanity* and *vain* and *vanity*.

## 12.1  English Stress

**Stress** is the term we use in order to refer to the comparative loudness with which vowels are pronounced in words. In words like *demon* and *lemon* the first vowel is pronounced more loudly than the second vowel. (A vowel stressed in this way will also tend to be slightly longer than one lacking such stress and it may also have a slightly higher pitch.) In a polysyllabic word we say that the most intensely pronounced vowel carries primary stress. Every word pronounced in isolation contains a vowel pronounced with such stress.

How many different degrees of stress are there altogether? One frequently proposed answer to this question is that we can distinguish four degrees of stress in English. *Demon* and *lemon* illustrate only two of these, actually the two extremes, a primary stressed vowel (marked ′) and an unstressed vowel (marked ˘): *démŏn* and *lémŏn*. If we add words such as *unlikely* and *dishearten* we can find still another degree of stress. The first vowel in each of these words is pronounced less loudly than the second vowel, the primary stressed vowel, and more loudly than the final vowel, the unstressed vowel. The same degree of stress seems to occur here as on the vowel in the second constituent of compounds, as in *ícebòx*, *hótdòg*, and so on. This degree of stress is sometimes called tertiary stress (marked ˋ) because it seems possible to find still another one between it and primary stress, one which is called secondary stress and is marked ˆ: *ùnlíkelỹ* and *dìshéartĕn*.

Secondary stress can be illustrated in phrases like *new books* and *old wine*. If we place primary stress on *books* and *wine* in each case, we will have a lesser degree of stress on *new* and *old*: *nêw bóoks* and *ôld wíne*. Of course, we can place primary stress on *new* and *old* if we want to emphasize these qualities. In this case we will have placed primary stress on the vowels in the adjectives and secondary stress on the vowels in the nouns: *néw bôoks* and *óld wîne*. In either case the secondary stressed vowels will be pronounced more loudly than either the first vowels in *unlikely* and *dishearten* or the final vowels in *icebox* and *hotdog*.

We therefore appear to be able to distinguish four degrees of stress as follows: primary (´), secondary (^), tertiary (`), and unstressed (˘). Here are some combinations of the various stresses for illustration:

| | |
|---|---|
| primary, unstressed | *wórkĕr, hópelĕss, cómmă, tíckĕt* |
| unstressed, primary | *ăbóut, rĕcéive, păráde, ă mán* |
| tertiary, primary | *dìsbár, pèrfórm, bègín, òbsérve* |
| tertiary, primary, unstressed | *ìdéă, bègínnĕr, òbsérvĕr, Nòvémbĕr* |
| primary, tertiary | *ícebòx, bús-stòp, cówbòy, cómpoùnd* |
| primary, tertiary, unstressed | *néwspàpĕr, síghtsèeĭng, skýscràpĕr* |
| unstressed, primary, tertiary | *ă blóod tèst, thĕ bús-stòp* |
| unstressed, secondary, primary | *ă nîce cár, hĭs ôld hóuse, thĕ nêw párt* |
| secondary, primary, unstressed | *gôod wórkĕrs, rûn smóothĕr* |

In this system of showing stresses *hotdog* and *hot dog* are distinguished from each other because the first is *hótdòg* and the second is either *hôt dóg* or *hót dôg* In the same way a *blâck bóard* may or may not be a *bláckboàrd*.

In syntactic arrangements primary stress typically occurs as follows:

| | | | |
|---|---|---|---|
| NP | *old mán* | Adjp | *very óld* |
| AdvP | *very cleárly* | VP | *go outsíde* |

In more complex arrangements we would then expect to find the following syllables to be stressed most heavily:

*very old mán*      *tell funny stóries*

We should note that while we have identified as many as four different degrees of stress, no more than three seem to occur within any one word. The distinction between primary and secondary stresses also seems to be entirely a syntactic matter. So while there may be four (or even more) distinguishable phonetic levels of stress, there appear to be no more than three (at the most) distinctive, i.e., phonemic, levels.

## 12.2  Stress Assignment

Native speakers of English know where to place the primary stress in individual words because for most English words such **stress assignment** is fairly easily predictable. Native speakers follow certain rules of stress assignment to the extent that they rarely have difficulty in correctly stressing English words. Occasionally they may apply one of the rules inappropriately but even in such cases follow stress assignment rules, however the wrong rules for the particular case. If a grammar of a language is a statement of the rules that speakers of that language follow, then we should try to state some of these stress rules in English. That is the task to which we will now turn.

English speakers usually assign primary stress as follows to words pronounced in isolation. The vowel in a monosyllabic word is always pronounced with primary stress:

> *héart, fáce, gó, pléase, friend*

A basic stress pattern for two syllable words of native stock or for words that have been thoroughly nativized is stressed syllable followed by unstressed syllable. (From this point on we will mark only the vowel carrying primary stress.)

> *bróther, búilding, córner, dínner, gárden, héaven, hónor, íron, ócean, pérson, ríver, wéather, táble, spírit, yéllow*

This pattern is mandatory when the second syllable is an inflection or *-ly*:

> *físhes, hóuses, láughing, stárted, smóother, bíggest, trúly*

Extensions of this pattern in which there are two or more unstressed syllables following the first stressed syllable can be found in words like the following:

> *árticle, énemy, béautiful, dángerous, líberal, índustry*

Another basic English pattern has an unstressed syllable followed by a stressed syllable (and possibly an unstressed syllable). This pattern usually begins with what appears to be a prefix. However, this prefix is not a "live" morpheme, but is a "dead" **etymological** prefix:

> *abóut, alíve, belíeve, begín, contról, contáin, deféat, detáin, excépt, expláin, forgét, forgíve, inclúde, indéed, prepáre, preténd, recéive, recórd, withstánd, withdráw*

For many English words the assignment of primary stress is made from the end of the word in accordance with the suffixes found there. Many such suffixes are etymological rather than morphological in nature. That is, the words may not be subject to the kind of morphological analysis discussed in the previous chapter. Primary stress is assigned as follows. It is assigned to the suffix itself in the following cases:

-éer    *auctionéer, enginéer, pionéer, profitéer, mountainéer*
-ée     *absentée, appointée, refugée, trainée, employée*

Other similar stress-bearing suffixes appear in the following words: *millionáire, convalésce, Chinése, statuésque, masséur, oblíque, and ballóon.*

In the following cases primary stress is assigned to the syllable that precedes the suffix:

-ic     *académic, aquátic, emphátic, fanátic, heróic, realístic*
-ical   *analýtical, arithmétical, theátrical, numérical*

(Note that stress assignment rules of this kind have occasional exceptions. For example, the stress pattern of *Árabic* is exceptional – compare *Islámic*.)

The syllable before the suffix *-al* carries primary stress if the vowel in that syllable is tense or a diphthong (*adjectíval, patricídal, anecdótal*) or is followed by a consonant cluster (*ancéstral, dialéctal, baptísmal*); otherwise it is the antepenultimate syllable of the derived word that carries primary stress (*proféssional, divísional, oríginal, medícinal*).

Primary stress is always assigned to the antepenultimate syllable in words with the following suffixes, each of which is considered for purposes of stress assignment to consist of two syllables:

-e/i/uous  *discóurteous, indústrious, ambíguous, supérfluous*
-e/ysis    *metáthesis, antíthesis, parálysis, análysis*
-graphy    *autobiógraphy, geógraphy, telégraphy, orthógraphy*
-ia        *ammónia, inértia, encyclopédia, Califórnia, Virgínia*
-ial       *artifícial, testimónial, influéntial, prejudícial*
-ian       *Canádian, physícian, musícian, Itálian, statistícian*
-ible      *convértible, digéstible, incrédible, irresístible*
-ient      *expédient, omníscient, resílient, impátient*
-ify       *eléctrify, persónify, indémnify, exémplify, ámplify*
-ion       *admirátion, prevéntion, proclamátion, abolítion*
-itude     *grátitude, plátitude, sólitude, solícitude*
-ity       *actívity, facílity, commúnity, matúrity, rárity*
-ium       *equilíbrium, potássium, gulgeránium, rádium*
-logy      *análogy, phraseólogy, theólogy, technólogy*

-omy        *appendéctomy, astrónomy, ecónomy, lobótomy*
-ual        *cásual, indivídual, evéntual, efféctual, rítual*

Primary stress is placed on the antepenultimate syllable in words which end with the following suffixes. In these cases the endings are single syllables:

-ate        *ádequate, degénerate, delíberate, prédicate*
-ize        *émphasize, homógenize, ímprovize, sýnthesize*
-graph      *áutograph, páragraph, télegraph, phónograph*
-ist        *ársonist, bígamist, philánthropist, dialectólogist*
-ous        *frívolous, décorous, ridículous, solícitous, anónymous*

In words which end as follows the stress is antepenultimate in words of three syllables and penultimate in words of two syllables:

-ane   *céllophane, mémbrane*
-ene   *kérosene, óbscene, hýgiene*
-ide   *cýanide, próvide, óxide*
-ine   *ásinine, féline, túrbine*
-ite   *érudite, pólite, térmite*
-oid   *ásteroid, týphoid, mástoid*
-ose   *grándiose, béllicose, láctose*
-ule   *mólecule, cápsule, schédule*
-ute   *cónstitute, déstitute, tríbute*

Many suffixes have no effect at all on the stress patterns of the words to which they are affixed, e.g., *achíevement, úgliness, matérialism,* and *efficiency*.

It is quite apparent that in words pronounced in isolation there may be more than two distinguishable levels of stress. In *nationálity* and *residéntial*, for example, while primary stress falls clearly on the antepenultimate syllable in each word (if we follow the convention outlined above that for stress-assignment purposes *-ial* be regarded as two syllables), the first syllable in each word is still more prominent than any other syllable except the stressed syllable. The first *a* of *nationality* is also pronounced [æ] and the first *e* of *residential* is also pronounced [ɛ]; such vowels often carry the kind of stress which we earlier called tertiary stress, a degree of stress that is also frequently found in prefixes: *ùndo, rèdo, dìsbar, nèo-Marxist,* etc. In general, vowels pronounced as schwa are unstressed, as are final vowels that have not been assigned primary stress. In the above words, therefore, we have the following stress pattern:

nàtiŏnálĭtў   rèsĭdéntiăl

Compounds have their own stress pattern. In *icebox* and *hotdog* the primary stresses on the independent words *box* and *dog* reduce to give us the stress pattern that occurs when *icebòx* and *hótdòg* are pronounced in isolation. We have this same pattern of stress reduction in other compounds like *rádio stàtion* and *wórks depàrtment*. Note that we can create further compounds from each of these: *icebox paint, hotdog vendor, radio station employee, works department manager*, and even *works department manager trainee*. What happens to the stress in constructions such as these is that a very precise pattern of stress reduction occurs. If we characterize the stresses in *hotdog*, etc., by using the superscripted number [1] for primary stress and [2] for this reduced stress (so as to avoid use of the terms *secondary stress, tertiary stress*, etc.), and if we ignore all other syllables, we have:

$$[h\overset{1}{o}t] \quad [d\overset{1}{o}g] \qquad [w\overset{1}{o}rks] \quad [dep\overset{1}{a}rtment]$$
$$\downarrow \hspace{5em} \downarrow$$
$$[h\overset{1}{o}td\overset{2}{o}g] \hspace{3em} [w\overset{1}{o}rks\ dep\overset{2}{a}rtment]$$

If we create further compounds in the same [1][2] pattern, e.g., *hotdog vendor* and *works department manager*, we might expect to find the following patterns of stress:

$$[h\overset{1}{o}td\overset{2}{o}g]\ [v\overset{1}{e}ndor] \quad [w\overset{1}{o}rks\ dep\overset{2}{a}rtment]\ [m\overset{1}{a}nager]$$
$$\downarrow \hspace{8em} \downarrow$$
$$*[h\overset{1}{o}td\overset{2}{o}g\ v\overset{2}{e}ndor] \quad *[w\overset{1}{o}rks\ dep\overset{2}{a}rtment\ m\overset{2}{a}nager]$$

However, this is not the stress pattern that actually occurs. Any existing stress in the first compound other than the first [1] must be reduced a notch. Consequently, the [2] on *dog* becomes [3], as does the [2] on *department*. The result is as follows:

$$[h\overset{1}{o}td\overset{3}{o}g\ v\overset{2}{e}ndor] \hspace{3em} [w\overset{1}{o}rks\ dep\overset{3}{a}rtment\ m\overset{2}{a}nager]$$

If we further compound *works department manager* with *trainee* to produce *works department manager trainee*, we get the same reductions. The further derivation is as follows:

$$[w\overset{1}{o}rks\ dep\overset{3}{a}rtment\ m\overset{2}{a}nager]\ [tr\overset{1}{a}inee]$$
$$\downarrow$$
$$[w\overset{1}{o}rks\ dep\overset{4}{a}rtment\ m\overset{3}{a}nager\ tr\overset{2}{a}inee]$$

In this case the overriding [1][2] pattern on *works* and *trainee* holds the total compound together, but, in doing so, it seems to create more than the four degrees of stress that we have needed previously because in the above discussion we have ignored other syllables with even less stress.

We also need to consider how stress patterns are associated with phrases and clauses. In *the old man* for example we can choose to place greater emphasis on *old* than on *man*, or vice versa. We can even choose to give greatest prominence to *the*. We can obviously use this last kind of stress in association with the compounds discussed above: *new hotdog vendor* can carry the greatest degree of stress on *new*, *hot*, or *vendor*.

One obvious conclusion we can draw from the above observations is that English stress is very complicated. We can take the view that there are only four distinguishable degrees of stress and give one possible account of English stress. However, if we also try to account for the knowledge that native speakers seem to have about stress in English, we find that we can use certain rules or principles to describe that knowledge. The issue then becomes one of deciding how much knowledge we should ascribe to native speakers. Do they have access to a system of stress assignment rules for words and phrases which requires only two stresses, stress and unstress, at some deep level, but which allows them to produce the various degrees of phonetic stress that we can observe? Might they even be aware – at some level at least – of how words are composed out of various types of **tense** and **lax** vowels, out of different types of consonant **clusters**, and with different affixes? And are they able to use this knowledge in assigning stress within words? We have been content here to show some of the stress patterns that exist and point out some of the consequences of different approaches. In the next section we will show how the qualities of certain consonants and vowels change in word formation and, in doing so, we will make a few more observations about stress.

## 12.3 Consonant Alternations

In the previous chapter we noted that many morphemes have more than one **allomorph**. We also showed that for many morphemes these allomorphs are **phonologically conditioned**, e.g., the regular "plural" and "genitive" morphemes for nouns and the regular "past" and "past participle" morphemes for verbs. We noted too some of the morphologically conditioned allomorphs of morphemes, e.g., the allomorphs of "wife" in *wife* and *wives*, and of "leave" in *leave* and *left*. What we will now do is look at some of these last differences in the consonant **alternations** we find in the allomorphs of morphemes in order to point out how systematic many of them are. We will also discuss these differences in terms of the phonological processes that are involved.

**Palatalization** is a process that occurs frequently. In palatalization the quality of a consonant is changed when it occurs before a high front vowel or glide. Sometimes the two merge to form a **strident**. In the following examples, palatalization occurs in the second word in each pair. The palatalizations are also categorized according to the consonants that are involved. We will also employ a phonetic notation.

[t] → [š]

| | | | |
|---|---|---|---|
| act | action | permit | permission |
| commit | commission | relate | relation |

[s] → [š]

| | | | |
|---|---|---|---|
| race | racial | grace | gracious |
| depress | depression | malice | malicious |

[t] → [č]

| | | | |
|---|---|---|---|
| cult | culture | Christ | Christian |
| digest | digestion | cent | century |

[d] → [ž]

| | | | |
|---|---|---|---|
| persuade | persuasion | corrode | corrosion |
| provide | provision | evade | evasion |

[z] → [ž]

| | | | |
|---|---|---|---|
| seize | seizure | use | usual |
| please | pleasure | enclose | enclosure |

Palatalization is a very interesting phenomenon in that speakers vary considerably in their use of palatalization. For example, words like *Indian, duke, gradual, associate, controversial, Christian, racial, picture,* etc. may be pronounced quite differently by different speakers and by the same speaker on different occasions.

The following two cases are slightly different in that they involve [k] in alternation with either [s] or [š]:

[k] → [s]

| | | | |
|---|---|---|---|
| medical | medicine | toxic | toxicity |
| fanatic | fanaticism | classic | classicist |

[k] → [š]

| | | | |
|---|---|---|---|
| physic | physician | pediatric | pediatrician |
| electric | electrician | magic | magician |

Another pattern of consonant alternation involves **voicing shifts**, either the shifting of a voiceless consonant to a voiced consonant or vice versa:

voiceless to voiced

| | | | |
|---|---|---|---|
| *wife* | *wives* | *wolf* | *wolves* |
| *south* | *southern* | *worth* | *worthy* |
| *louse* | *lousy* | *brass* | *brazen* |
| *sign* | *design* | *sound* | *resound* |
| *goose* | *gosling* | *proof* | *prove* |
| *glass* | *glaze* | *bath* | *bathe* |

voiced to voiceless

| | | | |
|---|---|---|---|
| *give* | *gift* | *bereave* | *bereft* |
| *drive* | *drift* | *leave* | *left* |

In the next category one allomorph – the second given – contains a consonant that does not occur in the pronunciation of the other allomorph. (We should note that the consonant does appear in the spellings of both allomorphs regardless of the pronunciation.)

| | | | |
|---|---|---|---|
| *sign* | *signal* | *prolong* | *prolongation* |
| *long* | *longer* | *knowledge* | *acknowledge* |
| *bomb* | *bombard* | *vehicle* | *vehicular* |
| *solemn* | *solemnity* | *hymn* | *hymnal* |
| *damn* | *damnable* | *paradigm* | *paradigmatic* |

While this last pattern is rather infrequent in English, voicing changes and palatalization are quite frequent. It is voicing, for example, that determines which of the regular allomorphs of the "plural," "past," etc. occur and which constrains the formation of certain **consonant clusters**. The palatalization process also results in different pronunciations of words in different parts of the English-speaking world. This variation is particularly obvious in words that contain, or contained, /yu/ after various **coronal** (i.e., tongue-tip) consonants. For example, varieties of English differ as to whether they have non-palatalized or palatalized pronunciations for words like the following: *Tuesday, duke, virtuous, nature, fissure,* and *obituary.* Since some varieties of English have simply dropped the /y/ in words like *news, tune, dew, Tuesday,* and so on, we can find several different acceptable pronunciations of such words depending on where we happen to be in the English-speaking world.

The existence of regular consonant alternations such as those we have just mentioned might encourage us to postulate that one alternant is more important than the other. For example, the [t] in *act* seems to be more important than the [š] in *action*, the [k] in *toxic* more important than the [s] in *toxicity*, the [v] in *give* more important than the [f] in *gift*, and so on. In such cases we might want to regard the more important sound to be the one most typical of the basic morphemic shape, i.e., to regard it as a **morphophoneme**. The [t] in [ækt] would therefore underlie the [š] in ['ækšən] and the [š] would result from a process of assimilation of that [t] before the high front vowel that underlies the suffix [-iən]. ['ækšən] is then the product of [ækt] plus [-iən]. *Toxicity* would be ['taksɪk] plus [-ɪti] to give us [tak'sɪsəti], and [gɪv] plus [-t] would give us [gɪft].

Similar reasoning would lead us to propose that the best representation for the "plural," "genitive," and "third person singular" morphemes in English would be [-z] and for the "past tense" and "past participle" morphemes would be [-d]. So *cats* [kæts] would come from [kæt] plus [-z] and *baked* from [bek] plus [-d].

Such examples as *solemnity* and *longer* are particularly interesting if we apply this concept of the morphophoneme to them. *Solemn* would appear to have to end in [mn] rather than in [m] alone, i.e., to be basically ['salɛmn] rather than ['saləm]. When the [-ɪti] suffix is added we get [sə'lɛmnəti] with the [n] actually realized. However, the realization of *solemn* ['saləm] requires dropping the final [n] because English words cannot end with [mn]. It also requires the reduction of [ɛ] to [ə].

The pair *long-longer* is interesting in a similar way. There must be a final [g] in the morphophonemic form of *long* because it is pronounced in *longer*. However, there is an additional issue here: *long* is probably [lang] rather than [laŋg]. In English a nasal before a stop in the same syllable is always homorganic with that stop, i.e., made in the same position in the mouth. So the actual pronunciation [laŋ] seems to derive from a basic form [lang] with first of all a change of [n] to [ŋ], giving us [laŋg], and then the deletion of the final [g] (in most varieties of English) except when the [-ər] suffix occurs. (It may be of interest to note that the rule for nasal assimilation just mentioned could also apply to words like *limp* and *stamp*, giving them the morphophonemic representations of [lɪnp] and [stænp] respectively!)

All the above examples have used phonetic bracketing rather than phonemic bracketing for observations about morphophonemes. This use is necessitated by the fact that all the observations are basically phonetic in nature – although some are quite abstract – and are rather different from the phonemic observations arrived at in chapter 9 through the use of contrastive pairs of words.

## 12.4   Vowel Alternations

**Vowel alternations** are perhaps even more pervasive than consonant alternations and are often quite systematic. Once again English spelling often preserves similarities between allomorphs that are not readily apparent in their actual pronunciations.

There are numerous alternations in English between a vowel other than schwa [ə] and schwa itself. The words in the second and fourth columns usually have a schwa where indicated in contrast to the words in the first and third columns:

| | | | |
|---|---|---|---|
| *cremate* | *crematorium* | *catastrophic* | *catastrophe* |
| *crematorium* | *cremate* | *catastrophe* | *catastrophic* |
| *telegraphy* | *telegraphic* | *melodious* | *melody* |
| *telegraph* | *telegraphy* | *repeat* | *repetition* |
| *particular* | *particle* | *demon* | *demonic* |
| *prohibition* | *prohibit* | *demonic* | *demon* |
| *academy* | *academic* | *Canada* | *Canadian* |
| *vehicular* | *vehicle* | *Canadian* | *Canada* |

One could, of course, simply list the allomorphic variants of each morpheme in such cases and say where each occurs, i.e., independently or with what affixes. However, it usually seems desirable to attach more importance to one allomorph than the other or others and to consider it to be the most typical instance of the morpheme or the shape from which any other allomorphs derive. Such an approach would lead to a preference for the forms without schwa because we know that in English unstressed vowels reduce to schwa in many instances rather than that unstressed schwas materialize as full stressed vowels in certain places in the language. But if we look at a pair of words like *catastrophe* and *catastrophic*, we will see that the best "basic" form might contain two instances of [æ], i.e., [kætæstr-]. However, we actually never get more than one instance of [æ] in any particular occurrence of the word. We must therefore postulate an abstract morphemic shape that never occurs. Just how far we should go in postulating such abstract forms is a matter of considerable linguistic controversy.

Let us look at some of the same issues by examining another set of data. There are pervasive patterns of vowel alternation in English. In the following examples the patterns of alternation are shown according to the spellings that exist in English.

*a* represents [e] and [æ]

| | | | |
|---|---|---|---|
| *sane* | *sanity* | *able* | *ability* |
| *urbane* | *urbanity* | *state* | *static* |
| *humane* | *humanity* | *angel* | *angelic* |
| *profane* | *profanity* | *fable* | *fabulous* |
| *explain* | *explanatory* | *radius* | *radical* |
| *glaze* | *glass* | *graze* | *grass* |

*e* (and sometimes *ee* or *ea*) represents [i] and [ɛ]

| | | | |
|---|---|---|---|
| *athlete* | *athletic* | *obscene* | *obscenity* |
| *meter* | *metric* | *penal* | *penalty* |
| *serene* | *serenity* | *supreme* | *supremacy* |
| *discreet* | *discretion* | *convene* | *convention* |
| *deal* | *dealt* | *clean* | *cleanse* |
| *leave* | *left* | *heal* | *health* |
| *sweep* | *swept* | *please* | *pleasure* |
| *breathe* | *breath* | *heath* | *heather* |
| *sheep* | *shepherd* | *zeal* | *zealous* |

*i* (and occasionally *y*) represents [aɪ] and [ɪ]

| | | | |
|---|---|---|---|
| *rise* | *risen* | *divide* | *division* |
| *decide* | *decision* | *collide* | *collision* |
| *provide* | *provision* | *mime* | *mimic* |
| *satire* | *satiric* | *wild* | *wilderness* |
| *parasite* | *parasitic* | *ride* | *ridden* |
| *type* | *typical* | *line* | *linear* |
| *sign* | *signal* | *virus* | *virulent* |
| *suffice* | *sufficient* | *Christ* | *Christian* |

*o* represents [o] and [a]

| | | | |
|---|---|---|---|
| *verbose* | *verbosity* | *mediocre* | *mediocrity* |
| *cone* | *conic* | *phone* | *phonic* |
| *mode* | *modesty* | *holy* | *holiday* |
| *tone* | *tonic* | *joke* | *jocular* |

*oo* represents [u] and [a]

| | | | |
|---|---|---|---|
| *goose* | *gosling* | *bloom* | *blossom* |
| *food* | *fodder* | | |

*ou* (with *u* as a variant) represents [aʊ] and [ʌ]

| | | | |
|---|---|---|---|
| *house* | *husband* | *abound* | *abundant* |
| *profound* | *profundity* | *south* | *southern* |
| *pronounce* | *pronunciation* | | |

Before commenting any further, we can note that the vowels in the second column occur in stressed syllables, which are often either antepenultimate syllables or syllables before a suffix such as -ic or a suffix that results in a final consonant cluster, e.g., *cleanse* or *stealth* There is a good historical explanation for much of this variation. Historically, the **Great Vowel Shift** that occurred some four to five centuries ago resulted in the raising of tense vowels and the diphthongization of the high front and high back tense vowels in certain circumstances. Tense vowels that did not undergo this process because they found themselves in other circumstances became like their lax counterparts. So whereas some [i]s eventually became [aɪ]s and some [e]s eventually became [i]s, other [i]s became [ɪ]s and other [e]s became [ɛ]s. One very dramatic consequence of the Great Vowel Shift was that morphemes often developed rather different allomorphs as these processes worked their way through the language, and produced many of the vowel differences noted above. There were other processes at work too. For example, vowels became lax in certain environments, e.g., before certain consonant clusters, accounting, for example, for the *deep-depth* alternation we see above.

These are historical facts about English. Are they in any way relevant to a structural statement about contemporary English? It so happens that it is possible to relate the above vowel alternations. For example, we can postulate that behind each of the pairs of vowels given above lies a single "abstract" vowel morphophoneme and that certain systematic changes occur during the process of affixation. By using a set of elaborate rules – unfortunately with many exceptions and qualifications – we can produce the actual vowels that occur phonetically. Such a treatment of the alternations also leads us quite far away at times from the actually occurring phonetic data; just how "real" it might be has also been a very controversial issue in recent decades.

Here are the "abstract" vowels just mentioned; they are given between the pairs of "phonetic," i.e., actually occurring, vowels they underlie and they also are shown with a macron [¯] to indicate their basic tenseness:

| | | | |
|---|---|---|---|
| [e] | [ǣ] | [æ] | *humane, humanity* |
| [i] | [ē] | [ɛ] | *obscene, obscenity* |
| [aɪ] | [ī] | [ɪ] | *rise, risen* |
| [o] | [ɔ̄] | [a] | *cone, conic* |
| [u] | [ō] | [a] | *goose, gosling* |
| [aʊ] | [ū] | [ʌ] | *south, southern* |

In this view the abstract phonological form underlying the second vowel in *humane* in both *humane* and *humanity* would be [ǣ]. The second vowel in both *obscene* and *obscenity* would be [ē], and so on. In certain prescribed environments the [ǣ], [ē] etc. would raise to [e] and [i] giving us the vowels we find in *humane* and *obscene*. In other environments there would be laxing to [æ] and [ɛ] giving us the vowels we find in *humanity* and *obscenity*.

Underlying high vowels like [ī] and [ū] would diphthongize and lax in the same way so that the underlying [ī] in *rise* and *risen* emerges phonetically as [aɪ] in the first word and [ɪ] in the second.

The above is a very abstract view of morphological relationships in the language. As we have seen, it can require the use of underlying forms that never actually occur. For example, it requires the form [absēn] to underlie both *obscene* and *obscenity*. In an alternative view such a form would be disallowed because it is not "real" anywhere in the language, i.e., it never occurs. Note that in this view both the "plural" [-z] and the "past tense" [-d] remain acceptable because they actually do occur somewhere, e.g., in [dagz] *dogs* and [sevd] *saved*. In such a view both *obscene* and *obscenity* would have to be derived from either [abˈsin] of [abˈsɛn] and the issues would be those of deciding which form to give primacy to and accounting for either [i] changing to [ɛ] or [ɛ] changing to [i].

What we have tried to show in this chapter is some of the systematic interplay that occurs between words and sounds in the language. As we have seen, such interplay involves matters of stress patterning and allomorphic variation. We can content ourselves with listing some of the structural varieties of these that occur in the language and we have listed many of them. We can also try to push our investigation a little further in order to see what kinds of underlying morphological and phonological structures we can postulate for words. In that way we might give our accounts more "depth." However, we have not gone on a search for such statements at any great length and depth since such a search would take us far from the data and well into speculation. (We may already have gone too far!) What we have seen though is that there are some very interesting structural patterns in the language. In seeing some of these patterns emerge, we should also have become aware that the English spelling system may not be quite as bad as many of its critics have said it is.

## 12.5  Exercises

1  Try to apply the system used for showing the relationship of stresses in *hotdog vendor* to the following structures. The first one is done for you.

(a)  National Mental Health Awareness Week
     (This is a week devoted to making people aware of mental health issues.)

     [national] [mental] [health] [awareness] [week]
     [national] [mental health] [awareness] [week]
     [national] [mental health awareness] [week]
     [national] [mental health awareness week]
     [national mental health awareness week]

    (b)   spaceship center maintenance coordinator
    (c)   Social Science Research Council committee
    (d)   African language literatures
    (e)   railroad station ticket taker

2   How might you account for the fact that some people stress the first syllable
    rather than the second in the following nouns?

    defence, Detroit, cement, police

3   Try to find further examples of the kinds of phonological relationships that we
    have discussed in this chapter. Here are a few.

    persuade, persuasion; opaque, opacity; fuse, fusion; part, partial; resign, resig-
    nation; phlegm, phlegmatic; presume, presumptive; damn, damnation; maniac,
    maniacal; doctrine, doctrinal; Johnson, Johnsonian; solemn, solemnize; hymn,
    hymnal

4   Not everyone agrees that we should attempt to postulate phonological relation-
    ships even in words that might appear to be related. Which of the following
    pairs would you consider to be related phonologically? The first two are done
    for you.

    cave, cavity (Although the vowels alternate as they do in *grave* and *gravity*, the
    difficulty resides in specifying what the *-ity* suffix could mean and how any such
    meaning relates to *cave* so as to produce *cavity*. However, if the vowel change
    is purely phonological mandated by the presence of the *-ity* ending, we have a
    pair of words just like *grave* and *gravity*.); site, situation (The vowel alternation
    is the same as in *rise* and *risen* and we also have the word *situate*. The *-ion* also
    commonly forms nouns from verbs. There is therefore considerable regularity
    here and even the *-u-* occurs elsewhere, as in *actuate* and *fluctuate*.); Michael,
    Michaelmas; grateful, gratitude; tyrant, tyranny; slow, sloth; long, length; glass,
    glaze; peace, pacifist; hole, hollow; throat, throttle; Jane, Janet; feet, fetters;
    dine, dinner; lyre, lyric; bone, bonfire

5   The Great Vowel Shift in English is mentioned in the text. What were the pre-
    Shift vowel pronunciations of each of the following words? The first three are
    done for you.

    meet ([ē]), house ([ū]), fill ([ɪ]), goose, bed, ride, drink, name, stone, help, sun,
    full, fast

# 13
# Sounds in Context

In this chapter we will be concerned with various aspects of the spoken language which have been given only brief mention elsewhere. Specifically, we will look at syllables, intonation, and some of the kinds of reductions and restructurings that occur in connected speech, particularly in allegro, or fast, speech.

## 13.1  Syllables

As we have previously noted, it is difficult to give precise definitions to terms like **sound, word,** and **clause** even though such terms are used quite freely in discussions about language. The term **syllable** is no less difficult to define. It may be tempting to say that there are as many syllables in an utterance as there are vowels but there is some difficulty in describing just exactly what **vowels** themselves are. In at least one system for describing vowels it is actually their ability to be "syllabic" that is the deciding criterion. Dictionaries do, of course, not only record syllables but even divide words into syllables both orthographically, i.e., in spelling, and phonetically. However, many of these divisions seem purely arbitrary, particularly the orthographic divisions. They often seem to have no function other than to tell you where to break a word if you run out of space on a line while you are writing that word.

We might want to make a distinction between phonetic syllables and structural syllables in the language. For example, certain allophones of phonemes always appear before stressed vowels, e.g., the aspirated allophones of /p/, /t/, and /k/. Consequently, if we find pronunciations such as [ə'pʰír], [ə'tʰæk], and [ə'kʰãʊnt] for *appear, attack,* and *account,* we may have good reason to assert that the syllable division (here shown as $) in such words occurs after the first vowel and before the first consonant: /ə$pír/, /ə$tæk/, and /ə$káʊnt/. Such phonetic facts might serve as guides in making decisions about structural facts; however, such a procedure would actually reverse the position we have adopted heretofore, the position that it is structural characteristics which are basic and that phonetic realizations derive from such characteristics.

Let us look then at some structural possibilities for English stressed syllables. First of all, we should note that English syllables can be either **open** or **closed**, that is, some syllables end in vowels and some in consonants:

open    *he, hay, you, so, high, cow, boy*
closed   *cat, thin, bake, glide, end, ode, eat, shout*

In words like the above it is also apparent that whereas all vowels (i.e., vowel sounds) can occur before consonants only tense vowels and diphthongs can occur in open syllables.

Let us propose that every syllable may have a syllable **onset** but must have a syllable **rhyme**. The optional syllable onset consists of one or more consonants with the possible sequences highly constrained (as previously indicated in chapter 9), e.g., /str-/ but not /*sdr-/, /kl-/ but not /*lk-/, etc. The obligatory syllable peak must have a vowel **peak** and may have a **coda**, which like the onset will consist of one or more consonants. So we have the following structure for an English syllable:

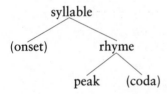

If we apply this structure to monosyllabic English words we have the following possibilities:

|        | onset | peak | coda |                            |
|--------|-------|------|------|----------------------------|
| *cat*    | *c*     | *a*    | *t*    |                            |
| *script* | *scr*   | *i*    | *pt*   |                            |
| *rates*  | *r*     | *a-e*  | *ts*   | (the *a-e* represents [e]) |
| *eat*    |       | *ea*   | *t*    |                            |
| *owe*    |       | *owe*  |      |                            |
| *though* | *th*    | *ough* |      |                            |

The system obviously works for monosyllabic words. However, there are problems with polysyllabic words. Where does one syllable end and the next begin? One possible solution is to say that in polysyllabic words all syllables are pronounced as though they were sequences of monosyllabic words. Each syllable would also have the maximum possible onset. The only exception to this principle is that an unstressed lax vowel, particularly schwa [ə], does not require a coda, as we saw in the above examples *appear*, *attack*, and *account*, and possibly *illegal* (*i-lle-gal*).

Dividing words in this way, we get the following results. (We must, of course, note that these divisions are structural and phonological and that the spellings that follow are restructured where necessary to reflect this fact.)

lax vowels

| | | | |
|---|---|---|---|
| *lemon* | *lem$on* | *polish* | *pol$ish* |
| *kitten* | *kitt$en* | *beckon* | *beck$on* |
| *rascal* | *ras$cal* | *master* | *mas$ter* |
| *cuddle* | *cudd$le* | *Coptic* | *Cop$tic* |
| *costly* | *cost$ly* | *rustproof* | *rust$proof* |
| *Wednesday* | *Wednes$day* | (when pronounced /wénzdi/) | |

In each of the above cases the consonant after the lax vowel would be the coda of the syllable containing that lax vowel. The lax vowel is checked.

tense vowels

| | | | |
|---|---|---|---|
| *demon* | *de$mon* | *Polish* | *Po$lish* |
| *station* | *sta$tion* | *bacon* | *ba$con* |
| *pupil* | *pu$pil* | *rooster* | *roo$ster* |
| *notice* | *no$tice* | *final* | *fi$nal* |
| *noisy* | *noi$sy* | *greasy* | *grea$sy* |
| *awful* | *aw$ful* | *idea* | *i$de$a* |
| *chaos* | *cha$os* | *furious* | *fu$ri$ous* |
| *hateful* | *hate$ful* | *moleskin* | *mole$skin* |
| *innocent* | *inn$o$cent* | *retroactive* | *ret$ro$ac$tive* |

In each of the above cases there is either no coda after a free tense vowel or diphthong or, if there is a coda, as in *hateful* for example, that coda is necessary because the next syllable cannot begin with a /tf/ onset. This principle works well but it is not without certain difficulties, for example, in a word like *writer* pronounced with a flap [ɾ] for the *t* we have a sound the quality of which is actually determined by its intersyllabic position. However, our rules require the word to be syllabified as *wri$ter*. Apparently certain consonants between vowels seem concurrently to be both codas of preceding vowels and onsets of succeeding vowels, i.e., they are **ambisyllabic**. One can argue that after either a lax or a tense vowel any consonant can be ambisyllabic, e.g., the boldfaced consonants in *waiter, better,* and *metric.* The /t/ in each case closes the first syllable and is therefore a coda but it is also the onset (or part of the onset) of the following syllable.

Failing to recognize the ambisyllabic nature of certain consonants seems to lead to unsatisfactory results in words like *able* and *apple,* because they are assigned the following syllabic structures: *a$ble* and *app$le.* Are such words really so different in their syllabic structures? A more telling criticism, however, has to do with such syllabications as *noi$sy* and *grea$sy* in the above lists and in the word *writer* syllabified as *wri$ter.* These syllabications violate the morphological structures of the words, which are *nois-y, greas-y,* and *writ-er* respectively.

An alternative view of syllabication takes into account this concept of ambisyllabic segments, i.e., the idea that certain sounds belong concurrently to two syllables and are both codas and onsets. This view makes no distinction between free and checked vowels. Since the /m/ in *lemon* and *demon* can be both an onset and a coda, it is assigned to both syllables and there is no clear syllable break in these words. In the words that follow similar ambisyllabic consonants are shown in boldface: *rascal, master, rooster, writer, able, apple, noisy, greasy, cinema, copy, debit, problem, secret, modesty, fairy,* and *Harry.* The ambisyllabic treatment of the consonants in *fairy* and *Harry* seems particularly appropriate because, in situations in which vowels neutralize before /r/, that /r/ must be part of the syllable containing the vowel but the /r/ also functions as part of the following syllable. (Note that the issue of ambisyllabicity does not arise in words like *account, alive, about,* etc. There is no reason to believe that the initial syllables of these words include consonants as codas.)

These are just two possible accounts of syllable structure in English. There are still other approaches, for example, one that places great emphasis on vowel quality and consonant clustering in determining syllable boundaries. In fact syllable structure is one of the current "hot" areas of linguistic investigation. Whatever the results we can be sure that English syllables are far from the entities described in traditional spelling-bound accounts.

English is also said to have a tendency towards being a **stress-timed** language rather than a **syllable-timed** language. By this we mean that English syllables vary in the length of time they take to utter, i.e., three syllables do not necessarily take three times as long to utter as one syllable. In many other languages all syllables do seem to take about the same length of time to utter. (Note that we can get some of this syllable-timed effect if we make up a sentence out of monosyllabic words and, in doing so, avoid words like *was, the, and,* etc.: *Those men bought six large red cars last week.*) If, in addition, some syllable-timed languages characteristically employ **open syllables,** we get patterns like the following in which C represents a consonant or consonant cluster and V a vowel:

CV$CV$CV$CV$CV$CV
CV$CV$CV$CV$CV$CV$CV$CV$CV$CV$CV$CV

Moreover, since the second of these utterances has twice as many syllables as the first, it will take about twice as long to utter. In contrast, in the stress-timed pattern of English, syllables are stressed at regular intervals and intermediate syllables are jammed between these stressed syllables. This results in many unstressed vowels being reduced to schwas or omitted entirely. If we use S to represent a stressed syllable and s to represent an unstressed or weakly stressed syllable, a characteristic English pattern may be shown somewhat as follows:

s s S  s  S ssssS  s s  sS  s s S  s  sS  S  s s  S

In such a pattern stressed syllables occur at fairly regular intervals, but the first half of this pattern – the section that includes the first four instances of S – contains 40 percent more syllables than the second half; however, each half of the whole utterance is of roughly the same duration in real time.

## 13.2  Intonation

Not only are English utterances characterized by their stress-timed rhythm but they also have typical patterns of **intonation**. The two major determinants of intonation are the placement of the most prominent stress in a clause and whether the pitch of the voice falls, rises, or stays level at the end of the clause.

Any constituent in a clause may be emphasized by giving it the most prominent stress, even an individual sound, as in the case of *t* and *d* below. In these examples the most heavily stressed constituent is shown in boldfaced capitals.

> *It's a **T** not a **D**.*
> ***HE** left yesterday.*
> *He **LEFT** yesterday.*
> *He left **YES**terday.*
> *I said **UN**happy.*
> *He read it **CLEAR**ly.*

We can see the same phenomenon in more complex structures in which more than one constituent can be stressed in this way:

*When he CAME, she TOLD him.*
*OBviously, he has the time to DO it.*
*JOHN, don't give it to HIM!*

However, in the typical English sentence the heaviest stress is likely to fall at or close to the end of that sentence on the main content word there.

The second characteristic of intonation that concerns us here is what typically happens to the pitch at the ends of clauses. We can observe that this final pitch may fall (↘), or it may rise (↗), or it may stay level (→). Falling pitch typically occurs at the ends (i.e., over the final word) of sentences that are not interrogative in purpose:

*He left yesterday.* ↘
*They cleaned up the yard.* ↘
*They signed it a week ago.* ↘

Falling pitch may also occur on interrogative sentences when these contain a clear interrogative structure, e.g., they have subject-verb **inversion**, or they are **tagged**, or they begin with a *wh*-word. Note that each of the following questions can be asked with a final falling pitch:

*Are you going?* ↘
*He's going, isn't he?* ↘
*Where's he going?* ↘

Rising pitch is, however, obligatory in **echo questions**:

*He's going?* ↗
*He recommended that book?* ↗
*He said what?* ↗
*He asked who to do it?* ↗

Many such questions are signaled entirely by intonation. We should note that other kinds of questions may also take final rising pitch. This additional feature seems to add to their interrogative force:

*Are you going?* ↗
*He's going, isn't he?* ↗
*Where's he going?* ↗

These questions sound much more inquiring than those given above with falling pitch; the latter may sound indifferent, detached, or even weary. Therefore, the two kinds of questions are likely to affect listeners somewhat differently.

Falling pitch and rising pitch signal sentence closure and are typically found at the ends of utterances. Within utterances there are often brief pauses, for example at clause boundaries, and it is at these pauses that we may also find level pitch:

> *When he did that,* → *I just stopped dead.* ↘
> *Actually,* → *he'll pay for it himself.* ↘
> *All things considered,* → *we didn't do too badly.* ↘
> *Peter,* → *stand up!* ↘
> *So,* → *are you going to do it?* ↗
> *Ready,* → *set,* → *go!* ↘

Note that in each of the above utterances if the speaker were to stop after the level pitch there would be a sense of incompleteness. We can sometimes deliberately seek this effect:

> *And then,* → (pause) *what?* ↗

The following three sentences show different patterns of use of these three pitch levels:

> *Would you like tea or coffee?* ↘
> *Would you like tea or coffee?* ↗
> *Would you like tea* → *or coffee?* ↗

The first sentence seems to be a rather half-hearted offer of refreshments to someone. The second sentence seems to contain a much warmer offer. However, in both cases the tea and/or coffee are probably not yet made. The third sentence offers a choice between tea or coffee: both are probably available. A possible answer to the first offer is *No thank you, don't bother*, to the second is *Perhaps tea*, and the third *Tea, please*.

No one has succeeded in arriving at an utterly convincing account of English intonation. Such an account would have to cover the various kinds of stress patterns that occur in English, both word stress and sentence stress. It would also have to deal with the matter of the stress-timed rhythm of English and the consequences of that rhythm for vowel reduction and the clustering of consonants. (We will have more to say about these matters in the next section.) It would also have to take into account the various ways in which speakers modulate the pitch levels of their voices in speaking English. What we have done here is indicate only a very few of the major structural features that must be accounted for and some of the more important issues that must eventually be resolved.

## 13.3  Allegro Speech

Most structural accounts of languages focus on individual utterances pronounced quite carefully and in complete isolation from one another. However, that is not how we normally use language. In normal use utterances are connected to one another in various ways and they are usually spoken quickly and casually without a great deal of attention being paid to many fine details in their production. Only when there is a lot of noise in the environment or if the occasion is marked in some way as being very formal do we pay much attention to such details. Indeed, those people who pay attention to these details all the time are likely to be fairly tiresome to listen to, and to strike us as being pedantic or to be performing in some way. Quite simply, everyday speaking does not require that kind of attention. We usually speak casually and rather quickly and are usually more attentive to what we want to say than to the way we say what we want to say. What happens, then, when we speak this way using **allegro speech**, i.e., ordinary, casual, rather quick, everyday speech?

One of the first things that we notice is that there is a considerable amount of **assimilation** in such speech, i.e., many sounds change to become like neighboring sounds in some respect. Such assimilation may be **progressive**, i.e., a sound takes on one or more characteristics of a preceding sound, or it may be **regressive**, i.e., a sound takes on one or more characteristics of a following sound.

We can see progressive assimilation in the following cases in which **palatalization** occurs:

> *Place your hand here.* [šyə]
> *Can't you do it?* [čə]
> *I'm glad you came.* [jə]
> *Had you not done it, we would.* [jə]
> *Do you know the date?* [jə]

An utterance like *Did you eat yet?* may even be pronounced as [jičet]. We can see regressive assimilation in the following reductions of *and* to *n*, and then of all the *n*s:

| | |
|---|---|
| *hit and run* | *hit'n' run* [ṇr] |
| *top and bottom* | *top'n' bottom* [m̩b] |
| *back and forth* | *back'n' forth* [m̩f] |
| *stop and go* | *stop'n' go* [ŋg] |

There may also be assimilation of the nasals in the following:

| | |
|---|---|
| *in case* [ŋk] | *ten pens* [mp] |
| *main gate* [ŋg] | *ten cups* [ŋk] |
| *in person* [mp] | *seven percent* [mp] |

Such assimilation is also present in the following examples in which a voiced phoneme is either realized by a voiceless allophone or replaced by its voiceless counterpart:

*five past* [f] before [p]
*love to sing* [f] before [t]
*she's tops* [s] before [t]
*have to go* [f] before [t]
*has to be there* [s] before [t]

Omissions are also extremely frequent. Unstressed vowels and syllables may be deleted:

| | | |
|---|---|---|
| *p(e)rhaps* | *p(a)rade* | *g(o)rilla* |
| *p(o)lice* | *t(e)rrific* | *b(e)lieve* |
| *b(a)lloon* | *c(o)rrect* | *s(u)ppose* |
| *(be)cause* | *(po)tatoes* | *(e)xactly* |
| *(Ha)s he been?* | | |

Consonants may also be deleted:

*I caught (h)er.*
*I caught (h)im.*
*I caught (th)em.*
*I'm going to (gonna) go tomorrow.*

Deletions and vowel reductions can produce a considerable number of variant forms and they do in some very frequently used – and very necessary – words in English. The parts of the verb *be* are used very frequently in reduced form, e.g., *I'm, you're, he's, she's, it's, we're,* and *they're*. We should note that *it's* is also a possible reduction of *it has*, as in *it's been a long time*. (The spelling *it's* always has either *it is* or *it has* as a possible substitute; *its* is the correct spelling only for the personal pronoun.) Auxiliary and modal verbs also have frequently used reduced forms, e.g., *She'd have said so* (*would*), *I'll go* (*will* or *shall*), and *I've been there* (*have*). (It is because these verbs are so frequently reduced that we find instances of such a spelling mistake as *He should of known about it* instead of the correct *He should have known about it*.) Allomorphic variants like *'m, 're, 'll, 've,* and *n't* which can occur only bound to another morpheme are sometimes called **clitics**. Third person pronouns are frequently reduced, being found with their consonants omitted and their vowels reduced to schwas. The articles *the* and *a* rarely occur as [ði] or [æ] (or [æn]) but most frequently as [ðə] or [ə] or [ən]. Common prepositions like *of*, *for*, *to*, *at*, and *from* are also frequently found with their vowels reduced to schwas or, as in the case of *for*, with the vowel omitted entirely. *Not* is almost invariably *n't* and *and*, as we saw above, can be realized in a variety of ways. One result of all the above is an extremely complex morphology for such morphemes as *of*, *have*, *you*, *is*, *not*, and *and* if we must account for everything that happens to these morphemes in both carefully enunciated speech and in allegro speech.

We can see the results of the various processes mentioned above if we compare slow and carefully enunciated pronunciations of the following utterances with the quickest pronunciations we can manage. There are likely to be considerable differences in the two kinds of pronunciations, particularly in the places marked by boldface type.

> The boy **and** girl probably should **not** have told her.
> **Did you** watch the parade with him?
> We **have exactly ten** minutes to catch ten cats.
> **Would you** go to the Yukon with us?
> **Can't you** eat it up?
> **Are you going to** ask him?

We must insist that there is nothing "wrong" with these allegro forms – they are perfectly good English. One set of circumstances will call for the slow, somewhat ponderous pronunciations; an entirely different set of circumstances will call for the allegro forms. And it would not be very wise to misidentify the circumstances and choose the inappropriate forms or to shift randomly from one kind of pronunciation to the other.

Finally, we should note that in allegro speech we may encounter sequences of sounds that are normally proscribed in slow speech. Structural statements usually describe the latter kind of speech so we must be prepared either to write a separate phonology for allegro speech or a set of adjustment rules to derive the allegro forms from the slow forms. The latter seems to be the better approach since we are not dealing with two entirely independent phonological systems. For example, we might be tempted to revise the rules postulated in chapter 9 to define permissible initial consonant **clusters** because we do find phonetic clusters of the following kinds in allegro speech:

| | | | |
|---|---|---|---|
| (I)s **that** | [#zð-] | ch(a)rade | [#šr-] |
| (I)s **Fred** | [#sf-] | ph(o)netic | [#fn-] |
| V(e)ronica | [#vr-] | (e)xactly | [#gz-] |
| b(a)nanas | [#bn-] | s(y)ringe | [#sr-] |

| | | | |
|---|---|---|---|
| (*I*)*t seems* | [#ts-] | *v*(*o*)*luptuous* | [#vl-] |
| (*E*)*xtremely* | [#kstr-] | *b*(*e*)*cause* | [#pk-] |

One solution is to say that we do have the kinds of restrictions on initial clusters that we mentioned in chapter 9. What we see here are the applications of certain adjustment rules that are necessary for allegro speech which allow for the phonetic sequences of the kind just noted. However, these are **phonetic clusters** and we might still wish to say that each would be an impermissible **phonemic cluster**.

What we also see in some of the allegro forms given in the last few pages are some good examples of how various structural aspects of the language come together. We do not interpret the utterances we hear by processing each utterance sound by sound before we try to work out what each utterance might mean once we have somehow decided what those sounds are. We hear each utterance in a meaningful context. As we listen to it, we process it concurrently for its sounds, its grammatical structure, and what sense it might have in the context of its utterance. Consequently, when we hear something like [tsimznat], we interpret the initial [t] as *it*, and may not even be aware that there was no vowel at the beginning. The rest we figure out as *seems not*, relying obviously on the context to help us as well as our knowledge that an initial *it* is usually followed at some point by a verb, and so on. In the same way we distinguish between such possibly confusable pairs (and one triple) as the following:

| | | |
|---|---|---|
| *pea stalks* | *peace talks* | |
| *I scream* | *ice cream* | |
| *house-trained* | *How strained!* | |
| *Why choose?* | *white shoes* | |
| *that stuff* | *That's tough!* | |
| *night rate* | *nitrate* | *Nye trait* |

We can note that these utterances may be almost undistinguishable phonetically, but it is difficult to see how they would be confused in actual use.

Finally, we can observe that often one of the clearest indicators of whether someone is a native speaker of English is the ability of that person to use allegro speech. Paradoxically, that is why some non-native speakers are sometimes said to speak the language "better" than native speakers. Actually, they do not speak it "better" at all: they just do not control the allegro possibilities, always produce the longer forms, but leave the impression of being more concerned than the natives about the "proprieties" of the language. Conversely, we sometimes come across individuals who have mastered certain allegro forms as they have acquired some knowledge of the language informally but have not acquired the full forms nor perhaps an extensive vocabulary or deep grammatical knowledge. Such individuals tend to sound like natives for a very short while only. And, of course, we all recognize that one of the greatest difficulties that native speakers – particularly young children – face is learning how to use in writing the full equivalents for the allegro forms they have been using all their lives.

# 13.4  Exercises

1   Use the syllabication rules given in this chapter to show the syllable divisions in the following words. Which consonants might you consider to be ambisyllabic?

losses, fixture, answered, facsimile, noble, idle, engineer, scramble, arise, equalized, evade, restore, tennis, biopsy, pity, detail, duty, petrol, practice, crackle, petroleum, parents, party, parade, exist, postal

2   What phonetic changes occur when you add *n't* to each of the following verbs?

must, do, will, can, shall, am

3   What do spellings like the following show about English pronunciation?

(a)  He could of done it.
(b)  Drinka pinta milk.
(c)  I hafta go.
(d)  Wanna go?
(e)  fish'n'chips
(f)  He's gonna do it.

# 14
# Further Reading

There are numerous introductions to linguistics. Hudson (1984) provides an excellent brief account of the concerns of the discipline. Perhaps the two best comprehensive treatments are O'Grady and Dobrovolsky (1992) and Finegan and Besnier (1989); Atkinson et al. (1982) and Fromkin and Rodman (1993) are also good introductory texts. Brown (1984) presents a more general treatment of linguistic issues. McArthur (1992) is a very useful general handbook on the English language.

The three grammars by Quirk and his associates are quite simply the best available reference grammars of English. They contain a wealth of information and vary mainly in size from the shortest account (1973), through a much longer account (1972), to the most recent massive volume (1985). Leech and Svartvik (1975) is also based on this work and approaches much of the data from a functional point of view. The *Collins Cobuild English Grammar* (1990) is also extremely useful. Aarts and Aarts (1982) provides a good simple account of English structure in much the same vein as Quirk and his associates. Huddleston (1984) and Huddleston (1988) are two other excellent sources of information; both contain very informed discussion of many issues that we have touched on. All these books deal with English morphology and syntax. Halliday (1985) offers an unabashedly functional approach to English syntactic structure.

Stockwell (1977) and Matthews (1981) provide introductions to syntactic theory. Brown and Miller (1980), Burton-Roberts (1986), Young (1980), and Thomas (1993) deal either mainly or entirely with English syntax in introducing the basic principles of syntactic analysis. Baker (1978), Culicover (1982), Brown and Miller (1982), and Radford (1981, 1988) are thoroughly transformational-generative in their approaches. Stockwell et al. (1973) is an older transformational-generative approach useful for its discussions of many issues that have been tackled from time to time. McCawley (1988) is a fascinating and comprehensive updating of many of these same issues and offers many intriguing insights into syntactic matters. Cook (1988), Cowper (1992) and Haegeman (1991) provide accounts of Chomsky's current view of language.

Matthews (1991) and Spencer (1991) provide introductions to morphology. Bauer's book (1983) on word formation contains a wealth of theoretical insights and information. Marchand (1969) is almost encyclopedic in its treatment of English word formation.

Hawkins (1984) and Lass (1984) are good introductions to phonological theory, Giegerich (1992) to English phonology, and Ladefoged (1975) and Mackay (1987) to phonetic theory. Clark and Yallop (1990) cover both phonetics and phonology. Gimson (1962) and Heffner (1950) contain a wealth of information on English phonetics.

Kreidler (1989) gives a good account of English pronunciation. Wells (1982) provides a comprehensive survey of the variety of ways in which English is spoken throughout the world. Wijk (1966) presents considerable information concerning the relationships between the sounds and spellings of English. Chomsky and Halle (1968) and Halle and Keyser (1971) are concerned with trying to account for various aspects of English pronunciation within the transformational-generative paradigm.

Aarts, F., and Aarts, J. 1982. *English Syntactic Structures: Functions and Categories in Sentence Analysis.* Oxford: Pergamon Press.

Atkinson, M., Kilby, D., and Roca, I. 1982. *Foundations of General Linguistics.* London: George Allen & Unwin.

Baker, C. L. 1978. *Introduction to Generative-Transformational Syntax.* Englewood Cliffs: Prentice-Hall.

Bauer, L. 1983. *English Word-Formation.* Cambridge: Cambridge University Press.

Brown, E. K., and Miller, J. E. 1980. *Syntax: A Linguistic Introduction to Sentence Structure.* London: Hutchinson.

Brown, E. K., and Miller, J. E. 1982. *Syntax: Generative Grammar.* London: Hutchinson.

Brown, K. 1984. *Linguistics Today.* London: Fontana.

Burton-Roberts, N. 1986. *Analysing Sentences: An Introduction to English Syntax.* London: Longman.

Chomsky, N., and Halle, M. 1968. *The Sound Pattern of English.* New York: Harper & Row.

Clark, C., and Yallop, C. 1990. *An Introduction to Phonetics and Phonology.* Oxford: Basil Blackwell.

*Collins Cobuild English Grammar.* 1990. London: HarperCollins.

Cook, V. J. 1988. *Chomsky's Universal Grammar: An Introduction.* Oxford: Basil Blackwell.

Cowper, E. A. 1992. *A Concise Introduction to Syntactic Theory: The Government-Binding Approach.* Chicago: University of Chicago Press.

Culicover, P. W. 1982. *Syntax.* 2nd edn. New York: Academic Press.

Finegan, E., and Besnier, N. 1989. *Language: Its Structure and Use.* New York: Harcourt Brace Jovanovich.

Fromkin, V., and Rodman, R. 1993. *An Introduction to Language.* 5th edn. New York: Holt, Rinehart and Winston.

Giegerich, H. J. 1992. *English Phonology: An Introduction.* Cambridge: Cambridge University Press.

Gimson, A. C. 1962. *An Introduction to the Pronunciation of English.* London: Edward Arnold.

Haegeman, L. 1991. *Introduction to Government and Binding Theory.* Oxford: Basil Blackwell.

Halle, M., and Keyser, S. J. 1971. *English Stress: Its Form, Growth, and Its Role in Verse.* New York: Harper & Row.

Halliday, M. A. K. 1985. *An Introduction to Functional Grammar.* London: Edward Arnold.

Hawkins, P. 1984. *Introducing Phonology.* London: Hutchinson.

Heffner, R.-M. S. 1950. *General Phonetics.* Madison: University of Wisconsin Press.

Huddleston, R. 1984. *Introduction to the Grammar of English.* Cambridge: Cambridge University Press.

Huddleston, R. 1988. *English Grammar: An Outline.* Cambridge: Cambridge University Press.

Hudson, R. A. 1984. *Invitation to Linguistics*. Oxford: Martin Robertson.

Kreidler, C. K. 1989. *The Pronunciation of English: A Course Book in Phonology*. Oxford: Basil Blackwell.

Ladefoged, P. 1975. *A Course in Phonetics*. New York: Harcourt Brace Jovanovich.

Lass, R. 1984. *Phonology: An Introduction to Basic Concepts*. Cambridge: Cambridge University Press.

Leech, G., and Svartvik, J. 1975. *A Communicative Grammar of English*. London: Longman.

Mackay, I. R. A. 1987. *Phonetics: The Science of Speech Production*. 2nd edn. Boston: Little, Brown.

Marchand, H. 1969. *The Categories and Types of Present-Day English Word-Formation*. Munich: C. H. Beck.

Matthews, P. H. 1981. *Syntax*. Cambridge: Cambridge University Press.

Matthews, P. H. 1991. *Morphology: An Introduction to the Theory of Word-Structure*. 2nd edn. Cambridge: Cambridge University Press.

McArthur, T. 1992. *The Oxford Companion to the English Language*. Oxford: Oxford University Press.

McCawley, J. D. 1988. *The Syntactic Phenomena of English*. 2 vols. Chicago: University of Chicago Press.

O'Grady, W., and Dobrovolsky, M. 1992. *Contemporary Linguistic Analysis. An Introduction*. 2nd edn. Toronto: Copp Clark Pitman.

Quirk, R., Greenbaum, S., Leech, G., and Svartvik, J. 1972. *A Grammar of Contemporary English*. New York: Seminar Press.

Quirk, R., and Greenbaum, S. 1973. *A Concise Grammar of Contemporary English*. New York: Harcourt Brace Jovanovich.

Quirk, R., Greenbaum, S., Leech, G., and Crystal, D. 1985. *A Comprehensive Grammar of The English Language*. London: Longman.

Radford, A. 1981. *Transformational Syntax: A Student's Guide to Chomsky's Extended Standard Theory*. Cambridge: Cambridge University Press.

Radford, A. 1988. *Transformational Grammar: A First Course*. Cambridge: Cambridge University Press.

Spencer, A. 1991. *Morphological Theory*. Oxford: Basil Blackwell.

Stockwell, R. P. 1977. *Foundations of Syntactic Theory*. Englewood Cliffs: Prentice-Hall.

Stockwell, R. P., Schachter, P., and Partee, B. H. 1973. *The Major Syntactic Structures of English*. New York: Holt, Rinehart and Winston.

Thomas, L. 1993. *Beginning Syntax*. Oxford: Basil Blackwell.

Wells, J. C. 1982. *Accents of English*. 3 vols. Cambridge: Cambridge University Press.

Wijk, A. 1966. *Rules of Pronunciation for the English Language*. London: Oxford University Press.

Young, D. J. 1980. *The Structure of English Clauses*. London: Hutchinson.

# Indexed Glossary

This glossary provides brief definitions of the terms used in the text together with one or more examples whenever appropriate. Reference is also made to pages in the text where further information may be found.

**acronym**  A word formed from the inital letters of a set of words: *AIDS, GNP*. p. 235

**adjective**  A typical adjective is a word like *big* or *beautiful* and can be found in either forms like *bigger* and *biggest* or after *more* or *most*, as in *more beautiful* and *most beautiful*. pp. 4–5, 20–3, 39–41, 46–9, 222–3

**adjective phrase**  A construction with an adjective as its head: *old* and *very old* are adjective phrases headed by *old*. pp. 39–41, 46–9

**adverb**  A typical adverb is a word like *wisely*, ending in *-ly*, and used to modify a verb. pp. 4, 23–5

**adverb clause**  A clause occupying the same position in a sentence as an adverb phrase: *because I ordered him to go* in *He left because I ordered him to go*. pp. 112–14

**adverb phrase**  A construction with an adverb as its head: *silently* and *very quickly* are adverb phrases headed by *silently* and *quickly*. pp. 60–4

**affix hopping**  The transformational process in which affixes are moved: *pres be -ing go* becomes *be pres go -ing*. pp. 146–8

**affricate**  A sound involving a complete stoppage of the airstream followed by an immediate turbulent release: the sounds at the beginning and end of *judge*. p. 189

**agentless passive**  A passive clause containing no mention of who or what performed the action of the verb: *The house was destroyed*. pp. 82, 120–1, 142–3

**allegro speech**  Fast speech typically characterized by the assimilation and elision of sounds. pp. 261–5

**allomorph**  One of the variants of a morpheme: the /-s/ of *cats* and the /-z/ of *dogs* are allomorphs of the "plural" morpheme. pp. 217–18, 245

**allophone**  One of pronunciation variants of a phoneme: [tʰ] and [t] are two of the allophones of /t/, as in *tot* [tʰat]. p. 201

**ambisyllabic**  A consonant that may belong to either the preceding or following syllable: the *t* of *waiter*. pp. 256–7

**appositive**  A restatement of some kind: *John Smith* is an appositive noun phrase in *my friend John Smith* and *that he confessed* is an appositive noun clause in *The fact that he confessed should count in his favor*. pp. 44, 111

**article**  A subclass of determiner: *the* is the definite article and *a* (or *an*) the indefinite article. p. 29

**aspect**   The use of *be -ing* (progressive aspect) or *have -en* (perfective aspect) in a verb phrase: *I am going* and *He has left.* pp. 53, 54–60

**aspirated**   A sound released with a small puff of air: the *t* at the beginning of *top* [tʰap] is aspirated. pp. 200–1

**assimilation**   A change in one sound to make it resemble another neighboring sound: in *it's* and *he's* the final sound is [s] after [t] but [z] after the vowel in *he.* pp. 204, 226, 261–3

**attributive adjective**   An adjective that occurs before a noun: *big* in *big shoes.* p. 22

**auxiliary verb**   A verb that accompanies the main verb in a clause: *can,* and *was* in *I can go* and *He was singing.* See also **lexical verb.** pp. 18–19, 53–5, 118

**back formation**   The derivation of a word like *peddle* from *peddler.* p. 235

**back vowel**   A vowel made in the back of the mouth: the vowels in *boot* and *bought.* p. 190

**bare infinitive**   The form of the verb that occurs without *to* or any kind of inflectional marking: *go* in *I can't go.* p. 17

**base**   A morpheme or combination of morphemes to which an affix can be attached: *do* in *does* and *undo.* pp. 217–18

**blend**   A word formed from the combination and shortening of two other words: *smog* from *smoke* and *fog.* p. 235

**bound morpheme**   A morpheme that must occur attached to another morpheme: the *-s* "plural" in *cats* and the *-kempt* of *unkempt.* p. 218

**cardinal**   A number word like *one, two,* or *three.* pp. 30, 38

**checked vowel**   A vowel which must be followed by a consonant: the vowels in *bit* and *beg.* p. 195

**citation form**   The pronunciation of a word in isolation rather than in context. p. 181

**clause**   A syntactic unit consisting of a subject and predicate: *Birds sing.* p. 70

**clipping**   The shortening that occurs in words like *(omni)bus* and *lab(oratory).* p. 235

**clitic**   A morpheme, such as *-n't* and *-'ll,* as in *shouldn't* and *I'll,* often frequently occurring in the language but always bound to another morpheme. pp. 222, 262

**closed syllable**   A syllable with a coda: *tap* or *script.* p. 255

**cluster**   A possible phonemic sequence: *script* begins with the consonant cluster /skr-/. pp. 193–5, 247, 263–4

**coda**   The consonant(s) following a vowel in a syllable: the *-p* of *tap,* the *-pts* of *scripts,* and nothing at all in *by.* pp. 255–6

**cognate object**   A kind of restatement of a basically intransitive verb in a following noun phrase: *He died a good death.* pp. 81–2

**comparative**   The *-er* inflection on an adjective: *bigger.* pp. 20–1

**complement**   A constituent required to complete a construction: *old* and *of chocolate* are complements in *The cat is old* and *They are fond of chocolate.* pp. 48, 49, 59–60, 62–3, 80–90, 166–9

**complementizer**   A word like *that* in *The book that I want is over there* and *The fact that you mentioned it should help.* pp. 104, 106–7, 110, 113, 151, 153–4, 167

**complex sentence**   A sentence containing one main clause and one or more subordinate clauses: *Birds can fly because they have wings.* pp. 114–15

**compound predicate**   A conjoined predicate: *swims and sails* in *Nancy swims and sails.* p. 114

**compound sentence**   A sentence containing two or more main, i.e., coordinate, clauses: *Birds fly and fish swim.* p. 114

**compound subject** A conjoined subject: *Jack and Jill* in *Jack and Jill went up the hill*. p. 114

**compound word** A word constructed from two bases: *blackbird* and *icebox*. pp. 231–3

**compound-complex sentence** A sentence containing two or more main, i.e., coordinate, clauses, and one or more subordinate clauses: *Birds can fly because they have wings but fish can only swim*. p. 115

**conjunction** A conjunction typically joins one phrase or clause to another: *and* in *Jack and Jill* and *because* in *He left because it was time to go*. pp. 4, 28–9

**conjunctive adverb** A joining word like *however* or *moreover* with considerable freedom of movement in the second of the conjoined elements: *He went; however, he should have stayed at home* and *He went; he should have stayed at home, however*. pp. 29, 63, 102–8

**consonant phoneme** A sound such as /p/ or /f/ which involves considerable interference with the airstream. pp. 181–7

**constituent** One of the parts of a construction: *the* and *man* are the constituents of the noun phrase *the man*. pp. 33–64

**construction** A syntactic arrangement of two or more constituents: a determiner and a noun in a noun phrase like *the man*, and a preposition and a noun phrase in a prepositional phrase like *to the top*. pp. 33–64

**conversion** The use of one part of speech in a syntactic position other than its usual one: *brother* in *Don't brother me!* pp. 233–5

**coordinate construction constraint** It is usually only possible to coordinate grammatical elements which are alike: a noun phrase with a noun phrase as in *John and his brothers*; a direct object with a direct object as in *Give me liberty or death!*; and a subject complement with a subject complement as in *He is wise and decent*. pp. 97–8

**coordinating conjunction** A conjunction that joins equal items: *and* in *Jack and Jill* and *but* in *He's tired but he's happy*. pp. 28–9, 97–103

**coordination** The joining of similar grammatical elements: *John and his mother*, *tired but successful*, and *Victory or death!* pp. 97–103

**correlating conjunctions** Conjunctions that work in pairs: *either* and *or* in *Either you go or I do*. pp. 29, 99

**countable noun** A typical countable noun takes the "plural" inflection – *cat* and *man* and *cats* and *men* – and can be used after *many* – *many cats* and *many men*. Contrast **mass noun**. pp. 9–10, 37

**dangling participle** A construction such as *Driving home, the car ran out of gas* in which no subject is present for the participle *driving*. pp. 27, 28

**dative movement** The movement involved in the following shift of the noun phrase *the boy* from *I gave the book to the boy* to *I gave the boy the book*. pp. 161–3

**d(eep) structure** The abstract structure of a sentence from which its actual structure, its s(urface) structure, may be derived transformationally. pp. 140–1

**demonstrative pronoun** The pronoun *this* or *that* (and their plural forms *these* or *those*) when used by themselves as noun phrases: *This is what I want*. p. 14

**deontic** The use of a modal verb to express necessity, obligation, possibility, etc.: *You must do it* (I insist). pp. 53–4

**derivation** A grammatical affix that changes the meaning and/or part-of-speech category of a word: *un-* in *unhappy* and *-ness* in *happiness*. pp. 6, 23, 217, 224–31

**descriptivism** An approach to language study which describes how speakers of a language actually use that language. pp. 1–2

**determiner**  A word like *the*, *this*, or *my*: *the book*, *this apple*, *my friends*. *My* is also sometimes called a **possessive pronoun**. pp. 14, 36–8, 137

**diphthong**  A vowel sound involving considerable movement of the tongue: the vowels in *boy*, *buy*, and *cow*. pp. 190–1

**direct object**  The object of a monotransitive verb: *the cake* in *I ate the cake*. Also the second object of a ditransitive verb: *the cake* in *I gave him the cake*. pp. 82, 119, 141–4

**disjunct**  An adverb phrase that provides a kind of "frame" for an accompanying clause: *naturally* and *obviously* in *Naturally, I'll do it* and *Obviously, they can't go*. pp. 63–4

**ditransitive verb**  A transitive verb that can take two objects: *give* in *I gave the boy a dollar*. pp. 85–7, 119–20

**do support**  The provision of *do* to carry an isolated tense so as to allow affix hopping to occur: *he pres n't know* becomes *he pres do n't know*. p. 148

**double genitive**  A combination of the periphrastic genitive and the genitive inflection: *a play of his*. p. 11

**echo question**  A question which echoes part of some previous utterance: *He wants what?* It often seeks confirmation of certain information. pp. 127–8, 148–9, 259

**ellipsis**  The omission of part of a structure: *He goes more often than she* (*goes*). pp. 11, 175–6, 235

**embedded clause**  A clause which is subordinated to another clause: a relative clause *that I want* in *The book that I want is over there* is embedded into *The book is over there*, its matrix clause. pp. 103–15

**embedded question**  A clause such as *who had left* in *I asked who had left*. pp. 110, 149–52

**emphatic pronoun**  See **intensifying pronoun**.

**endocentric compound**  A compound like *blackbird* which describes a kind of bird. p. 232

**epistemic**  The use of a modal verb in a context in which the truth or falsity of the proposition is an issue: *Can he speak French?* (yes or no). pp. 53–4

**equi deletion**  The process which accounts, among other things, for *I* being the subject of both *want* and *go* in *I want to go*. pp. 167–9

**exclusive *we***  The *we* that excludes the listener (I and someone else but not you). p. 13

**exocentric compound**  A compound like *loudmouth* which describes not a kind of mouth but a kind of person. p. 232

**expletive *it***  The use of *it* for purely grammatical, i.e., meaningless, purposes: *It's cold today* and *It's good that he's coming*. pp. 74–5, 77, 172–3

**expletive *there***  The use of *there* for purely grammatical, i.e., meaningless, purposes: *There's a man outside*. pp. 74–5, 77, 165–6

**extrapositioning**  A clause movement of the following kind, of *That he should go was decided* to give *It was decided that he should go*. pp. 76, 109–10, 172–3

**finite verb**  A verb form marked for either present or past tense: *I go, I went*. pp. 51–2

**flap**  A quick tap of the tongue on the alveolar ridge as a realization of certain *t*s in some varieties of English: [ɾ] for the *t* of *writer*. pp. 203, 211–12, 256

**flat adverb**  An adverb lacking the *-ly* ending: *slow* and *tight* in *Drive slow!* and *Hold tight!* p. 25

**free morpheme**  A morpheme that can occur by itself: *the* or *cat*. p. 218

**free vowel**   A vowel that may occur either before a consonant or finally in a word or utterance: the vowels in *beet* (*bee*) and *goat* (*owe*). p. 195

**fricative**   A sound that involves the turbulent release of air: the sounds at the beginning and end of *fish*. p. 189

**front vowel**   A vowel made in the front of the mouth: the vowels in *bit* and *bet*. p. 190

**genitive**   The *-'s* inflection on a noun or pronoun: *cat's* and *yours*. Sometimes called possessive. pp. 8, 10–11, 42, 106, 218–19

**gerund**   A verb with the *-ing* inflection used in a syntactic position characteristic of a noun: *swimming* in *Swimming is good for you*. p. 26

**get passive**   A passive formed with *get* rather than *be*: *He got hurt*. pp. 122–3

**glide**   A sound having characteristics of both a consonant and a vowel: the beginning sounds of *yet* and *well*. p. 189

**gradable adjective**   An adjective capable of taking the "comparative" and "superlative" inflections: *big, bigger, biggest*. pp. 20–1

**Great Vowel Shift**   Some five hundred years ago English tense vowels moved to higher positions in the mouth and the highest such vowels became diphthongs, so [e] became [i] and [i] became [aɪ]. p. 251

**group genitive**   A genitive in which the *-'s* ending actually attaches to a whole phrase rather than to a single word: *the Prince of Wales's son*. p. 11

**high vowel**   A vowel made in the upper part of the mouth: the vowels in *beat* and *boot*. p. 190

**homonym**   A word that is pronounced the same as some other word but has a quite different meaning: *bank* in *a savings bank* and *the river bank*. p. 215

**homorganic**   Made in the same position, as are /t/ and /s/, and /p/ and /f/. p. 192

**idiom**   A group of words with a meaning unique to that group: *kick the bucket* with the meaning "die." pp. 122, 216, 236

**imperative**   A clause lacking a subject and beginning with an uninflected verb: *Go back!* pp. 123–4, 145–6

**inclusive *we***   The *we* that includes the listener (you and I). pp. 13, 124

**indefinite pronoun**   A pronoun like *anyone, something*, or *nobody*. pp. 15, 41, 105, 107, 123

**indirect object**   The first object after a ditransitive verb: *him* in *I gave him the cake*. Sometimes also applied to *him* in *I gave the cake to him*. pp. 85–7

**inflectional affix**   A grammatical affix that attaches to a word to mark it as a particular part of speech: the "plural" *-s* noun ending of *cats* or the "past tense" *-ed* verb ending of *begged*. pp. 6, 217–23

**intensifier**   A word like *rather, quite*, or *very*. pp. 7, 22, 47

**intensifying pronoun**   A pronoun ending in *-self* or *-selves* used as follows: *I myself told him*. Compare **reflexive pronoun**. p. 14

**interjection**   A word like *Ouch!* or *Oh!* p. 4

**International Phonetic Alphabet**   A standard system used to transcribe the sounds of languages. p. 200

**interrogative pronoun**   A pronoun like *who* or *which* used to introduce a question: *Who wants it?* Also called a **wh- word**. p. 15

**intonation**   The overall pattern of stresses and pitches with which an utterance is pronounced. pp. 126, 127, 258–60

**intransitive verb**   A verb like *come* or *go* which does not take a direct object. pp. 81–2

**intrusive r**  In some varieties of English an *r* is inserted to link a word that ends in a vowel to one that begins with a vowel: *Cuba-r-and Spain*. p. 210

**inversion**  The reversal of normal subject-verb word order: *Is he there?* and *Can he go?* pp. 76, 131

**inverted question**  A question employing inversion: *Can you go?* with its inversion of *you* and *can*. pp. 76, 125–7, 259

**irregular inflection**  An inflection which does not follow strict phonological rules and is to that extent idiosyncratic: the "plural" *men* and the "past tense" *went*. See also **regular inflection**. pp. 8–9, 218–23

**irreversible binomial**  An expression like *cup and saucer* and *fish and chips* in which the order of the coordinated elements cannot be reversed (*\*saucer and cup* and *\*chips and fish*). p. 100

**lateral**  The sound represented by the *l* in *led*, made by forcing air around the sides of the tongue. p. 189

**lax vowel**  A vowel produced without muscular tension in the tongue: the vowels in *bit* and *bet*. p. 190

**lexeme**  The type of word a dictionary records. pp. 214–16

**lexical verb**  The main verb in its clause: *go* is the lexical verb in *I can go* and in *I was going*. See also **auxiliary verb**. p. 18

**linking r**  In non-rhotic varieties of English a final *r* in a word is pronounced only before a following word beginning with a vowel: both *here* and *there* are pronounced *r*-less in isolation or before words beginning with a consonant but in *here and there* the final *r* is pronounced in *here* but not in *there*. p. 210

**linking verb**  A verb like *be*, *appear*, or *seem*: *He is old*, *They appeared calm*, and *You seem to be tired*. pp. 80, 87–8, 123

**location genitive**  A phrase like *at Peter's*. p. 11

**low vowel**  A vowel made in the lower part of the mouth: the vowels in *bat* and *bought*. p. 190

**marked infinitive**  The form of the verb preceded by *to* as in *to go*. p. 17

**mass noun**  A typical mass noun does not easily take the "plural" inflection: *wine* and *courage*. It can also appear after *much*: *much wine*. Contrast **countable noun**. pp. 10, 11, 37

**matrix clause**  A clause into which another clause is embedded: in *The fact that you mentioned it is interesting*, *that you mentioned it* is a noun clause embedded within the matrix clause *The fact is interesting*. pp. 103–4

**minimal pair**  A pair of words showing a single phonological contrast: *bit* and *pit*, and *bit* and *bat*. pp. 180–1

**modal verb**  A verb like *can*, *may*, *shall*, or *will*. pp. 18–19, 118, 222

**modality**  The meaning expressed by a modal verb. pp. 53–4

**monophthong**  A single vowel sound: the vowels in *bat*, *bit*, and *beet*. p. 190

**monotransitive verb**  A transitive verb that takes a single object: *eat* in *He ate the cake*. pp. 82–5

**morpheme**  A basic unit of meaning in a language: *unhappiness* contains three morphemes *un-*, *happi* (*happy*), and *-ness*. pp. 216–18

**morphological conditioning**  See **irregular inflection**.

**morphophoneme**  A postulated underlying phonological representation of a phoneme when there are different surface realizations: the /-z/ "plural" underlies the /-z/ of *dogs*, the /-əz/ of *judges*, and the /-s/ of *cats*. pp. 245–52

**nasal**  A sound which involves the escape of air through the nose: the sounds at the beginning and end of *man*. p. 189

**negation**  The introduction of a negative, particularly *not*, *n't*, or *un-*, into a construction: *He can't go* and *It's not unlikely*. pp. 59, 130–3, 160–1

**negative raising**  The *n't* in *I don't suppose he knows that* appears to originate in the embedded clause: *I suppose he doesn't know that*. pp. 170–1

**neo-classical compound**  A compound with its parts drawn from Latin or Greek: *anglophile, homophobe*. p. 233

**neutralization**  The loss of a phonological contrast in certain environments: /i/ and /ı/ contrast in *beet* and *bit* but not before the /r/ of *beer*. pp. 195–6, 210, 257

**non-finite verb**  A verb form not marked for tense, i.e., a participle or an infinitive: *dancing* in *They were dancing* and *to go* in *He wants to go*. pp. 51–2

**non-restrictive**  An appositive that supplies extra, therefore omissible, information: the appositive *the capital of England* is extra information in *You should visit London, the capital of England*. pp. 44, 108, 111–12

**noun**  A typical noun is a word like *dog* which can be found in other forms: *dogs, dog's,* and *dogs'*. pp. 4, 8–12, 218–20

**noun clause**  A clause that fills a position in a sentence usually filled by a noun phrase: *that I should go* in *He said that I should go*. pp. 109–12

**noun phrase**  A construction with a noun as its head: *John, the man,* and *the old man* are all noun phrases with *John* and *man* as their heads. pp. 36–46, 137

**object case**  The form of the personal pronoun that occurs in object position: *me* and *him* in *She hugged me* and *Give it to him*. pp. 12–14, 105, 220

**object complement**  The noun phrase or adjective phrase that follows an object in certain constructions: *president* and *very happy* in *They elected him president* and *It made him very happy*. pp. 89–90, 119

**object to subject raising**  *John* in *John is difficult to please* is both the object of *to please* in the embedded clause and the subject of *is difficult* in the matrix clause. See alo **raising**. p. 170

**onset**  The beginning of a syllable: the *s-* in *sap*, the *scr-* in *scream*, and nothing in *ate*. p. 255

**open syllable**  A syllable which lacks a coda: *by* or *tree*. p. 255

**ordinal**  A number like *first, second, third,* etc. p. 30

**palatalization**  The modification of a consonant by a following high front vowel: *tune* pronounced *chune*, i.e., /tyun/ like /čun/. pp. 245–6, 261

**part of speech**  One of the various categories into which we can fit the words of the language; noun, verb, etc. pp. 4–8

**particle**  A word like *up* or *over* used as part of a phrasal verb: *They took up a collection* and *We looked over the plans of the house*. pp. 90–3

**passive**  The rearrangement that occurs when the direct object of a transitive verb becomes the subject of that verb: the change of *John ate the cake* to *The cake was eaten by John*. pp. 55–7, 82–7, 118–23, 141–4

**past participle**  The following *-ed* (or *-en*) inflection on a verb: *begged* and *written* in *I have begged* and *He has written*. pp. 16, 54–7, 221–2

**past tense**  The following *-ed* inflection on a verb: *I begged*. pp. 16, 52–3, 221–2

**peak**  The vowel and any following consonant(s) in a syllable: the *-op* of *stop*, the *-ipt* of *script*, and the *-oy* of *boy*. p. 256

**periphrastic genitive**  The use of a prepositional phrase headed by *of* in a phrase like *the end of the war*. p. 11

**periphrastic modal**  One of a set of complex modal verbs: *be able to, be about to,* etc. p. 54

**personal pronoun**  A pronoun like *I, you, he,* etc. pp. 12–14, 220

**phoneme**  A basic sound in a language: *pens* has four phonemes /p/, /ɛ/, /n/, and /z/. pp. 180–5

**phonological conditioning**  See **regular inflection.**

**phrasal adjunct**  A construction headed by a participle used to modify a noun phrase in another clause: *Being quite tired* modifies *the boys* in *Being quite tired, the boys rested for a while.* See also **dangling participle.** p. 59

**phrasal verb**  A verb accompanied by a following particle which may have possibilities of movement: *took off* in *The plane took off,* and *take down* in *She took down the curtains* and *She took the curtains down.* pp. 82–3, 90–3, 119

**phrasal-prepositional verb**  A verb-particle-preposition combination: *get away with* in *He got away with murder.* pp. 93, 119

**phrase**  The smallest syntactic unit, often, though not necessarily, more than one word: *John, the boy,* and *the young man* are all noun phrases in *John left, The boy left,* and *The young man left.* p. 133

**plural**  The *-s* inflection on a noun or pronoun: *cats* and *these.* pp. 8–9, 218–20

**polysemy**  The different, but related, meanings of the the same word: *play* in *Shakespeare wrote plays* and *The children are playing outside.* pp. 215–16

**possessive**  See **genitive.**

**possessive pronoun**  See **determiner.** p. 14

**postdeterminer**  A word like *other* or *only* in *the other day* and *my only chance.* p. 38

**predeterminer**  A word like *all* or *such* in *all the books* and *such an effort.* p. 38

**predicate**  The part of a clause which excludes the subject: *dances regularly* in *Sally dances regularly* and *ate all the candies* in *The child ate all the candies.* p. 70

**predicate adjective**  An adjective that occurs after a linking verb: *active* in *She was very active.* pp. 22–3

**predicate adjunct**  An optional element in the predicate of a clause: *on Tuesday* in *We are going on Tuesday.* pp. 59–60, 62, 64, 112–13

**preposition**  A word like *in* or *at* which heads a prepositional phrase: *in the house* and *at the back.* pp. 4, 29, 49–51

**prepositional phrase**  A construction with a preposition as its head: *to* and *over* head the prepositional phrases *to the store* and *over my head.* pp. 49–51

**prepositional verb**  A verb and preposition combination: *comment* and *on* in *They commented on the budget* in the sense of "made observations about." pp. 92–3, 119

**prescriptivism**  An approach to language study which tries to tell speakers of a language how they should use that language. pp. 1–2

**present participle**  The *-ing* inflection on a verb: *baking* in *I was baking.* pp. 16, 221

**present tense**  The third person singular *-s* inflection on a verb: *She studies.* pp. 16, 53, 221

**pronoun**  A word, which although not a noun itself, typically appears in a position filled by a noun phrase: *he* in *He goes.* pp. 4, 12–16, 220

**proper noun**  The name of a specific entity: *John* or *London.* pp. 10, 37

**pseudo-transitive verb**  A verb which although followed by a direct object cannot be passivized: *They have a nice house* but not *\*A nice house is had by them.* pp. 88, 121

**raising** The process which accounts for how a grammatical element may be said to function in two different clauses: *him* in *I want him to go* as both the subject of the verb *to go* in the embedded clause and the object of *want* in the matrix clause. pp. 73, 169–72

**reciprocal pronoun** A pronoun like *each other* or *one another*. p. 15

**reduplication** A word containing some kind of repetition: *mishmash* and *zigzag*. pp. 235–6

**reflexive pronoun** A pronoun ending in *-self* or *-selves* and used as follows: *I hurt myself*. Compare **intensifying pronoun**. pp. 14, 122, 163–5

**regular inflection** An inflection which follows strict phonological rules: the "plural" *cats* and the "past tense" *begged*. See also **irregular inflection**. pp. 8–9, 218–23

**relative clause** A subordinate clause that modifies a noun phrase: *who built it* in *The people who built it live down the street*. pp. 43–4, 104–9, 111–12, 152–6

**relative pronoun** A pronoun like *who* or *which* in sentences like *I know the man who did it* and *The ship which sank belonged to him*. pp. 14, 104–9

**replacement allomorph** An irregular inflection in which a replacement of phonemes occurs: in *feet* the *ee* vowel replaces the *oo* vowel of *foot* to mark "plural." pp. 219–20

**restrictive** An appositive that supplies information which cannot be omitted: the appositive *Fred* in *my cousin Fred* is key information. Compare **non-restrictive**. pp. 44, 108, 111–12

**retroflex** The sound represented by the letter *r* in *red*, made by curling back the tip of the tongue. p. 189

**rhetorical question** A question structure used for rhetorical effect rather than for information-gathering purposes: *Who really believes such things?* p. 130

**rhotic variety** A variety of English in which the *rs* in words like *car* and *cart* are pronounced. p. 1

**rhyme** The peak and coda, if there is one, of a syllable: the *-ipt* of *script* and the *-oy* of *boy*. p. 255

**role** The relationship that a noun phrase has to a verb: *John* has an agent role in *John kicked the ball* and *the ball* has a patient role. pp. 70–3, 120–1

**round vowel** A vowel produced with concurrent lip rounding: the vowels in *boot* and *boat*. p. 190

**sentence adjunct** An optional element attached to a clause or sentence: *Very quietly* in *Very quietly, he left the room*. pp. 62, 112–13

**sentential relative clause** A relative clause attached to a whole sentence: *which was a good idea* is attached to *He kept his mouth shut* in *He kept his mouth shut, which was a good idea*. p. 109

**simple sentence** A sentence containing a single clause, therefore a main clause: *Birds sing*. p. 114

**stative verb** A verb which does not usually occur with the progressive aspect *be -ing*: *I know* and *I understand* but not *\*I am knowing* and *\*I am understanding*. p. 55

**stem** A morpheme or combination of morphemes to which an inflection can be attached: *cat* and *unfasten* in *cats* and *unfastens*. p. 217

**stop** A sound requiring a distinct interruption of the airstream: the sounds at the beginning and end of *dip*. p. 189

**stress** The relative intensity with which vowels are pronounced. pp. 127, 130, 203, 239–45, 258–9, 260

**subject** Usually the initial noun phrase in a clause and in a clause with a finite verb the noun phrase to which that verb agrees in number: *John* in *John goes* and *Was John there?* pp. 70, 73–8, 105, 144

**subject case**   The form of the personal pronoun that occurs in subject position: *I* and *he* in *I go* and *He sings*. pp. 13, 220

**subject complement**   The noun phrase or adjective phrase that follows a linking verb: *a baker* and *very wise* in *He is a baker* and *She is very wise*. pp. 87–8

**subject to object raising**   *Him* in *I want him to go* is both the subject of *to go* in the embedded clause and the object of *want* in the matrix clause. See also **raising**. pp. 169–70

**subject to subject raising**   *John* in *John is eager to go* is the subject of both *to go* in the embedded clause and *is eager* in the matrix clause. See also **raising**. p. 170

**subject-verb agreement**   The inflectional marking required by a finite verb because of its subject: *I go* but *he goes*, and *John sings* but *The boys sing*. pp. 75, 78–9, 144, 166

**subjunctive**   The uninflected form of the verb found in certain contexts: *go* and *forbid* in *I insist he go* and *God forbid!* pp. 19, 110

**subordinate clause**   See **embedded clause**.

**subordinating conjunction**   A conjunction which subordinates one clause to another: *because* in *He's going because I asked him to*. pp. 28–9, 112–13

**superlative**   The *-est* inflection on an adjective: *biggest*. pp. 20, 107, 222–3

**suppletion**   An inflectional change involving a complete change in the underlying word: *go* to *went*, and *good* to *best*. pp. 17, 20, 24, 221–2

**s(urface) structure**   The actual structure of a sentence, which may be derived transformationally from an abstract or d(eep) structure. pp. 140–1

**syllabic consonant**   A vowel-consonant combination produced as a single sound unit: the final combinations in *battle* [ḷ] and *redden* [ṇ]. pp. 204–6

**syllabic nasal**   A vowel-nasal combination produced as a single sound unit: the final *-en* in *redden* [ṇ]. p. 205

**tag question**   An inverted construction attached to a clause mirroring certain characteristics of that clause: *didn't he?* in *He did it, didn't he?* pp. 76, 125–7, 149, 171, 259

**tense vowel**   A vowel involving considerable muscular tension in the tongue and its controlling muscles: the vowels in *beet* and *boat*. p. 190

***there* insertion**   The process by which there is introduced into a sentence like *There's a man here to see you*. pp. 165–6

**third person singular**   The *-s* inflection on a verb: on *swims* in *Sally swims regularly*. pp. 16–17, 221–2

**tough movement**   See **object to subject raising**.

**transformation**   One of the processes involved in changing a d(eep) structure into a s(urface) structure. pp. 140–1

**transitive verb**   A verb that can take a direct object and be passivized: *steal* in *He stole the money* and *The money was stolen*. pp. 55, 80, 82–7, 118–23

**ungrammatical**   A form or arrangement that the language does not allow: */parzt/ and *He not can't go*. p. 5

**unround vowel**   A vowel produced with spread, i.e., unround, lips: the vowels in *bit* and *bat*. p. 190

**verb**   A typical verb is a word like *bake* which can found in other forms: *bakes*, *baked*, and *baking*. pp. 4, 16–20, 221–2

**verb phrase** A construction with a verb as its head: *can go* and *has been dancing* are verb phrases headed by *go* and *dancing*. Also used to describe *ate the apple* and *left suddenly* in *He ate the apple* and *The visitors left suddenly*. pp. 57–60, 137

**vocal tract** The anatomical features involved in the production of speech. p. 188

**voiced sound** A sound such as the vowels in *beet* and *boot* or the consonants in *bag* which involves vibration of the vocal cords. p. 187

**voiceless sound** A sound such as the consonants in *sip* which does not involve vibration of the vocal cords. p. 187

**vowel phoneme** A sound such as /i/ in *beet* or /u/ in *boot* which is produced with unimpeded airflow. pp. 184–7, 254

*wh-* **question** A question seeking information and having a characteristic initial *wh*-word: *What do you want?* pp. 127–30, 149–51

*wh-* **movement** The movement of a *wh-* word to the front of its clause: *pres can he eat what* to *what pres can he eat*. p. 151

*wh-* **word** A word like *who* or *which* used to introduce a question: *Who is there?* pp. 128–9, 133

*yes-no* **question** A question that can be answered either *yes* or *no*: *Can you go?* or *He did it, didn't he?* pp. 125–6, 149

**zero allomorph** The failure to take an inflection: *sheep* has no overt "plural" in *two sheep* and therefore has a "zero" marking for "plural." p. 221